FACTORY FOLKWAYS

FACTORY FOLKWAYS

A Study of Institutional Structure and Change

BY JOHN S. ELLSWORTH, JR.
Assistant Professor of Sociology, Yale University

New Haven: Yale University Press

LONDON: GEOFFREY CUMBERLEGE, OXFORD UNIVERSITY PRESS

First published, November, 1952; Second printing, February, 1953
Copyright, 1952, by Yale University Press.
Printed in the United States of America by Vail-Ballou Press, Inc.

CONTENTS

Introduction

The purpose of this book is a twofold one. It aims, on the one hand, at testing and clarifying certain sociological theories, and on the other hand, it is interested in applications of social science. Hence it is adressed both to sociologists, who are interested primarily in general explanations and interpretations of human behavior, and to practical people, who are faced with directing behavior or solving problems connected with human activity. It may be, of course, that in attempting to ride the two horses—theory and practice—the book falls between them, but the writer is convinced that the common attempt to separate theory and practice is not necessarily wise. "Pure science" doubtless has its virtues, but on the level of industrial human relations the marriage of theory and practice promises great rewards for both sociology and industry. Each party can learn from the other. For industry, the principles of social science can provide useful analytical tools and profitable guides for activity. For sociology, industry provides not only a fruitful field for studying organized behavior but, beyond that, a chance to see principles tested through application.

In approaching this dual purpose, the book includes as its first section a reasonably complete history and description of a single plant. This is presented so that the reader can analyze it for himself, if he cares to, and can use it as factual material with which to check conclusions offered later. Following this descriptive section, other parts of the book are devoted to exposition of theoretical material and to applying this to an explanation of developments in the plant under scrutiny. By this means, it is hoped, the utility of the theoretical approach is demonstrated and the need for certain revisions and elaborations of the theory is made clear.

Back of this attempt to apply social science to industrial activity lies the assumption that an industrial plant is a social organization. Countless writers have, in the past 20 years or so, stressed "the human factor" and rebelled almost too shrilly against the older, rationalistic theories of industry. These writers, however, have been concerned largely with elaborating the list of motivations which inspire industrial workers by adding needs for such things as prestige and security to the desire for "maximization of income," which was once regarded as an all-sufficient drive. They have also noted, sometimes with an air of delighted surprise, that human beings react toward each other as human beings and not as machines. In doing so, however, they have overlooked what is perhaps the crucial point.

This point is that the plant, the office, or whatever is an institution in the fullest sociological sense of the term. Therefore, although this book is concerned mostly with a single factory, its subject is social structure—the elements and conditions which are always present when people work together to accomplish their purposes and to satisfy their needs. In this sense, one might almost say, as one elderly worker did, that the subject is a "home."

"I have two homes," this man said, "my home where I live and my factory home where I work."

By this, although he could not have gone on to put his thought in words, this man meant more than that he, in common with millions of others, spends a large part of his life in a factory. He meant, in part, that the hopes, aims, and fears of factory people are keenly alive during working hours as they are after they "punch out" in the evening, that human needs are not left behind at the time clock in the morning. To be sure, some workers speak in stereotypes which make of the factory no more than a job and of themselves no more than commodities. Frequently they talk as though all their grievances could be cured by money, but the essential point is that by their behavior they make of industry as vital a nexus of human relationships as the family, the church, the school, and the other institutions of which the fabric of society is woven.

This means that any given industry is a complex of structural elements and interacting forces, and it means further that attempts to isolate factors and to interpret them apart from their settings is bound to fall short of full understanding. Just as the attempt to explain industrial behavior solely in economic terms was inadequate, so are attemps to do so simply in terms of such things as non-economic motivations or communications. These are important in context, but by themselves they are of limited significance.

It is natural, one supposes, to seek quick and easy solutions for human and other problems, to look for and seize upon the formulas which have worked for others—the suggestion system, the organi-zation chart, or the like in industry. Certainly it is easier to do this than to unravel the complexities of human situations and thus to diagnose the problems which exist in a given place at a given time. The burden of the argument here, however, is that it is unsafe to make predictions or to create policies without explor-ing every area of pertinent information which exists in an organi-zation.

To this, no doubt, many industrialists, including especially those who have adopted the other fellow's gadget and found it worthless, would agree. What is not so easy, however, is to state the principles for making a diagnosis, to outline the theoretical basis which will serve as a blueprint for investigation. This is, nevertheless, the sub-stance of this book's purpose. The author intends to draw from the theoretical storehouse of social science some of the principles which seem to apply to industry in order to test and sharpen them by application and, equally, to suggest that they are the principles by which social organization can best be comprehended.

To be sure, as the notion of testing suggests, these principles cannot be offered as perfect. Social science has little which ap-proaches the precision of physical science. Nevertheless, some of the concepts of sociology are ready for practical application. They are not perfect, but that is not necessarily a bar to their use. Busy people can seldom afford to wait for the best which may be devel-oped someday. They must use what is at hand today, and through use they may well come upon improvements. As operating men say, you do not get the "bugs" out of a new product until you put it into production. Just so with sociological principles—practical application will show up their imperfections and sharpen their strong points. The practical man wants something to work with now, and the scientist wants practice to test his theories. The writer sympathizes keenly with both points of view. More than half his adult life has been spent working for people and supervising people. The rest has been spent as a sociologist trying to make sense out of what he has learned by experience. He has suffered from the mistakes of poor bosses, and he has made his share of similar mistakes. On the whole, he thinks that sociology has helped or might have helped him to avoid some pitfalls, and he is also convinced that sociologists can learn a great deal from the intelligent people in industry who, after all, are manipulating the very thing sociologists try to study—that is, human behavior.

The most important of the theoretical devices to be presented here is Malinowski's concept of institution. Incidentally, it should be apparent, especially in connection with this "theory of institutions," that the words "test" and "testing" are here used very broadly. This "theory" is actually a kind of check list, a set of categories which are intended to include all the elements which make up a social organization. As such it serves both as a system for classifying data and as a constant reminder of all the areas of information which must be explored. It is, then, an analytical tool and as such can be "tested" only in the pragmatic sense that it can be shown to be useful for diagnosis and as a basis for the further steps of science. These steps would include the development of measuring devices of the greatest possible precision and, as the ultimate goal, the formulation of theories to describe what is generally true of a given class of facts and to express or explain the relationships among phenomena. In this connection Malinowski's concept is particularly valuable because it is not confined to any particular kind of institution such as American industry but, rather, makes it possible to use the same terms in discussing organized human activities of all kinds in both primitive and civilized societies. Or at any rate one of the purposes of this book is to show that this is so, that a concept conceived in studies of primitive tribes and of contacts between primitive and civilized societies applies readily to modern industry.

Of his concept, Malinowski, who was by no means a rash or foolish man, said,

> Each institution, that is, organized type of human activity, has a definite structure. In order to observe, understand, describe, and discourse theoretically upon an institution, it is necessary to analyze it in the manner here indicated, and in this manner only. This applies to field-work and to any comparative studies as between different cultures, to problems of applied anthropology and sociology, and indeed, to any scientific approach in matters where culture is the main subject. No element, "trait," custom, or idea is defined or can be defined except by placing it in its relevant and real institutional setting.[1]

These are sweeping statements. They mean that no student of human affairs can dispense with the theory. They mean also that no administrator or executive can really know what he is doing unless he follows the principles laid down in the theory. Actually, however, the assertions are not quite so radical as they sound. To some extent these principles are used all the time. The most successful leaders, more or less intuitively, probably use all of them. Others seize upon one or another. Hence, on the whole, they have a commonplace ring. They are plausible because they are realistic. For the same reason they are hard to apply. Real life almost never yields to quick and easy analysis. The facts in any situation are hard to get, hard to assess, and hard to interpret. Worse, it is hard to know what facts are relevant, how to classify the facts, and how to relate them to each other. The institutional theory is of assistance on all these points. It is, in a way, a kind of guide for research. It says, "You have to know about this, this, and this, and you've got to know how these elements effect one another." Conscientiously

1. B. Malinowski, *A Scientific Theory of Culture,* p. 54. Inasmuch as any orderly behavior is cultural in nature, the full scope of this statement is readily apparent.

followed, the theory is a stern taskmaster which seems to require more work than less systematic approaches. On the other hand, it consistently points in the direction of genuine solutions whereas random activity more often than not wanders into dead-end streets and not infrequently complicates the very problems it is intended to simplify. It is, of course, by no means an all-purpose tool. Its strength is that it clearly designates all the elements which enter into organized activity. It tends to prevent limited approaches and to force the investigator to consider all relevant factors. Alone, however, this concept is static rather than dynamic; hence other concepts are needed. Some of these are set forth and used in this book. Others, notably the very valuable contributions of psychology, are neglected here.

This neglect is intentional and unavoidable. Industry knows a good deal more about psychology than it does about sociology. In fact, it sometimes appears that industry expects psychology to solve, ultimately if not right away, all its problems. This psychology cannot do. It might if it were possible to psychoanalyze every individual in industry, but psychoanalysis would still be worthless without some knowledge of the cultural milieu in which individuals operate. Even then, the task would be so time consuming and expensive that it would be out of the question. What industry and other kinds of institutions need is some way of getting at human behavior en masse, of understanding social structure as such, and of attacking group problems on the group level. Doubtless such an approach will always leave some individuals who need special attention, exceptions to whom the exception principle can be applied. Given a reasonably functional social system, however, most people get along fairly well and do not cause each other too much trouble. The few who cannot are problems for the psychologist. But if a social system is so disorganized that many people cannot adjust themselves to it the fault is likely to lie with the system rather than the individual personalities, and it is to the system that attention should be directed.

Parenthetically, it should be noted here that psychology contributes more than a basis for dealing with abnormal individuals. Through job placement, for example, it can be helpful in putting individuals into positions suitable to their personalities, that is, in relating different kinds of "normal" individuals to specific parts of the social structure. Parenthetically also, it may be remarked that, as the preceding sentence suggests, sociology and psychology are not independent sciences. They stand at different points on a continuum concerned with behavior, and they constantly have to call upon each other. Hence psychological considerations, by implication at least, are to be found in any discussion of social functions.

Ideally not only sociology, social antropology, and psychology but all the principal disciplines of social science should be employed to yield a complete analysis of any complex social situation. In the ensuing chapters the psychologist will unquestionably find many points which could be further developed by means of his techniques and theories, and doubtless psychological field work would have explained many matters of theoretical and practical interest. It might, for example, have shown more definitely why certain individuals emerged as union leaders while others were passive or why certain executives persisted in behavior which workers found consistently irritating. Moreover the techniques of attitude testing might well have aided materially in revealing the system of values and ideas which played such a marked part in the developments described in later chapters. To the same end and perhaps others, the methods of small-group study might also have been helpful. Equally it is obvious that the economist has a very special field of interest in an industiral institution. Nevertheless, because Malinowski's concepts make it possible to describe and analyze "the relevant and real setting," they have a kind of temporal priority. They delineate the structure in which the psychologist finds individuals operating and which supplies elements which the economist must frequently assume.

Certain assumptions are implied when one chooses a single case as the basis for a broad discussion. It is assumed, for example, that some uniformities pervade the whole class of phenomena being investigated. In this instance the assumption seems to be justified for the following reasons:

First, no factory in our culture operates in a vacuum. The people who run it and those who work in it know about other factories and about the cultural theories concerning what a factory is supposed to be. Hence they try to use the common knowledge which is available to them and to some degree make their own factory resemble others.

Second, information concerning other factories and factories in general demonstrates that the factory used as a sample here conforms in many respects to typical factory patterns. Such information in this case comes from three principal sources: from industrial literature; from people in industry including employees and executives in other factories, union officials, and specialists in trade associations; [2] and from observation of other industrial establishments. Indeed it is probably safe to go further and say that many of the patterns are shared not only by factories but by economic enterprises of other kinds.

Finally, application of sociological generalizations to this factory suggests the view that this particular social unit conforms to principles observable in any social unit. Malinowski's institutional theory was developed largely from studies made in the Trobriand Islands and of societies in Africa. The great disparity between such societies and the industrial phase of our society reinforces the conclusion that the theory is sound, since it applies so readily to both.

Nevertheless it should be emphasized that the particular factory which supplies, so to speak, the working model that illustrates the various points discussed is of no special importance except to the people connected with it. Any experienced industrialist will recognize familiar elements in it and, also, elements which are peculiar. Like every other factory it is, in some respects, unique. The workman who called it "home" would not feel quite at home in any other. The personnel, despite their knowledge of the world at large, have their own values, traditions, and history. The location of the factory is uniquely its own, and even some of the machinery, tech-

2. For instance, the American Management Association and the National Industrial Conference Board. This list of informants could be expanded considerably to include government officials, social scientists, and others whom the writer has heard speak or with whom he has discussed the subject.

niques, and practices are not precisely like those to be found anywhere else.

The warning contained in the last paragraph may not be necessary. No sensible person would expect any one case to be identical
with others. If one wanted to build a bridge, he would not suppose
that he could overlook local conditions like terrain, the traffic the
bridge would be expected to bear, and so on. On the other hand,
he would not expect to forget the scientific principles which govern
bridge building. It is not uncommon to meet industrialists who
think they can transport something intact from somebody else's
plant to their own. They think, for instance, that if a union contract
works well for somebody else it will do as well for them. On the
other hand, another familiar person is he who says, "That may work
for them, but we are different." There is something to be said for
both views. One man wants to rely on generalization, the other on
discrimination. Both processes are useful. Suppose one has three
aces in a game of poker. By generalization from other poker games,
from things he has heard other players say, and maybe even from
books, he knows three aces make a good hand. But does he bet in-
discriminately? Some players do, but suppose a usually cautious
chap raises the first bet. Then discrimination is in order: the situation differs from the average one in which three aces are likely to
win. Or suppose there are six wild cards in the game. It hardly seems
necessary to labor this point. It is a good idea to know what poker
hands are usually worth. It is also smart to keep alert on every hand
in order to be able to work from the general to the particular.

Any book which pretends to be scientific should include some
statement of the methods used in collecting data and some indication of the qualifications of the author. The reader should be given
an opportunity to discriminate, that is, some basis other than plausi-
bility and internal consistency for evaluating the material he is
examining.

Most of the information on the New Freedom Products Company
was obtained during eight years of "participant observation" as an
employee. This procedure is admittedly the reverse of what is considered orthodox by those who believe that data should be gathered

according to a carefully prepared schedule so that no pertinent material will be overlooked. Recognizing that this point of view has validity, it is arguable nevertheless that the method followed has an advantage in that the author was at the factory as an "insider" who came there to work without any preconceived notion as to what he was setting out to discover. Moreover, although, as already stated, the participant observation from which the material here presented has been drawn is in a great part retrospective, the author supplemented this information by visits to the factory and numerous interviews undertaken after he had terminated his employment and after the present study was conceived and outlined. Experience at the factory was preceded by two years of graduate work in sociology which certainly sharpened the author's interest in the institution as a social unit and also, perhaps, provided some degree of objectivity.

The experience which comprised the original "field work" consisted of a period spent as a sort of executive apprentice, during which the author learned to "make the product" under the tutelage of plant workers and foremen. While this education was superficial, it did include operation of most of the important machines in the three production departments, and, more important, it provided an opportunity for hours of conversation with many workers. Subsequently the author worked in the laboratory, the time-study department, the accounting department, the traffic department, and the payroll department and as administrative assistant to several of the officials. The last-named post was nebulous in definition but invaluable for experience, since it was a catchall for miscellaneous assignments. Among these were partial supervision of tenement maintenance; purchasing of materials and supplies; study of personnel problems; conduct of training courses; field trips to observe the use of the product; special assistance to the management engineer who devised the new organizational scheme in 1942; a study of the administration of the state unemployment compensation act and of the Fair Labor Standards Act; and attendance at meetings of the American Management Association, the National Industrial Conference Board, and two trade associations to which the company belonged. During the spring of 1941 the writer served on a special committee of personnel executives for the state

manufacturers' association to study employment problems related
to war production and later worked with the first state panel of the
division of the Office of Production Management which later became Training Within Industry. In 1942, the author became manager of training, office manager, and chairman of the suggestion
committee. During his last 14 months with the company he was
personnel manager in charge of employment, personnel services,
training, and labor relations. During that period the union was
organized, a contract was signed, and the pattern of union-management relations began to appear.

Such a background raises the question of bias. May not the
writer's point of view be influenced by his close association with
management and circumscribed by provincialism resulting from
long absorption with the problems of a single small plant? Every
effort has been made to eliminate these possibilities and to achieve
scientific detachment. In field trips to the factory after this study
was begun, informants were sought from among employees who
seemed likely to represent typical points of view and from among
those who had given some evidence of rebellion against the management. Three of them were union officers. The president of the
union brought plainly into the open the question of the author's
possible bias on the side of management. He asked whether the
author had really severed all connections with the company. When
assured that the author expected never to return, he offered to
give freely any information desired. He told many details about the
inception of the union organization and also provided invaluable
information about the Italian immigrant workers. The union vice-
president signified his confidence by saying that he wished the
author was still on the management's contract-negotiating committee because "we all knew the way you looked at things." Other
informants included all of the company officials (one of whom had
interested himself for 40 years in collecting company memorabilia),
all of the production executives, and numerous other employees
in both the plant and the office. Every effort was made to secure a
proper representation of informants in accordance with years of
service, ethnic background, and special points of view. Some selec-
tions were made because information from employees suggested

that certain others could corroborate or contradict data already collected.

It is worth noting that the work of the personnel manager differs from that of other executives in that he often acts as the workers' advocate. He acts frequently in the role of an employee's confidant and is in an advantageous position to gain the confidence of workers. Perhaps because in previous employment the author had been a wage earner himself, he found the role of worker advocate especially congenial.

One source of information was, unfortunately, not tapped. In the course of years a number of employees had left the company, some of them because they were dissatisfied with treatment they received there. A few ex-employees were interviewed, but none of these expressed serious criticism of the company. None was found who was still disgruntled. A chance talk with a man who had been discharged for drunkenness revealed resentment directed primarily at one executive but not at the company.

On the point of possible provincialism in the author's point of view because of his long affiliation with a single factory, it may be said that before he entered employment at the New Freedom Products Company he made investigations of several other factories, and later, in preparation for writing this book, he examined a wide range of industrial literature. Furthermore, he has sought opinion and comment from numerous workers, executives, and scientists who were not connected with this factory.

The problem of methods is a peculiarly interesting one. At what point does intimacy with a subject preclude objectivity? Contrariwise, at what point does objective detachment cause the observer to miss pertinent facts? One can but admire the field worker who has his project so well in hand before he goes to the field that he can follow a rigid schedule, obtain all the data he requires, and return to his desk with everything he expected to obtain before he left it. To the subject of such studies, however, the results may be less than impressive, for the methodical worker may come away from the field with *only* what he expected to find, leaving behind him data of great intrinsic worth. On the other hand, the observer who achieves intimacy with the group may become so absorbed in detail that he loses perspective. Hence, he too may overlook pertinent material.

As has been noted above, the present investigation was begun upon a foundation of material already gathered as a member of the social group under analysis. A preliminary examination of this previously acquired information was made in the light of sociological theory. Gaps in the information soon became apparent, unconsidered details gained significance, and some problems which had seemed of great magnitude assumed lesser proportions. With this new perspective as a guide, field trips with specific purposes in mind were undertaken. Even on these trips, however, formal questioning proved to be less valuable than mere listening. As one informant remarked, "All you got to do is turn 'em on and let 'em run. They'll tell you everything if you give 'em time." This was true of workers, foremen, executives, and "officials" alike. They all seemed to enjoy talking; and it was noticeable that as they talked they sometimes became so immersed in their subject that they appeared to be reliving the incidents related. For example, an employee with 50 years of service started an interview with a pleasant account of his early recollections. At first his mood was one of affectionate loyalty for the company, but, as he recalled other happenings, he became bitter and angry and revealed material which more than rewarded the interviewer's patience. In other interviews unexpected sidelights on the attitude of immigrants toward authority turned up and helped to explain certain apparent inconsistencies in the study. In such cases previous plans had to be discarded so that new areas of information could be explored. Finally, some interviews suggested others. For instance, an employee might recall events which involved other people who were still available, and this made it possible to check the first account by allowing others to relate the same incidents. Accounts of specific episodes, moreover, were often more informative than generalized memories of conditions, although in most cases these accounts tended to confirm the memories. Thus the employee who remembered being asked to be on the watch for officials with whom other workers wanted to talk lent validity to the general statement that in the old days officials often came to the plant and conversed with workers.

In all of the interviews the author's familiarity with the plant and the personnel was extremely helpful. There was no need to learn the plant's own language of technical terms, and local allusions struck familiar chords.

In approaching the subject of change at the factory, it was found useful to set as a base period that representing conditions as they existed about 40 years ago. To reconstruct these conditions it was necessary to rely largely upon the memory of persons who were then in the employ of the company. Such historical reconstruction is admittedly hazardous, and it is not claimed that a full and accurate picture of the institution as it was four decades ago was obtained. One fact seems to be well established, however—namely, the existence of frequent personal contacts between the officials and the workers up to World War I and that this "personal system" was the fundamental basis of organization. This was corroborated by repeated statements of representatives of both groups and documented by anecdotes in which such contacts figured.

It is likely that the "golden-age fallacy" influenced the reminiscences of the older employees, and some of this has probably crept into the historical sections of this book. Whether or not the "good old days" were as pleasant as nostalgic memories suggest cannot be demonstrated. Very likely they were not. After all, the base period used here as a point of reference for measuring subsequent change is arbitrary. The company had been growing and changing for more than 60 years before that, and there is no reason to suppose that life within it had been unvaryingly happy and harmonious. On the other hand, throughout the first 60 years or so of its existence the company was small, and workers and officials saw each other often and intimately. The evidence indicates clearly that the frequency of these contacts diminished gradually but steadily during the past 40 years and that such developments as organization of the union cannot be understood except in relation to this change.

An especially pleasant task is to record indebtedness to the many people whose generosity and acumen made writing this book possible. Many "Teasville" people, in and out of the company, had a hand in the work, although most of them did not know it. Many will know who stands behind the pseudonym, "A. D. Perkins." To my mind he was a great man, very much like those who made the eighteenth century the Age of Enlightenment. Jack of many trades, master of several, he mastered life in a way which qualified him for the title of philosopher in the finest, traditional sense of that word. The assistance and friendship of the union president and vice-president were a source of pleasure and profit. I hope the other "New Freedom Products Company" people who were so helpful will not mind my mentioning these three separately; every employee I asked gave me freely of time and knowledge. Raymond Kennedy sweated over nearly every line here printed (except these) and a good many which went into the wastebasket. He was not responsible for what is said, but if the words make sense the credit belongs to his memory. I must acknowledge also the help and inspiration given to me by my other colleagues at Yale and by my teachers there, especially during the preparation of the doctoral dissertation upon which much of this book is based.

The name here used for the factory is fictional. Employees and executives alike have freely given information which they considered confidential in nature. Hence it seems no more than courteous to protect them as far as the disguises here employed can do so. Names of places, of individuals, of products, and of some materials have also been disguised, but nothing has been done to alter the essential nature of facts. Consistency of this disguise has required concealing the true names of such documents as the company's history. In such cases they are referred to under disguised names as though these were the real names, and occasionally quotations have been altered to the extent of substituting fictional names for real ones. No specific notes have been made to show where this was done, but the reader will probably be able to detect such changes wherever they occur.

In summary, this book deals with a single factory as an institution. Its implications, however, are not limited to this factory. It attempts to demonstrate the utility of certain sociological theories, especially Malinowski's concept of institutions, for analysis of organized groups of people of all kinds. Further, it is an essay into the important field of industry, into the basic maintenance ways of our society. This particular factory has changed from a primary group in which social control and the satisfaction of numerous needs were accomplished through personal contacts to one in which important contacts were depersonalized. From a single, closely interlinked hierarchy of owners and workers, there has developed a complex administrative organization. A union has been organized. No sociologist needs to be told that depersonalization has created serious individual and personal problems, that modern problems of social control and administration are as pressing as any with which mankind is faced, or that relations of management and labor have repercussions which affect all society. This book does not propose to solve these broad problems. It does attempt, however, to show how social science can be used in an attack on some of them.

SECTION ONE

*History and Description
of the New Freedom
Products Company*

CHAPTER ONE: *The Town and the Shop*

TEASVILLE. Teasville is, in the opinion of the people who live there, a small town. Its 4,000 inhabitants live on scattered farms and in small communities in the valley of the Dillingham River. Through the valley runs a busy highway. Two ridges, known locally as mountains, stand like walls on the eastern and western boundaries of the town. The road to the nearest large city, 15 miles away, climbs over one of these ridges.

The flat river bottom is composed of fertile, sandy loam. This supports broad tobacco plantations—the most important of which are now owned by large, out-of-town corporations—dairy and poultry farms, market gardens, and apple orchards. Teasville center, with its bank and several large stores and service establishments, draws trade not only from the whole township but from neighboring towns as well. Three other smaller centers—Hall's Corners, West Teasville, and the Flats—have post offices and stores of their own. One of these centers has a small factory, its own fire department, water district, grammar school, and churches. The others are much more closely integrated with the life of the Teasville community.

The New Freedom Products Company, a manufacturing enterprise, is the largest single employer in the town. About 300 Teasville residents work in its plant and office. Nevertheless, many local people would resent having Teasville called a one-factory town. The tobacco plantations provide work for many, and other agriculture, including dairy and other farms, is an important enter-

prise. In addition Teasville is the dwelling place for numerous
people who work in the city. Service institutions, including stores,
garages, the bank, the electric company, and the schools, among
which are two private boarding schools, employ considerable numbers. Figures detailing the distribution of employment are not
available, and local citizens vary in their opinions of the relative
importance of various occupations. Some think of the community
as primarily residential; others look upon it as a manufacturing
town; still others regard it as most important agriculturally.

Upon reflection many describe it as a diversified, prosperous, independent Yankee village—Yankee, even despite the fact that many
citizens were born in or trace their immediate ancestry to Poland,
Lithuania, Italy, Germany, France, Sweden, Ireland, and other
European countries. That, Teasville feels, is the way of New England towns, and on the whole Teasville considers itself fortunate
in the quality of its immigrant population. By common consent,
Teasville's "foreigners" have proved, with some exceptions, to be
good, industrious, sensible people who make good citizens.

Outsiders, as Teasville calls people who do not live there, often
remark that they find it a "sleepy," isolated place. As they come
over the mountain from the city, they feel they are leaving the busy,
modern world and entering a pleasant, distant valley. To some
extent this impression is an illusion. About 70 per cent of the local
young people find husbands or wives in other towns, often in the
city but almost always within 20 miles of home. Many Teasville
people shop in the city or drive there to the movies in the evening.
Some wealthier people have winter homes in Florida or summer
homes "at the shore"—that is, on Long Island Sound. Trips to
Boston or New York are frequent, and before World War II longer
trips—to Mexico, Canada, California, or Europe—were not uncommon. Nevertheless the feeling of isolation or, as Teasville
people prefer to call it, "independence" persists.

The New Freedom Products Company reflects this feeling. Officers and employees alike smile complacently when outsiders tell
them that their company is "unique." Both executives and workers
have knowledge enough to assess the accuracy of this phrase. Nevertheless, they tend to interpret it as a compliment. Officers take active

interest in a number of state and national trade associations, try to keep abreast of modern industrial developments, and from time to time apply borrowed techniques to their problems. The workers belong to a C.I.O. union and look to it for guidance. Foremen and minor executives also keep in touch with the world through professional or semiprofessional organizations and technical or industrial publications. Sometimes both executives and other employees complain that the company is behind the times. Sometimes they feel that they have solved problems more quickly or more effectively than have most industries.

Company officers and most of the employees identify themselves closely with the town. For generations the officers have lived close to the factory, which is half a mile from Teasville center. The majority of the employees live within a mile of the factory—most of them in factory-owned houses. It is company policy to keep its buildings from becoming a local eyesore, to keep them inconspicuous, and as far as possible to make them an asset rather than a liability to the appearance of the town. Outsiders passing the factory occasionally mistake it for a school.

As the largest single employer and property owner, the company is, of course, a tremendous factor in the life of the town. It owns approximately 180 dwelling houses in Teasville in adition to its factory buildings. Occasionally the company is criticized for "trying to run the town." On the other hand, although executives are encouraged to undertake public duties, the company refrains from influencing them in these activities. Care is taken to avoid the appearance of bringing undue weight to bear on the community.

Five miles from the main plant, in the neighboring town of Herford, the company has a branch which manufactures some of the same products and employs between 60 and 70 people. This was originally a competitor, but it was absorbed into the New Freedom Products Company early in the present century and now is so closely integrated with the rest of the company that it might almost as well be another department in Teasville. Being small, the Herford plant is less important in the life of the town in which it is situated, although there is something of the same interdependence between the factory and the community. There is little rivalry between the two plants, but employees are frequently shifted from one to the other, and in several cases some members of a family work in Teasville while others work in Herford. The main office is in Teasville, and in most respects the two plants can be regarded as one. When the union was organized, activity was apparently equal in both plants, and in choosing officers the members seem to give little weight to the plant a person works in. In another company, this geographical separation might be significant; in this case there is no reason to believe that it warrants much special attention.

In addition to its houses in Teasville, the company has about 70 in Herford. Ninety per cent of the employees live in these two towns. Ten per cent live elsewhere. Before World War II only a handful lived in other towns, and even these had homes within ten miles of one or the other of the plants. Today the two communities no longer supply all the employees the company needs.

THE COMPANY—1945. The company's principal product is special equipment for certain basic industries. This product incorporates highly inflammable materials, and its manufacture requires special technical knowledge. Manufacturing techniques have been developed to such a high degree by the company that for the past 30 years it has been virtually alone in its field. Direct competition is at a minimum.[1] A device not manufactured by the company, however, is used for the same purposes as the company's basic product. This competition makes it necessary for the company to maintain maximum quality and prevents it from charging monopoly prices. It is possible that ultimately the company will lose its market for this product. In addition the company manufactures a textile product, primarily for its own use and secondarily for sale to manufacturers of certain consumer goods. The textile mill employs approximately one-third of the factory employees. Another textile was manufactured by the company for its own use until 1932. This material is now purchased from southern mills. Some of the executives believe

1. Three other companies manufacture the same product, but two serve different geographical areas and the third is so small that it offers no effective competition.

that it would be more economical to purchase the textile now manufactured, but others think this product is needed to support the
company's overhead and to ensure quality. The company is seeking
additional products to manufacture. The principal products, with
small modifications, have important military uses. In both world
wars production expanded greatly.

During the decade preceding World War II, employment stabilized at approximately 360 (295 or so at Teasville, 65 at Herford),
including executives and office and plant employees. This figure is
now used as representing "normal" employment, although when
the company returned to peacetime schedules after the war the
payroll remained near or above 400, and there was need for about
25 more workers. Salaried employees (not including foremen) rose
steadily to 76 in 1944 and dropped only to 71 after the war.

Of the 240 employees who pay rent to the company for their
houses, 68 live in Herford and 172 live in Teasville. These
tenants, in some cases, have wives or children who also work for
the company so that the figures do not represent the total of employees who live in company houses. Unfortunately separate
figures to give this total are not kept by the company. In Teasville
there are five principal housing areas. Two of these are preferred
by office employees and foremen. Until about 1930 one was reserved for Italians and another for Slavs, but today this ethnic
segregation seems to be disappearing although the neighborhoods
retain some ethnic character. The houses are mostly four- or six-
room, wood, frame structures, although those of the president and
some others are larger. Basic rents for employees are $20 a month
for four-room houses, $24 a month for six-room houses, and up to
a total of $30 or even more per month, depending upon such
"extras" as oil-burning furnaces and hot-water heaters, most of
which are optional with the tenant. Houses are reserved for employees but are occasionally rented to nonemployees at a rental
50 per cent higher than that for employees. It is customary to
raise rents only when there is a change of tenant. Hence some
employees who have been in their houses many years are paying
as little as $10 or $12 per month. The company's books show a
substantial loss on tenements each year.

It is a policy of the company to give preference in employment to residents of the towns in which its plants are located and especially to relatives of employees. It is also a policy of long standing to give special consideration to long-service employees. In the company's employee manual a special point was made of the number of long-service employees on the payroll: "At the present time [January, 1945], there are one hundred and twenty-four employees on the payroll who have been with the company more than twenty-five years, sixteen who have been here over forty years, and three who have received awards for fifty years service." The heading above this statement is "A Good Place To Work."

Prospective employees come first to the office. The main entrance to this is a pretty arched doorway with a fanlight above it. A picture of this door is used on the employees' manual and other company publications as a symbol for the official "open-door policy." Symbolically the door is always open to any employee who has a problem which he wishes to take up with the company's highest officials.

Inside the door is a lobby which used to be one of the three main rooms where all office and executive work was performed. At the rear of this lobby is another door, a closed door, which was put there to prevent the officers from being disturbed by the noises made by people outside. This door, too, is a symbol. It seems to shut the officers away from the rest of the company. It was not there when the building was built many years ago. It was not there 40, 20, or even ten years ago. It was put there in 1944—about the time the employees voted to organize in a local of the Textile Workers Union, C.I.O. There was considerable executive debate before the door was installed. It was feared by some that it would symbolize a barrier between the employees and the officers. It does do that.

Traditionally the "open door" still exists, although employees of all ranks have commented that the union closed the door. One company officer even wanted its picture removed from the cover of the employee manual, which is called *Working Together*. Historically the open-door policy worked. It worked largely because the company owners and officers went out through the door to the plant almost every day—frequently several times a day. It was convenient for employees to stop the officers and ask them questions, get solutions for problems, obtain favors, praise, and satisfaction—to get, if nothing more, definitive, trustworthy answers to their queries.

Some of the older employees still think of the door as being open even though they do not like to go into the "nice, clean offices" in their "dirty working clothes." But most of the employees either do not think about the door at all or, when they do, do not believe that it is really open—not open in any important sense. They have been told that the management wants them to place their problems before foremen or lesser executives, and they know that the union contract provides that problems having to do with "hours, wages, and conditions of work" must be handled through channels which only in rare instances lead to the officers' sanctum.

Nevertheless the two doors retain their symbolism. The open door recalls days when the company functioned as a primary group, primary in the sense that Cooley emphasized when he said such groups were characterized by intimate, face-to-face association and cooperation, with intimacy and "fusion of personalities" as the essential factors.[2] Cooley included men and women brought together by their occupation in his list of primary groups. He believed, moreover, that with "a little common interest and activity, kindness grows like weeds by the roadside." Despite its sentimental flavor, perhaps because of it, this idea of Cooley's is pertinent here. Perhaps a majority of New Freedom Products Company people would agree with him. Today some older employees make remarks like the following: "It used to be fun going to work. But nowadays you hate to get out of bed in the morning and go down there." On the other end of the scale, company officers who are nearing retirement sometimes wonder: "If we had a real shirt-sleeve ownership—four or five men who would get down to work early and stay late, who would get out in the plant and see to things themselves—if we had that I'll bet we could do away with a lot of the departments we have now and still get along better than we do."

2. C. H. Cooley, *Social Organization*, p. 23.

The symbolism of the two doors is emphasized here because they represent the basic change which has occurred in this company. In the transition to a formal, impersonal organization from one which was closely knit by frequent, consistent, intimate, face-to-face contacts between individuals on all levels of status, several processes familiar to sociologists are revealed.[3] In addition some of these processes are illuminated in ways which are not so familiar but which are nevertheless significant. Today the company is an institution in which there are several levels of status—officers, executives, foremen, and operators—and in which communications from those on the lower levels must pass through those on intermediate levels. Much of the transition was unconscious. Changes in the roles filled by those on various levels occurred not because they were desired or foreseen but because they were automatic consequences of other changes which appeared desirable. To say that the union closed the open door is not true. In a more real sense the organization of the union was an effort on the part of employees to re-establish effective contact with the "officials" who retained control. On the other hand, the company's formal reorganization chart, prepared in 1942, was an effort to establish patterns for relationships between various statuses in the hierarchy. This hierarchy developed with increased size, increased complexity, and altered conduct on the part of the occupants of certain roles.

3. "Status" refers to the position of an individual in the organized system of relationships of his social group, in this instance of the factory personnel. Thus the owner-management group, called "officials," constitutes one status, while the workers constitute another. The phrase "level of status" refers to the ranking of positions in the prestige system of the group.

"Role" represents the dynamic aspects of status. It is what the individual has to do to validate his occupancy of a given status. To some extent the personality of an individual may influence the way in which he performs the role. In some circumstances an individual may concentrate on some aspects of the role to the exclusion of others. There is a permissible range of freedom in interpretation of the role, but variation cannot go beyond this range without affecting other roles and thus disturbing the organization of the group.

Cf. Ralph Linton, *The Study of Man*, p. 114, and *The Cultural Background of Personality*, pp. 76–78. See also C. S. Ford, "The Role of a Fiji Chief," *American Sociological Review*, 3, No. 4 (Aug., 1938), 541–550.

The alterations in these roles, notably in the roles of the company officers, are a most important key to understanding all the changes which occurred. Until about 30 years ago, the officers' roles included activities which facilitated face-to-face personal relations. The roles of the employees included corresponding activities which depended upon the activities of the officers. The officers made regular trips into the plant and frequent visits to the company housing areas. The employees utilized these opportunities to gain various satisfactions: answers to questions, consideration for requests, commendation, and the like. Through these mutually dependent activities the workers were bound closely to the company. They felt security in the personal interest of important company functionaries. Their desires for information and prestige were gratified, and they received direct, authoritative attention for their requests for such things as more pay, housing repairs, financial assistance, and promotion. Through casual talks they learned "from headquarters" whether the company was prosperous or not, and they felt, as many of them still recall, "that they belonged." Beginning about 30 years ago, officers commenced to give more of their time to other activities and less to their plant visits. Their roles included fewer and fewer opportunities for personal contacts with plant employees. This meant that the activities of the employees which depended upon these contacts became, to an increasing extent, senseless. Their roles included useless parts, and for a long time no adequate substitutes were supplied. Moreover, although the need for utilizing the personal contacts was intermittent, it was a strong need when it was felt, and absence of ways to satisfy it was also disturbing.

As will be shown later in this section, no dramatic outburst signalized the changing relationships. There was, instead, a slow, groping, cumulative uneasiness. *Anomie* [4] may be too strong a

4. Cf. Émile Durkheim, *De la Division du travail social,* pp. 397 ff. Durkheim describes *anomie* as occurring in growing industries when changes in relationships between employers and employees place strains upon the workers. He says that such conditions demand new organization of the group but that when changes continue rapidly interests in conflict do not have a chance to find a mutually satisfactory relationship. Elton Mayo develops the same thought and relates it to American industry in *The Social Problems of an Industrial*

term to apply. The situation was, however, anomic in character.
There were repeated individual frustrations, occasional more or
less aimless attempts to establish new patterns, and several efforts
by management to create substitutive expedients. The latest and
most comprehensive of these efforts was, as has been said, the reorganization of the company. The most drastic effort by the employees was the establishment of the union local.

The chart which outlines the company's functional reorganization is presented opposite. It constitutes a formal statement of
rules governing interstatus relationships in the organization.[5] The
lines indicate the channels of communication, authority, and
responsibility. The boxes indicate the persons through whom
communications are supposed to flow. For example, an operator is
supposed to bring all questions to the attention of his foreman,
who may either make a decision and thus dispose of the matter or
take it to the next higher member of management, and so on up
the line. Strictly interpreted, this means that on any subject im-
plying dealings between the management and the individual
factory worker contact may be made only through the person
indicated on the chart.

Attention should be called to the relationships between the
operators and the persons above the long horizontal line which
separates the policy-making group from the other executives. The
policy-making group consists of persons known in plant parlance
as "officials." The officials have traditionally been the owners and
managers of the company. At present they effectively represent the
ownership and are the "top management." They represent the
ownership in two senses. First, even to the few employees who may

---

Civilization (especially pp. 9–15). Mayo believes that modern industry has
largely passed from the stage in which "effective communications and collabora-
tion were secured by established routines of relationship" (p. 13).

5. Cf. Geneva Seybold, "Company Organization Charts," Conference Board
Reports; Studies in Personnel Policy No. 64, p. 3: "An organization chart is a
diagram of relationships and interrelationships within an organization, as of a
given date. It shows lines of authority, responsibility and control . . . Frequently company charts indicate the major duties or activities concomitant to
each office or position."

CHART I. ORGANIZATION CHART

THE NEW FREEDOM PRODUCTS

COMPANY

Notes: Most of the higher officers are descendants of John Drew or relatives. These relationships can be discerned from the names given in the appropriate boxes. In addition, half a dozen relatives occupy lesser managerial positions.

Several names, notably those of B. D. Perkins and F. F. Perkins, appear in more than one position. At the level of manager, four other individuals hold dual posts. Three of these are indicated by enclosing pairs of boxes in rectangles. In the fourth instance, the manager of the textile mill is also manager of textile sales.

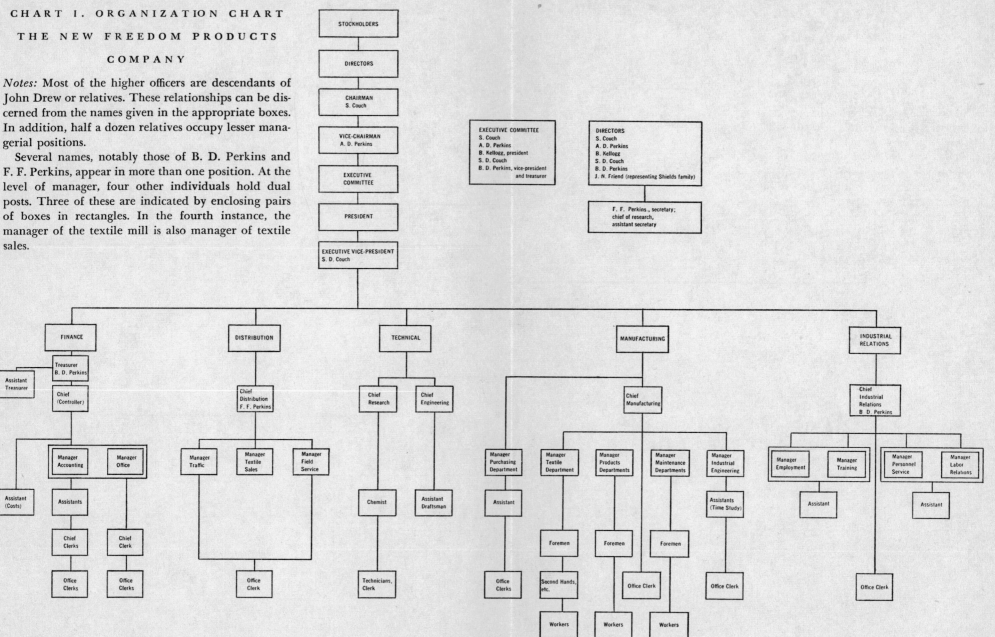

know that the present officials do not actually own a majority of the stock, they stand as surrogates for the owners. Most employees do not know whether the officials own full control or not but apparently assume that they do. Second, the officials evidently enjoy the full confidence of all stockholders: there has been no effort on the part of the absentee stockholders to dictate or question company policy. The officials have posts which, the company's history indicates, can be disturbed only by death, retirement, or promotion.

In the light of these facts the box representing the stockholders can be disregarded in further analysis of the institution. The same is true of the box representing the directors. Five of the directors are members of the executive committee, that is, of the group which effectively comprises top management. The sixth director represents the ownership interests of the Shields family, which until six years ago was the dominant branch of the founder's descendants in both ownership and management. This director is not a resident of Teasville and appears at the company offices only occasionally and briefly for directors meetings. If he participates actively in management decisions, his influence is not apparent to the rest of the personnel and is reflected only through the activities of the officials.

Two of the officials—the chairman and vice-chairman of the board of directors—now are in a semiretired status. They come to the office irregularly and are seen by the employees infrequently. They no longer have specifically assigned duties in active management, except that they participate in the deliberations of the executive committee. They are regarded as "elder statesmen." Because of their age and the state of their health, they are not expected to be active.

The other three officers—the president, the executive vice-president, and the vice-president-treasurer—are the active officials. The relationship of the first two is clearly expressed on the chart. The relationship of the vice-president-treasurer is less clear, since his functional assignments fall below the line between officials and other executives. His post on the executive committee, however, is the key to his technically higher status. Incidentally,

the individual who occupies the post has three distinct roles. The
first is that of an official, the second is that of head of the finance
division, which is not very different from the first, and the third
is that of acting chief of the industrial relations division. This
last role is on a quite different plane, and the incumbent feels
that the tendency to confuse the two levels of status represented
by his roles is a disadvantage. Sometimes it is hard to tell whether
he is acting in his official or his executive capacity.

The status of the remaining officer of the company, the secretary,
is difficult to describe. The title carries some prestige and implies
some duties in connection with the executive committee and the
board of directors. It does not, however, include policy-making
authority, and thus it differs from the other officer posts. This difference seems to be a real one in practice. Hence, despite the title,
this individual may be regarded primarily as one of the divisional
chiefs.

The titles of assistant officers—assistant treasurer and assistant
secretary—have some prestige value but aside from that are practically meaningless. The assistant secretary is chief of research, and
his role depends upon that fact. The assistant treasurer has no
other title, but his status is equivalent to that of the divisional
chiefs.

The divisional chiefs may be called "upper middle management" [6] as compared with the managers, who are "lower middle
management," and the foremen, who constitute what could be
called "lowest management." [7] The controller is one of the di-

6. The terms "upper middle management," etc., are not intended to be
technical in nature, although "middle management" has been given some
standing by Mary Cushing Howard Niles in her book, *Middle Management*.
According to Miss Niles (p. 1), "Every organization of several hundred persons
has a group of junior administrative officers . . . They are subject to pressure from above by their chiefs in top management . . . from below by the
supervisors . . . and sideways by colleagues whose departments . . . are interrelated . . . with their own . . . These officers comprise middle management."

7. Foremen are so viewed by top management, and most of them seem to
identify themselves with management, although this identification is recent
and not complete.

visional chiefs. The position of the treasurer between him and
the official group is a hang-over from an earlier conception which
had an officer assigned to each of the divisions.

While each of the divisional chiefs has other employees in line
of authority under him, the important line organization [8] is the
manufacturing division. With only a handful of exceptions, all
plant employees are in this division. Therefore, it is on the manufacturing division and the industrial relations division that attention is here focused. These two divisions are technically
supposed to handle all the relationships between the officials and
the factory employees.

Under the chief of the manufacturing division are four managers, three of them continuing the line authority, the fourth
acting in a staff relationship within the division. The first of the
line managers, the manager of production, is in charge of two
manufacturing departments and the shipping department. These
include the provinces of a number of foremen. The manager of
maintenance is in charge of seven so-called "service departments"
like the machine shop, the plumbing shop, and the auto and outside department, with the foremen attached to them. The manager
of the textile mill has only the textile department under him,

8. Cf. the following definitions of line and staff organizations by Geneva
Seybold, "Company Organization Charts," pp. 4–5: "By line organization is
meant that authority and responsibility flow in an unbroken line from the
highest executive through the various lower levels to the employee who has
least responsibility in the organization and no authority over others . . . the
staff relationship appears when managerial functions become complex enough
to require the need of assistants who will [aid] the executive by investigating
problems for him, assembling information, developing plans and providing
advice. The responsibility of doing remains with the line man . . . Staff
services are supplied both by individuals and by units or groups . . . In addition to the Personnel Department, other departments in manufacturing
companies usually regarded as staff units are the Purchasing Department, Public Relations Department, and the centralized Research Department. Within
each of these departments there is line authority, but from the standpoint of
. . . other departments, all members of the staff departments are staff
men . . ."

See also Elmore Petersen and E. Grosvenor Plowman, *Business Organization and Management,* pp. 101, 181–182.

but this is the largest unit in number of employees and it has the most complex internal organization. The industrial engineering department makes all time studies, is concerned with the job-evaluation system, and engages in various activities designed to promote efficiency.

The industrial relations division serves in a staff capacity in the entire organization, but its work is primarily devoted to services for the manufacturing division. As a staff function, it has no direct authority over workers, foremen, or others in the manufacturing division. Its duties are carried out through programs and advice requested and, in strict theory, authorized by the manufacturing division. Under the chief of industrial relations are four departments—employment, personnel service, labor relations, and training. The first three of these are headed by the manager of personnel, the fourth by the manager of training. An assistant to the manager of training also does most of the employment interviewing and introduces new employees to their jobs. A young woman acts as assistant to the manager of personnel, and there is a clerk who serves all four departments. In practice the manager of personnel has a relatively free hand, since the divisional chief has several other duties which require his time. Typical of the duties officially assigned to these departments are:

Employment: recruitment; placement and induction of new employees; employee records

Personnel service: hospital; clinic; safety promotion; group life, hospital, and disability insurance; workmen's compensation; recommendations on pensions; cafeteria; tenement standards and allocation; recreation and entertainments; suggestion system; and merit rating

Labor relations: wage surveys; collective bargaining; labor laws

Training: apprentice school; educational programs; foremen's meetings and training; Training Within Industry program [9] (adopted as permanent by the company)

All of these executives, their assistants, and the clerical staff of

9. This program consists of brief courses for supervisors on job instruction, improvement in job techniques, and handling grievances. During World War II it was created and sponsored by the federal government.

the company are housed in the office, in the laboratory across the lawn from the office, or in the office annex close to the factory gate. There are 76 office employees, half of whom are officers, executives, assistants, or technicians. The rest are clerks, bookkeepers, stenographers, and secretaries whose jobs include varying degrees of responsibility.

The offices of the personnel departments and of the manufacturing and maintenance executives are in the basement of the main office, which has doors on the factory side. The factory hospital is also on this floor. Thus employees tend to use doors other than that pictured on the manual when they come to the office.

THE PLANT. Beyond the office, about 200 feet from the highway, is the main factory gate. It is guarded by an old man, who is supposed to control parking, assist visitors, admit authorized persons, and see that no one occupies spaces reserved for officials. Inside this gate are the buildings which house the manufacturing and maintenance departments. Well-kept lawns, shrubs, trees, and vistas of the factory brook make scenes of surprising beauty.

These buildings are nearly all one-story structures built of the same native red sandstone as the office. They are scattered over several acres in order to reduce the hazard inherent in the nature of the materials used. Some buildings are busy. Others are at times practically deserted, since brands of the product for which they were originally used are now seldom manufactured. In some rooms, where the danger from inflammable materials is greatest, women work alone and have signal flags which they can hang outside their doors to summon the foreman. In other rooms groups of operators tend their machines. In the textile department many men and women work in the main building. In nearly all cases each operator has his own job or battery of machines for which he is individually responsible. Thus the application of the individual incentive system is relatively simple. Each employee's own work is easily measured.

Automobile trucks, which supplanted horse-drawn wagons less than ten years ago, move materials and products from building to building. A messenger makes regular rounds carrying papers and notices for the bulletin boards. All departments are interconnected by telephone. These channels and the travels of minor executives and foremen are the principal means of communication. Only infrequently does one of the company officers "make the rounds."

Each of the maintenance and production departments has a foreman directly in charge of the workers. Some of the foremen are called "general foremen." This is a relatively new title which had more meaning during the rush days of World War II than it now has. Technically a general foreman is in charge of more than one department or shift. The foreman of the boiler room, where there are night as well as day shifts, also superintends the watchmen and gatemen. On the other hand, the foreman of Department No. 2 attained this title when his department was operating on several shifts and retains it now that it has only one. In practice, the prestige of the foremen seems to depend more upon age and ability than upon title.

The situation in the textile mill demands special attention. The manager of this department, which includes approximately 80 employees, is primarily interested in technical aspects of manufacturing and in markets. While he stands in a line relationship to the employees under him, in practice this relationship is frequently by-passed by the general foreman, who often reports directly to the chief of manufacturing. Under the general foreman is a foreman through whom all relations with the workers are supposed to flow. Under this man are two second hands, a third hand, an instructor, and the "head fixer." The second hands have their time assigned almost equally between maintenance work and supervision of operators. The third hand has about a quarter of his time assigned to supervision and the balance to machine maintenance. The "head fixer," who ranks with the second hands, is primarily a mechanic with a very few employees working under him. He and the instructor act in strictly staff capacities in the mill. While the situation in the mill is not clearly defined, the second and third hands are supposed to give direct supervision to the employees in their respective areas. This creates

a somewhat anomalous situation, however, since these minor
supervisors are classed as workers, not as part of management, and
are represented by the union. One of them is a union steward.

CHART II. TEXTILE MILL ORGANIZATION

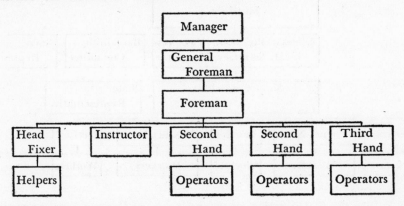

This chart has not been officially drawn up; it represents what is apparently
the formally approved organization. However, both the foreman and the
general foreman have direct contacts with workers, and, to represent the organization correctly, lines by-passing intermediate boxes would have to be
drawn from each of these positions to positions lower down. The same might
be said of the manager, but in this case relationships are contrary to official
policy and are actually informal responses to convenience and personality.

In some respects the situation in the textile mill is analogous to
that which obtained formerly in the company as a whole. The
foreman has direct, face-to-face contact with all the operators as
does the assistant foreman, and the lines of relationship are thus
multiple, running from the workers directly to each supervisor and
also through the various lesser supervisors to the general foreman.

Charts I and II outline the company's formal rules governing
interstatus relationships of the personnel. As might be expected,
activities do not always conform to rules. Some of the deviations
will be treated elsewhere in this study.

One important addition to the official pattern is to be found in
the relationships with the workers through the union. These have
acquired official character, despite the fact that they are not noted

on the organization chart. They are codified in the union's agreement with the company.

CHART III. UNION ORGANIZATION

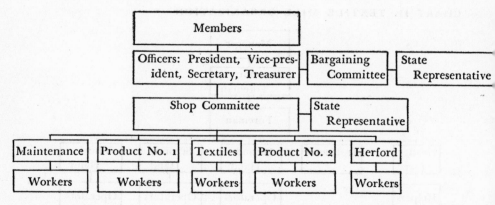

While the organization of the union local has not been formally plotted, Chart III closely approximates the relationships which are supposed to exist within the local. The workers appear at the top of this chart as the group which, in a democratic organization, holds the final authority. They appear again at the bottom as the individuals for whom the authority is exercised.

The stewards are the direct representatives of various groups of workers in presenting grievances. They are not precisely subordinate to the shop committee, but the shop committee is the next group which handles grievances. The officers exercise executive authority, subject to the sense of the meetings of members.

The manner in which the union integrates with the technical organization of the institution is indicated by the official grievance procedure as outlined in the union contract: Grievances are presented by employees to foremen, with or without the assistance of the steward in charge of the employee's department. If the grievance is not settled at that stage, it is discussed by the steward and the department manager. The next step is a discussion between a member of the union shop committee and the director of manufacturing. The final step, before the matter is sent to outside arbitration, is a meeting of the management committee and the union shop committee. The management committee consists of the director of manufacturing, the director of industrial relations, and the manager of personnel. Because he is an officer of the company and believes it a mistake for an official to participate in such deliberations, the chief of industrial relations does not ordinarily attend these meetings. In point of fact, only two such meetings were held in the first six months after the first union contract was signed. No grievance has gone so far as outside arbitration.

The union also participates in the officially recognized organization in two other ways. The bargaining committee exists temporarily to negotiate contracts with the management committee, and the officers of the union frequently confer with the manager of personnel or with him and the chief of manufacturing regarding proposed decisions with respect to wages, hours, or conditions of work. Proposals of both union and management have led to positive action and, in one case, to joint action.

Perhaps the most important current deviations from the prescribed norms which are summarized above are those which tend to by-pass the foremen and the line executives and to beat a path to the personnel department. Many employees take their problems directly to the personnel manager. He in turn often handles these problems, makes decisions, or obtains answers, except in cases which should be handled through the union grievance procedure. He and the chief of the industrial relations division even encourage these contacts, since they tend to strengthen their relationships with workers. On the other hand, such contacts also tend to weaken the position of the line functionaries. Hence they might in time weaken the organizational structure. Problems so handled frequently have to do with housing, sickness, requests for financial aid, or other personal matters. One such problem was of wider significance. In this case the foremen expressed a desire to establish closer personal contacts with the officials. They approached the manager of training on this point, and through him periodical dinners were arranged at which foremen could mingle with officers and other high executives.

CHAPTER TWO: *History of the Company*

It is practically impossible to draw a diagram of the technical organization of the company prior to the preparation of the chart described in Chapter 1. Relationships and responsibilities were not defined. So many permissible paths of interrelationship existed—many of them duplications—that attempts to chart them would produce a tangled spider web. It is not surprising that when the increased activities of war were added to this situation it was found necessary to reorganize.

FIRST PERIOD—1836–1866. The company was founded in 1836 as a partnership between an English firm and Henry Trotter, a Yankee resident of Teasville. Trotter had read of the invention of the product which the English firm manufactured and arranged with them to manufacture the same product in the United States. In 1839, dissatisfied with reports from the American venture, the English concern sent John Drew to Teasville to represent their interests and to keep the books. Drew soon became the dominant figure in management. His descendants continue to operate the company, and relationship to his family has been and still is important in determining the prestige accorded executives.

Relationships between employees and the partners were intimate and informal, as the following excerpt from the company's history shows:

. . . the original operations were conducted in a small plant improvised from some of Trotter's farm buildings . . . the workers were gathered up from the neighboring farms. They were all of Yankee stock and their fathers had probably fought in the Revolution. When an order was forthcoming the hands were called in, the product made up, and the workers went back to their farming . . . [Some of them evidently resented the British connection and], being bred of hard pioneering life on self-sustaining farms, they [tried to learn how to make machinery and manufacture the product on their own. This shortly led to competitive manufacturing.] Another Yankee characteristic of the early days was that of considering the small factory as merely the complement to farming operations. Accounts were not always strictly segregated, tools were freely borrowed back and forth, and in the busy sowing and harvesting seasons the manufacturing business took a back seat.

Although he was sent from England to introduce more businesslike methods, it is significant that Drew himself fostered the completely personal ways of the day. He had been a licensed preacher in England and soon was preaching more or less regularly in Teasville and neighboring communities. He also acquired a farm of his own. The following quotations from a paper written years later and given to one of Drew's daughters by one of the dozen or so early employees is a clear description of the employer-employee relationship. This woman wrote:

I was forchinate in my life at the age of 20 in giting occupation in manifactrin establishment it gave me work for a number of years. it was not far from home in The Flats east side the river my father and mother was well pleased that I was so forchinate.

I commenced work April the first 1843 I bordid in the the family of Mr. Drew as he was agent of the company and gave me imployment. they had 4 little children john jenny mildred Molly. I liked the family vary much. Mrs. Drew was a vary nice lady and vary good.

I got a long good with my work and all my friends thought
a grate deal of Mr. Drew as a good person and a sitisen.

The balance of this "parchment" tells how Drew took its author and one of his daughters to the city and helped the employee
establish a savings account, which made her "a little proud but
not haughty pride for haughty pride is gust before a fall I did not
wont to fall for I had money in the bank." It also relates the death
of the first Mrs. Drew and reveals that "Aunt Jennifer," as this
woman was known to Drew's descendants, became almost one of
the family.

This first formative stage of the company lasted until 1866. During this time Drew became sole managing partner and personally
attended to every phase of the business. His earliest assistant in
accounting and financial matters was one of his daughters. Later
John Turner became his office assistant. Samuel Knowlton, who
came to the company to help set up the first machinery, acted as
superintendent and engineer. Sales, employment and employee
welfare, and public relations were entirely in Drew's hands. Probably employee welfare and public relations would have been more
or less meaningless phrases to him, but there is evidence that his
activities included many duties now given such titles.

The relationship between Drew and his employees continued
on a purely personal basis—very much like that between a farmer
and his hired hands or a country storekeeper and his clerks. Drew,
in the words of one of his grandsons, "hired, fired, advised, and
helped, not only the workers but their families. He took a leading
part in civic matters and religion."

The factory in the Flats burned down in 1851, and a new factory was built on the present site in Teasville. According to the
company history, many of Drew's

> . . . old factory people followed him . . . There was
> "Auntie Knowlton" with her sons, . . . The payroll book
> lists other familiar names: "Aunt" Jennifer Stevens, John T.
> Drew [a son], Mildred Drew [a daughter], Henry Wilson [a
> stepson]. All the Drew children at one time or another took
> temporary employment in the shop, usually during their

summer vacations from school. This custom has been carried
on with each succeeding generation . . . At that time there
were about 28 employees, who averaged 41⅔ cents per day
in pay. William Knowlton was high paid man at fifty cents a
day, while young Wilson, Drew's stepson, received twenty-
five cents a day. Drew's son John was a machinist. Drew's own
salary was $500 per year, plus a share of the profits.

The fire had an additional effect:

> For the first time it began to dawn on the busy and harassed
> Drew that hand in hand with expanding sales and—produc-
> tion should go careful attention to safety measures and plant
> cleanliness . . . [He] revamped his new factory and employed
> thereafter stone and brick in all new construction, thus laying
> the foundation for the present character of the plants . . .
> Increasingly from 1859 on, all operations were decentralized
> into small one-story buildings well separated from one an-
> other. Plant cleanliness became more and more a corner-
> stone of the company's manufacturing policies, because not
> only was human life and safety involved but it was early
> realized that careful attention to such details bred in the em-
> ployees an equal care at their work, which resulted in a better
> quality product.

SECOND PERIOD—1866–1887. After the Civil War it became obvious to Drew that he could no longer continue his single-
handed management. Business was expanding, and the number of
employees rose from 50 to 75 and so on year by year until the
payroll stood at 100 when Drew died in 1887. Three sons-in-law
provided the managerial assistance which Drew, whose own son
died in the Civil War, needed. All three eventually became partners and as a triumvirate managed the company after Drew's death.

Until Drew died, however, he, his eldest son-in-law, and William Knowlton, the superintendent, were the management as far
as the employees were concerned. Knowlton was a son of Samuel
Knowlton, who came with Drew to Teasville. A fair inference,

borne out by recollections of old employees, is that Knowlton's prestige was similar to Drew's. Very likely it depended upon tradition and the long association of his father and himself with Drew. Knowlton's authority, however, did not equal that of Drew; he could not fire or hire without Drew's permission. But he was "much beloved by the help" and had a good deal of influence regarding transfers, promotions, and discipline. Thus, while the relationships between the employees and the management were no longer with a single man they continued to be fundamentally the same. There were only two status levels—the owner-management trio and the employees. Interstatus contacts were frequent, face-to-face, and personal.

Incidentally, while it is obvious that any person now living who worked under Drew would have had to be young at the time, it is interesting that he is recalled as a sort of paterfamilias. One pensioned employee remembered him clearly and reminisced at some length at the company's "Long Service Award" party in 1945. He said, "And there was an old feller named Drew there then. I remember one day he came in where I was working and took me by the ear. 'See here,' he says, 'You get on out to that ball lot and play for an hour. After that you come back and work.' Yes sir, that was a long time ago. Won't never be anybody run up a record for service like I done. I started work when I was twelve. They got laws that'd prevent anybody from getting an early enough start these days."

THIRD PERIOD—1877–1907. Between 1877 and 1907 Drew's three sons-in-law were the management, with T. J. Shields as managing partner. Shields' son was also added as a partner during this period. Two other members of the family followed this young man into the company and were given miscellaneous plant and office jobs in preparation for later elevation to management. The partners all had duties which took them into the plant regularly, but toward the end of the period they began to feel the increasing pressure of office duties. As an earnest of the kind of progress which ultimately had profound influence on the company, the younger Shields introduced (and kept) the company's first double-entry bookkeeping system and operated the first typewriter. Unlike their predecessors, the third generation of officials were all college graduates.

The fact that in a partnership each partner is liable and hence feels responsible for the whole company had a strong influence. Each believed that he had to be familiar with and participate in all phases of the business. The prospective young executives were expected, through their own initiative, to make places for themselves. In so doing they tended to encroach upon territory regarded by the older members as their own. Friction and confusion therefore characterized managerial operations. The fact that management was housed in a three-room office and that all occupants of the office were usually within speaking distance of each other meant that informal conferences were in session nearly all the time. Through these, differences were resolved and confusion was kept within bounds. Employee relations were still on a completely personal basis, and the employees knew which of the members of management could most advantageously be approached on various problems. For example, if an employee wanted higher pay or "to get away with something," he would go to the official who could be expected to give a generous and perhaps hasty decision. If he was in trouble and wanted "evenhanded justice," he would see another official. If he desired promotion, personal favor, or financial aid, he would speak to still another.

The working foremen began to play a more important role, but they could only recommend disciplinary action. The employees relied on the partners for decisions in all matters of importance. Moreover, since the partners were frequently in the plant and since some of them made it a custom to take Sunday walks through the housing districts, they were easily available in case questions arose. Disciplinary action with respect to an employee was taken only after a conference of the partners.

Working conditions were in sharp contrast to those of the present day. Hours were long—from 7 A.M. to 6 P.M. on weekdays and from 7 A.M. to 3:30 P.M. on Saturdays. Pay ranged from 75 cents a day for youngsters in their early teens to sums of $1.00 to $1.25

per day, which were common for grown men. Foremen might receive $2.00 per day. Older employees recall leaving their work to go out and play ball or go swimming "two or three times a day" or clambering up to a loft to box in a ring they had set up. One even remembers going to the office to get money from an official to buy a new baseball to replace one lost in the brook. Such activities were, of course, "extralegal." Workers were presumably paid to work all day. Unofficial but well-recognized standards of what constituted a day's work existed, however, and were enforced by the workers themselves. Provided these standards were met, employees felt safe in enjoying themselves. This was somewhat less true in the textile departments, where continuously operating machinery kept turning out materials which had to be handled as they came. Even in these departments, however, there was plenty of time for "chasing the girls," sliding up and down aisles, or learning new jobs by watching others work.

Business expanded rapidly after 1900, and buildings and equipment were added to keep pace with it. The first of the modern immigrant group, a Pole, arrived in that year, soon to be followed by others. Neither management nor employees recall any marked change in employee relations. In the opinion of one officer, however, the seeds of change had been sown. He recalls that officials were beginning to feel the increased load of administrative work and believes that the incoming immigrants were making it a little harder to maintain close acquaintanceship with all plant workers.

THE CORPORATION, EARLY PHASE—1907–1917. The company was incorporated in 1907, and official titles given to the officers represented the first formal division of authority. This division, however, was more formal than real. The partnership state of mind persisted, and management was shared as it had been before. Every one of the six officers was a member of the Drew family, and all were accorded full official prestige by the employees.

In the office the staff was enlarged to include two assistant bookkeepers and a stenographer, under the direction of Drew's old office assistant.

In the plant William Knowlton remained superintendent until he was succeeded by his son, J. R. Knowlton. A second superintendent was added shortly before World War I. He was instrumental in increasing worker output during the war. His method was "mainly persuasion and reason," and an officer who worked with him recalls that "after all, people will work if there's work to be done and you ask them in the right way. Dave had a great way with the help, and there was plenty of work." No longer were there ball games or other such obvious pastimes. Continuous application to work was more definitely insisted upon, although work was by no means so steady and arduous as it was 20 years later. Neither was it so well paid. In 1914 top day rates for workers were $4 for a plumber, $3.50 for a carpenter or a machinist, and $3 for one of the men in the power plant. Top foremen's rates were $6 per day for the foreman of the larger textile department, $4 for the other textile foreman, and $4 for the foreman of the machine shop. Male operators' and laborers' rates varied from $1.20 to $2.75. The highest female rate was $1.75. Workers were at the plant an average of nine hours a day, six days a week. While records of output are not available, subsequent studies indicate that the pace was slow and that there were plenty of opportunities for relaxation and gossip.

With the increasing number of persons on the management level and the diversification of managerial duties, contact between the officials and the employees decreased, but in other respects relationships remained largely unchanged. Officers continued to discharge plant duties and to make regular visits to the housing areas. Even the fact that during World War I employment rose to approximately 700, divided between the two plants, did not seem greatly to alter the personal nature of the contacts between the officials and the workers. Employment at Teasville just before that war was approximately 300.

Employees recall with approval the close contact they had with officers. One of them, now a foreman, relates numerous incidents which illustrate the situation more effectively than reminiscent appraisals of it could. He recalls that before World War I the younger Shields personally discussed job transfers with him and arranged increases in his wages. The following occurred in 1916, when the company was extremely busy:

> I remember not long after I went to X room. Old Mr. McGuire,[1] Jim McGuire's father, used to make spools, and he was getting to be a pretty old man. He'd go over to the storage bin, and sometimes he'd only bring one spool at a time. And he'd kind of stagger, and I was afraid he would fall into one of the machines. Used to carry one of them red bandana handkerchiefs sticking out of his side pocket, and more than once I picked up one of them blue tipped matches. Didn't have signs up all over the way they have today. Well finally I spoke to Franklin [one of the two superintendents], and I guess he mentioned it in the office because Mr. Shields' come out. He got me and Mr. McGuire together, and he said, "We have decided that you have worked long and hard. And you always done good work too. And we think it is time you had a rest. So we have decided to pension you, and we will give you $55 a month, and you can have your house free as long as you live. But that doesn't mean that your wife can have it free after that."
>
> "Now," he says to me, "Johnny, is that a fair proposition?"
> "Yes, it is," I says, "very fair."
> So the old man was pensioned off. You know, it's a funny thing about them pensions. Practically everybody that gets one dies pretty soon after.

This informant also relates that at an earlier date William Knowlton

> was really part of the officials. One time the girls in the textile mill was asking for more money. Few days later William Knowlton come out. He had a way of carrying his head on one side, and he had a white beard. The girls was sitting around talking and some of them was doing fancy work of their own.

1. This use of title and last name probably results from the fact that McGuire and Shields were older men and are now dead. Age and, especially for Catholics, death both influence the use of the word "Mr."

Wasn't a one of them working. Well Mr. Knowlton stood there watching and pulling on his beard. Then he says, "Well, looks as if everybody's working fine today. I suppose tomorrow you'll all be asking for more money."

Looking back on the period, older officers of the company do not appear to believe that the personal relationships were quite so close as they had been previously. They believe that the presence of immigrants who spoke little or no English was a barrier. The immigrants themselves tend to contradict that opinion. They believe that the officials knew them well and were interested in them.

The first Pole, who came to the company in 1900, later became a leader in the Polish community and often acted as interpreter between officials and his non-English-speaking countrymen. Hence, although he is so intensely loyal to the company that he will say nothing which might cast discredit upon it, his testimony is of some value. Especially valuable is his naïve phrasing. He regrets that the officials do not come into the plant and talk to the employees as often as they used to: "It is good for them to come out. *The master should see the servant.* That way it makes good feelings."

Evidently his people expected to respect their employers and were grateful for whatever attentions they received. This estimate is corroborated by younger Poles, who believe that their elders were, perhaps, too respectful—until the children came home from American schools and explained democracy to them.

A similar picture is drawn by Italian immigrants, who started coming to the company in 1910 or 1912, ten or a dozen years after the first Poles. The present president of the union, who came to the company directly from Italy in 1916 when he was thirteen years old, discussed the situation with some of the older Italians and analyzed it for the author as follows:

In those days when one of the children of an Italian family went to work his family would tell him to "look up to the boss, to honor the boss, and do exactly as he said because he was the boss." This was because in Italy no one questioned superiors. "You were not part of the government. The government, the king, owned you, It was that way in schools, which were run by the government. The teacher told you what to do and what to believe and you were supposed to ask no questions . . . After a while the kids would come home from school here and tell the old folks they were wrong: it was not that way in America."

These reports indicate a docility on the part of many employees which must have simplified management of a large percentage of workers. Of the approximately 300 employees in 1914, 122 had Slavic names and 26 had Italian names. Thus well over half the workers were immigrants from southern and eastern Europe.

The Italians, like the Poles, vividly remember personal contacts with the officials. The informant mentioned above recalls advice as to how to approach different officers and which ones to avoid. Moreover, he says, older Italians greatly liked the officials "because sometimes they would come around and shake them by the hand or pat them on the back and *call them by name.* They say it was wonderful to have somebody like that call them by their own names when they were 'so far away.' " This man's evidence is particularly valuable for several reasons. Because he came here as a boy, he speaks both English and Italian well and stands midway between the first- and second-generation immigrants. Also he is intelligent and perceptive, and he sought information directly for this study at the writer's request.

It is interesting that the most severe instance of friction between employees and the management occurred soon after World War I. This is still referred to as "the strike," although it was participated in by only a few employees and they stayed off the job only a few days. Significantly, these employees were almost all what might be called "old Americans" or "old immigrants" rather than Poles or Italians. It is said that the strike quickly collapsed when two of the instigators sought to curry favor with management by returning to work. The one effect observable 20 years later was the unpopularity of these two. It is notable that the older employees rather than the immigrants were those who seemed to be most sensitive to changing relationships between themselves and management. The immigrants regarded their contacts with the officials as better than anything they expected.

THE CORPORATION, SECOND PHASE—1918–1936. The history of the company up to this time was one of close personal relationships between the employees and the small group of men who, through executive control, ownership, and family affiliation, represented "the Company" to the entire personnel. Certain trends which tended to modify the consistency of these relationships have been noted. The number of officials increased. The introduction of such administrative devices as double-entry bookkeeping and cost accounting complicated office duties. The number of employees increased. Foremen and superintendents appeared, to begin the creation of a hierarchy of positions between the employees and the officials. To a limited extent the hours spent by officials at the factory began to differ from the working hours of the plant employees. Nevertheless, the roles of the officials still included activities which bound the personnel to the institution by personal ties. The idea of giving special attention to "personnel" or "industrial relations" occurred to no one. The economic interests of the employees and their needs for recognition, prestige, and security were, in the main, satisfied. Moreover, the tradition of personal cooperation, neighborliness, and friendliness, which was rooted in the community mores, was unaffected.

There is no evidence that this tradition was weakened very much for at least another ten years, and there is evidence that to some extent it still exists. On the other hand, the activities which supported it commenced to alter with growing rapidity. Thus, while an arbitrary date may obscure the gradual progress of the change, it is probably safe to set the year 1928 as confirming the transition from personal to impersonal relationships between the officers and the factory workers. In that year a modified Bedaux incentive system was installed, and to the employees "the system" symbolizes the change from one era to another.

The sons-in-law who succeeded Drew had all died or retired by
1919, but, with one exception, their successors were close relatives.
This exception, moreover, became such an intimate family friend
that he acquired what amounted to family status. Two fourth-
generation descendants of Drew were graduated from college and
came to the company in 1926. They became assistant officers in
1929 and fullfledged officials a few years later.

By 1938 policies and administrative decisions were determined
at meetings of the officials called irregularly by the president instead of in the frequent informal meetings facilitated by proximity
in the old three-room office. It was still traditional, however, for
all officers to keep their doors open, and the partnership idea—
that all officers participated in all phases of the business—remained strong. There was no logical division of executive duties,
and as time went by even the subordinates became conscious of
friction and inefficiency.

The elaboration of office and technical duties is reflected in the
growth of the salaried personnel, exclusive of foremen. There were
23 such employees in 1922 including the officers, 25 in 1927, 37 in
1930, and 39 in 1935. Purchasing, sales, and administration were in
the hands of the officers. Other office personnel were grouped into
the traffic, accounting, and payroll departments. The employment
of a trained chemist in 1917 paved the way for the research and
engineering departments. After 1928 the standards department,
which controlled the incentive system, was added to the office payroll.

With the establishment of the standards department in 1928, its
head was given supervisory duties and the title of assistant superintendent. It was characteristic of the anomalies which could develop that he was in some respects subordinate and in others
superior to one of the two older superintendents. Here, as elsewhere on the managerial level, friction developed, and only intimate contacts with officials prevented such sore spots from
becoming dangerous to the organization.

Final authority with regard to employees remained in the hands
of the officials. Foremen and superintendents could recommend

employment of individuals, discharges, and discipline, but action required approval from the officers. An effort was made to maintain personal contacts with the employees, especially through the younger officers, but the situation became less and less what the officials liked to believe it was. In retrospect older officers are now amazed that the personal relationships were maintained as well as they were. In 1942, however, when the reorganized management chart was produced, and even in 1944 when the union was organized it was impossible for some officers to believe that they no longer had close personal friendships with a large proportion of the workers. For their part, employees continued to classify the officials with respect to the type of problem about which they preferred to consult each one. Opportunities to see these men without going to the office, however, became progressively fewer. Some employees did, of course, come to the office, and some made opportunities to see officers at their homes or on the street. The open door existed, but officers did not go out through it so frequently as they formerly had.

The Teasville payroll reached its highest point in 1918 when there were 508 wage earners—more than there were at any time during World War II. From this point the wage-earner payroll dropped to 354 in 1922, rose to 464 in 1927, dropped to 339 in 1930 and thence to the depression low of 239 in 1933. It then stabilized at approximately 260 until the effects of World War II were felt. Herford's payroll went from 211 in 1918 to 130 in 1920, up to 168 in 1927, down to 97 in 1930, and from there declined steadily to 61 in 1940.

Before discussing further the influences which tended to destroy the old personal organization of the company, it should be noted that severe symptoms of disorganization did not appear until after 1936, except on the upper management level. The employees gave no marked signs of dissatisfaction and, although they now trace ensuing dissatisfaction to the incentive system, they do not recall specific instances until some years after "the system" had been in operation. The following statement by an officer of the union summarizes recent interviews with a number of employees:

I would say that the help have lost confidence in the company. You know, they don't believe the company when they say a thing any more. You remember when they gave that 10-cent raise just before the union election? Well, it was right after that that a lot joined up with the union. They thought the company just did it to fight the union even though they [the company] said they didn't . . . It came on gradually. The help used to feel close to the management. It really started with the point-system.[2] Henry [the chief of production] might have called Delio [Tiani, the union president] a liar about that, but there was cases where rates were cut. Maybe not very many, but there was cases, and that was enough . . . If they'd left that system the way Dorff [the representative of the firm who installed the system] set it up, they would be all right. But they didn't . . .

This informant and others agree that distrust is directed not so much at the officials as at lesser executives and time-study men.

Evidently forces which delayed the effect of the disorganizing influences were at work, or, to phrase the matter differently, conservative forces remained strong enough to withstand the pressures created by various changes.

One of these conservative forces was to be found in the old partnership idea. This was not only maintained in certain practices of the officials but was justified verbally as well. Management was said to be based upon "cooperation," and reference was occasionally made to a letter written by the English partners in 1837 to outline the form the partnership should take. This said, in part, ". . . our hope and earnest desire has been and is, to benefit all parties and to set out in a manner that will conduct us to a happy issue a healthfull and prosperous business by securing the hearty cooperation of all concerned." The phrase "the product family" was used in various ways. The product family was construed to mean the descendants of John Drew, especially at occasional dinner parties attended by executives and their wives. At other times it meant the friendly relationships maintained be-

2. That is, the incentive system, which is described more fully later in this chapter.

tween the company and other manufacturers, domestic and foreign, who made the same basic product. Finally, it was used to refer to the close relationships between employees and officials, and a point was made of the fact that not only the official family but many employee families as well had several representatives in the company's employ.

Other conservative forces were to be found in the traditional respect of the immigrants for authority, in the fact that H. S. Shields, while he was president, continued the practice of Sunday walks through the employee housing areas, in the fact that many employees maintained the appearance of tradition, and finally in the fact that the depression, commencing in 1930, provided an opportunity for the last important functional expression of the personal relationships and also created a situation in which employees hesitated to press for advantages.

There can be no doubt that Shields' influence was a strong one. During his last illness, which lasted for nearly five years, employees constantly inquired about him in terms that showed affection and respect. In 1937, for example, a sixty-nine-year-old woman, still active as a worker, said, "How's Harry Shields? I went to school with Harry, and for all his money I wouldn't change places with him now. It's too bad. He's a good man, and I wish he was back with us." At his funeral long lines of employees filed by the coffin, and many, both men and women, wept. They said of him, even as late as 1945, "He was all right. *You could talk to him.*" Following Shields' retirement in 1935, inability to get direct attention for housing problems contributed materially to the sources of employee dissatisfaction.

Reference has already been made to the respectful attitude of immigrants. An incident which occurred in 1935 emphasizes this point. At that time several employees were sent to train operators in the new plant of the Mexican subsidiary. One of these, an Italian, became homesick and came back to Teasville. Soon afterward he came to the office and asked to be sent back to Mexico. Later it was reported that the older Italians had met, censured this man, and directed him to make his request so that the Italian community's prestige would not be damaged.

With respect to tradition, the observations of three young men who were employed "to learn the business" and presumably become executives in 1937 are pertinent. All three of these men had had experience in other companies, and all three were impressed with the loyalty and understanding of many of the older employees who instructed them in various plant operations. All three, it should be noted, were also impressed with the fact that many employees were dissatisfied and that harmony was by no means so characteristic of relations with employees and even foremen as the officials asserted. Nevertheless, the remarks of an Italian, who had been with the company 25 years, to one of the new men are significant. Using nicknames, he inquired for H. S. Shields' daughter and for the two newest family executives. "I know them since they are so high. Sammy, he'sa got a littla boy now. That'sa good. He grow up to be president of company like his'a gran'-fadder."

Employees were and still are heartily agreed that the company handled matters excellently when it was necessary to lay off employees during the depression. Workers were treated as individuals. As few were laid off as possible, and these were chosen from families which had other members working for the company. Hours were cut and cut, until at one time some employees were working only 21 hours every other week. Employees believed, however, that this was better than not working at all. A welfare committee, headed by H. S. Shields, gave assistance in cases of unusual hardship, and here again the importance of personal factors was stressed.

It will be noticed that these conservative forces represent attitudes based on the past. The activities which supported these attitudes were by this time weak and intermittent. The officers did not maintain close, intimate, and continuous personal contacts with the employees. They were either busy at their desks or, frequently, away from the plant. Moreover, it is questionable whether they could have known so many employees as well as their predecessors knew the relatively few who worked for the company a generation before. In addition, although the open door was intended to maintain direct lines of communication between the

officials and the workers, there was a growing hierarchy of intermediate statuses. Finally, an impersonal device, the incentive
system, had put one important set of employee interests on an
automatic rather than a personal basis.

THE CORPORATION, THIRD PHASE—1936–19——.
The first attempt to organize managerial duties on a logical basis
followed the retirement of H. S. Shields in 1935. The new president, A. D. Perkins, a grandson of Drew, believed that the elements
of confusion were so strong that the company had been held together principally by Shields' powerful leadership. This, he
realized, was enforced by an unusual personality and backed by
the largest share of ownership. Perkins thought that the company
should be so organized that it would not be dependent upon the
strength of a single individual.

His plans included gradual reassignment of duties on a depart-
mental basis: coordination of executive activities by regular,
formal committee meetings; standardization of operational activities through special committees; and training of new young men
for executive positions.

Although meetings were placed on a regular schedule, several
committees established, and three young men, all related to the
official family, employed for executive training, the fact that the
partnership idea still remained basic prevented much progress
toward functional reorganization. Each officer still believed that he
should participate in all phases of the business, and as a group
the officers were unwilling to delegate executive authority to subordinates. The two branches of the official family were divided on
policy: one tended to cling to the older methods, the other to look
for new means to efficiency. Appeals to traditions of cooperation
and friendliness were frequent.

For several years these appeals were sufficient to prevent extreme disorganization, but when the wartime rush of business
arrived the organization was unable to stand the strain. In the
meantime the weak spots steadily became more apparent. Individual officers hesitated to make decisions without consulting

others. Subordinates were unable to take action without consulting an officer, and often the officers were not available or postponed decisions. At times subordinates were forced to wait for
hours or even days for superiors who were tied up in meetings
or away from the factory. This was especially discouraging to
men directly concerned with personnel problems. Every new employee hired had to be approved by an officer as did every
employee's physical examination, every granting of special overtime, every change in a manufacturing or maintenance schedule,
every assignment of a house, every important disciplinary action,
every time study, and many more details. These delays inevitably
reacted upon the people in the factory—both foremen and
workers.

The confusion inherent in the organization was not entirely
evident to anyone but A. D. Perkins. Most of the personnel experienced momentary irritations but failed to attribute them to
the failures in the organizational system. Doubtless the slow pace
of business throughout most of the 1930's obscured the situation.
The official personnel remained about as it had been, except that
Shields was forced by illness to retire. Office personnel increased
from 39 in 1935 to 47 in 1940, even though the volume of business
changed relatively little. When business reached towering heights
during the war, the number of office employees soared to 76.

The company history, printed in 1936, paints an ostensibly
pleasant picture, but its complacent recording of managerial assignments inadvertently reveals a number of troublesome inconsistencies. The following excerpts are useful because they illustrate these, because they reflect official attitudes, and because they
outline policy on employee relations:

> . . . operating details are largely in the control of Mr.
> Samuel Couch, assisted by Mr. Kellogg and Mr. S. D. Couch.
> Certain important raw materials . . . are purchased by the
> Messrs. Couch. All general purchasing is done by Mr. Hatch
> [and some purchasing was done by two other officers] . . .
> The care and upkeep of plant, grounds, tenements, and
> [material storage areas] are a matter of general executive

concern but the service departments in the main come under the eye of Mr. Samuel Couch, assisted by his son and by Messrs. Hatch and B. D. Perkins. Company financial affairs are similarly a matter of general concern . . .[3]

Perhaps the most important work revolves around the standards and planning department . . . [which establishes the bases for the incentive system and standard costs, prepares] production schedules for all foremen and actively follow[s] the carrying on of service and maintenance work . . . accident prevention and safety work.

The plants are run by superintendents and . . . foremen . . . There are nineteen trained foremen—men of long service and experience and thoroughly equipped to handle men and machines. Upon them devolves the full responsibility for conducting their departments in such a way as to produce a quality product efficiently, safely and economically . . . In recent years efforts have been made to increase a sense of responsibility in the foremen by holding general foremen's meetings every two weeks . . .

Directly under the foremen come their assistants and the wage-earning employees. From the earlier days when there were some two dozen of these, largely Americans, with perhaps a few Irish names, today there are over three hundred regular employees, a substantial share of whom are either foreigners or whose parents were aliens. The latest figures follow: out of a total of 323 employees (wage earners) there are two hundred and fifty-eight at Teasville and sixty-five at Herford. Of these twenty-nine percent are females and forty-five percent are foreigners of whom the largest group are Italians followed by Poles and Lithuanians. About fifty-four percent of the employees live in company tenements. The largest percentage of employees fall into the age group from forty to fifty years although it is interesting to note that the greater number of women workers are between twenty and thirty. Approximately seventy percent of all employees range

3. The proper names here are not important, except that all the men named were company officers.

between thirty to sixty, and eleven percent are over sixty. The average age of the employees is steadily increasing and now is forty-five. This is the outgrowth of a highly stabilized force which has come about largely through retrenchment and by not rehiring [this evidently means not hiring replacements] when workers have left . . .

With a force of this size it is quite possible to maintain a friendly, family spirit. All foremen and superintendents are urged to know the family history and background of employees. There are few employees whom the executive officers do not know by name and it is somewhat a matter of pride to be able to call them by their first names.

The care and health of employees are entrusted to Dr. Carter at Teasville and Dr. Reynard at Herford. Both of them are assisted by trained nurses . . .

All the officers are expected to be cognizant in a general way with all the company affairs and to share mutually in the responsibility for their management. For instance, all incoming mail is never delegated to clerks to handle but is opened and perused by such officers as are on hand before final distribution.[4] Opportunity is thus afforded for asking pertinent questions about each executive's assignment; it is one more example of the idea of "check and double check," and it made more reasonably certain that all views on the matter have been properly reconciled before final decisions are made. These daily "round table" discussions are supplemented by regular weekly meetings of the executives [officials]. All decisions are minuted and assignments of problems to the various men for handling to completion are made . . .

A tremendously important part of general management policy today is that of employee relations and services. It is first of all an established principle in the business that employees should have free and easy access to any executive

4. This ritual proved a stubborn stumbling block when management was reorganized in 1942. It was the last symbol of the partnership idea, and attacks upon it were resisted by all the older officers, although it obviously slowed up handling of important work.

officer without prejudice to his status with his foreman or superintendent. This right of appeal is believed to be a great factor in the friendly relations with the help. The second principle has been one of liberal wages and, wherever possible, the granting of extra compensation for extra effort either by way of improved quality or improved output. The maintenance of a complete housing group for employees on liberal rental terms is of great financial advantage to those employees who accept company houses, and the management has always regarded the cost of running its tenements as an indirect labor bill and a supplement to employee wages.

Hiring and "firing" is carefully scrutinized by the officers. Insofar as practicable it is desired to have employees be old established residents in a ten-mile area with the plant as a center. In this way a more stabilized force is obtained in which the traditions of steady work and community friendliness are well understood. New employees are carefully selected by the officers from names and applications on file. After their medical examination they are placed in an apprentice school in which a series of interviews regarding certain company ideals and policies are given, followed by job instruction. [This "apprentice school" is actually a record-keeping term. Job instruction is given by an experienced employee on the job.] The power to discharge workers resides with the superintendents with final approval of the officers. [Superintendents actually played almost no part in the few discharges which occurred during this period.] The usual causes are infractions of company rules over such matters as carrying matches into the factory, refusal to obey orders, poor workmanship, dishonesty, or continued interruption to work from irresponsible behavior at home. It is a rare occasion when such drastic action has been taken, the usual company discipline being in the nature of temporary layoffs for minor disregard of company regulations.

Among the many employee services the following may be enumerated: Group life insurance paid for by the company, group disability insurance paid for by the employee, com-

pensation insurance carried by the company and an informal
pension plan to care for disabled employees or aged workers
of long service in the company. Company land is set aside and
prepared for employee gardens and in distress periods workers
under company supervision are allowed to obtain wood for
fuel from the company's wood lots. Besides the usual services
of the company doctors and nurses in the event of accident or
injury during working hours, there is a weekly clinic to treat
minor ailments of employees and their families. A plant welfare
committee is available to arrange for assistance for employees
based always on the work or "self-help" idea. A suggestion
system with awards for acceptable ideas from employees has
been instituted. The thought behind employee services and
relations has been primarily a friendly, neighborly one in
which every effort is made to teach them to help themselves
by work and extra effort and to share with the company in
the benefits of employment, rather than be in a position of
pampered dependence . . .

In the olden days the small scope of the business permitted
an intimacy between factory and office that best promoted
careful workmanship. Today, however, the problem is quite
different and factory operation becomes a combination of
strict discipline, definite assignments of work and responsibility, greatly increased output and efficiency, and continuous
scientific check on the appearance and performance of the
resulting product . . .

Every effort is made to plan production well forward in
order to keep operations on an even level to avoid unsettling
employment by altering hours of work . . .

It is factory policy to establish reasonable working hours
and to confine operations to one shift. From the old fifty-four
hour week in late years hours have been reduced successively
to fifty and recently to forty hours. [This refers to the standard
work week. As a matter of fact, during this period hours often
went below forty per week.] The office operates also on a five-
day week. Rather than make wholesale discharges in de-
pressed times only a few selected younger employees or others

who had other means of support were released, and all operations were curtailed to as low as necessary to fill orders. For
several months in 1932 only twenty-one hours every other
week were scheduled, yet the employees accepted this result
of "work sharing" without complaint.

These excerpts from the company's history are reproduced at
some length because they give a rather complete picture of the
company's operations and employee relations as seen by the officers at the time. The book was written by one of the younger
officers and, in accordance with policy, was approved by all before
it was published. Both its tone and its content are significant.

While a quick reading may produce an illusion of orderly
organization, a closer perusal will indicate the extent of the "matters of general concern." Also it will be noted that operating
departments are described as being managed by officers and run
by superintendents, while later it is said that upon the foremen
"devolves the full responsibility for conducting their departments
in such a way as to produce a quality product efficiently, safely,
and economically." At the same time the standards department
made up the production schedules. The confusion which existed
can now easily be seen in these paragraphs. At the time it was not
apparent to the personnel.

Comment should be made on the paragraph dealing with the
foremen. As may be imagined, they did not feel that they had any
such clear-cut authority as this paragraph indicates, and it is interesting to note that ten years later training of foremen was considered the greatest task of the training department. Moreover,
some of the men here described as "thoroughly equipped to handle
men and machines" were regarded years later as particularly deficient in solving personnel problems. Finally, the freedom of discussion in foremen's meetings may be questioned. Many of these
men were reticent, and some foremen now state that only recently
have the majority of their colleagues cared to express themselves
without restraint.

The rest of the account is reasonably accurate, although certain
discrepancies such as that between the friendly family spirit de-

scribed on one page and the modern system of "strict discipline" on another may be observed. This was doubtless an unconscious inconsistency and one which reflected the growing contrast between the traditional ideal and the new conditions. Employee services were all that the account indicates. Workmen's compensation was and continued to be more generous than the law required. The pension plan was formalized in 1944. The suggestion system was revised in 1942 to include a worker and a foreman as members of the committee. Most awards are near the minimum, but they have been as high as $500 for a single suggestion. The welfare committee disappeared during the prosperous wartime period.

By 1940 an increasing number of minor incidents and complaints indicated employee dissatisfaction, and there was some evidence that even the more conservative officers sensed the growing distance between them and the employees.

An example illustrating both points of view is to be found in the special training sessions held for several years for about seven textile-mill second hands and maintenance men. Some officers consistently opposed these meetings because they believed they might train the men in concerted action. As a matter of fact, they did provide a means for the men to express their opinions and make requests as a group, and it is interesting to note that one of their number later became the president of the union. It is doubtful, however, whether the men actually used the training as a basis for future organization. The meetings were presided over by one of the three new executives and frequently attended by an officer. In time the men at the meetings asked that the officer, described as "that son of a bitch," be kept away. On the other hand they welcomed the infrequent presence of A. D. Perkins because "he doesn't try to shove words down your throat, and he will get you a decent answer to a question." Of their foreman they said, "What's the use of talking to him? He's only an errand boy anyway—always has to run to the office before he can make up his mind."

Ultimately this group organized what they called a "kangaroo court" which functioned in the mill. Their understanding was that each would abide by the will of the majority. Finally they took up questions, usually concerning time studies, as a group and once approached one of the officers on one of these with some show of pressure. Soon afterward, when a different type of sub-foremanship training had been arranged, the textile-mill sessions were discontinued. The kangaroo court, however, continued, although few but its members knew of its existence.

Once, on Christmas Eve, an officer went to one of the departments to wish the employees a Merry Christmas. Many were so disgusted at this apparently artificial display of good feeling that they hid behind machines to avoid him. Their attitude was, "Does he think he can make up for practically years of neglect by coming out here this way?" As jobs became more readily available elsewhere, several employees left, some after as many as 20 years of service. One man quit because he believed he was the victim of an unfair time study and could not get proper attention to his complaints. His foreman, incidentally, agreed with him but could get no more attention than he did. Another complained that when "people from the office" passed by they spoke to the man in the next room but no one ever looked in on him. A third felt that his abilities were being overlooked and that he did not care to wait longer for answers to questions and requests he had made months before. An officer who made a tour of the plant during a World Series baseball game was bitterly accused of spying to see whether the employees were on the job or trying to get the scores.

Foremen, too, reflected dissatisfaction. Many refused to speak in foremen's meetings. "Why," they asked, "should we stick our necks out and get our ears pinned back?" They recalled that originally it had been promised that executives would not be present at these meetings, and they wondered whether the head of the standards department and other "people from the office" were not just as undesirable. In an essay contest in 1940, one foreman wrote at length on the virtues of the company but expressed alarm over the future. His prescription was that younger executives should try to follow the ways their fathers did before them. When slide films designed to teach the rudiments of personnel work for foremen were introduced, some complained privately that the films were pointless: "We don't know where we stand. You say we ought to take responsibility. But if we do do something, we get it in the neck. If we don't, we get it in the neck. So what the hell?"

Most of these symptoms seem to be trivial. They were, however, regarded with concern because they were not consistent with the way people thought things ought to be. Certain types of grumbling were expected; others, which to an outsider might have seemed no more significant, were not. No one was greatly concerned when an operator complained because another was selected for a desired transfer. When, however, a point was made that officers forgot to do something about a funeral in the family of an old employee, there was uneasiness.

The wartime growth in company business commenced in the summer of 1940. As the number of new employees increased, it quickly became evident that officers could not "carefully scrutinize" each applicant. Preliminary interviewing was turned over to one of the time-study men, but officers still insisted on a brief interview before an applicant was officially placed on the payroll. Often applicants had to wait for hours or even return the following day for this formality. The picture of the interviewer nervously darting to official doors to see whether conferences had ended became a standing, humorless joke in the office. This time-study man was made superintendent of personnel and time study later in the year when his fellow time-study man was made superintendent of production to succeed one of the old superintendents who retired.

By the fall of 1941 the situation became intolerable. Suggestions for facilitating the work in the office were, however, consistently turned down because, as one officer said, "You will never get agreement until someone comes in from the outside to set up the scheme for us." Consequently a highly recommended management engineer was employed early in 1942. Much of his time was spent in persuading individual officers that there was need for changes in management organization and that they would profit individually by the changes he proposed. His plan was adopted, with modifications, and announced to the employees in September, 1942.

Reorganization was based on functional division of activity and upon delegation of authority and responsibility by the officers to lesser executives. Almost a year went by before many of the persons involved—officers or others—became reconciled to the changes and began to make them operate as they were supposed to. Some of the office personnel still complain bitterly of the new arrangements.

Indirectly, the new management chart officially confirmed the separation between the officials and the workers. Although the open door was still official policy, there were chiefs, managers, and foremen, now officially recognized as responsible members of management, between the workers and the important, policy-making family members who still were, in the eyes of many employees, *the* company.

The plant workers were, of course, affected by the influences that led to the revision of management's official organizational scheme, but they waited a little longer before attempting a drastic reform. A year or so after the new organization chart was promulgated, a group of plant men approached a national union and requested it to organize the work force. This request was refused, possibly because the union was afraid that such an attempt would fail. The depth of the workers' dissatisfaction can be judged, nevertheless, from the fact that they persisted in their efforts and went to another union, the Textile Workers Union of America, C.I.O., with the same request. Not until late in 1944 did the management become aware of this move, and by then the campaign for members had been in progress for months.

After some preliminary maneuvering the union was recognized when an election, held somewhat ironically on Valentine's Day in 1944, resulted in an 80 per cent vote in favor of the TWUA. This vote, moreover, clearly demonstrated that officials were wrong in attributing the union success to the influx of more or less temporary war workers, for employees who had been with the company for five years or more voted as wholeheartedly for the union as did the relative newcomers. And it is significant that, with one or two minor exceptions, older employees were those who sought the union, worked for it, and became its local officers.

At the time it was felt that worker-management antagonisms had reached explosive proportions. No explosion resulted, however, and in the years which have followed relations between the union and management have been smooth, not to say pleasant. On occasions the union has made it plain that it has no intention of sacrificing gains it has made or of ceasing to work for more, and it is also reasonably plain that it could muster plenty of strength to press demands forcefully. So far, however, there has been no real need to do this, and as yet there is no indication that differences with management will not continue to be worked out in peaceful negotiation.

CHAPTER THREE: *Factors Which Marked the Change*

The preceding account has been concerned primarily with a chronological description of developments in the company. The following paragraphs describe some of these in more detail.

THE "SYSTEM"—1928. To present-day employees the most significant date in the company's history, at least until 1945 when the union was established, is 1928 when the incentive system was installed. To them this date marks the end of the era of close, personal relationships with the officials.

Precisely how the system was received by the employees in 1928 is difficult to determine today. Those who installed it assert that it aroused comparatively little opposition, and even employees who do not like it believe that its alleged evil effects did not become apparent for some years. Evidently the officers and others who promoted the system were pleased that there was less trouble than they expected, although there was resistance and some employees left the company because they did not like the new scheme.

Even some of the officials regarded the new idea with suspicion, and those who promoted it had "a difficult selling job" on their hands. Some officials continued their distrust, despite obvious advantages in control and efficiency. It is interesting to note, however, that during the period of installation the jealously guarded power of discharge was temporarily delegated to others by the officials for the first time. The outside engineer who made the original

studies and H. J. Murphy who was assigned to assist him and to
learn to manage the system were given absolute disciplinary powers.

The essence of the system is extra payment, on a piecework
basis, for all work performed beyond an established minimum.
Hourly base rates are paid to all employees, whether they reach
the minimum or not. Additional work is rewarded with a "premium." Inasmuch as all productive jobs of the company are easily
measured on an individual basis, each employee can readily be
so rewarded for his own work. Maintenance and supervisory employees receive premium payment on the basis of the work performed by the productive operators in their respective departments. Theoretically, they can facilitate "high point hours" by
keeping machines in good running order, seeing that supplies are
always available, and in other ways.

The theory underlying such incentive system is that human work
can be measured in units, just as can electrical or other energy,
regardless of what particular job is being performed. These units
are called "points" (in the Bedaux system, "B's"). Trained time-
study men measure each job with stop watches and construct
"studies" which define the amount of specific product for any
given job which is equivalent to a point. Sixty such points produced in an hour represent the "normal" amount of work for
which the base rate is paid. Any points produced beyond that normal are called "premium" points and are paid for per point. At
present the amount paid for each point is $\frac{1}{60}$ of the base rate, but
until 1942 the amount paid per point was 75 per cent of $\frac{1}{60}$. The
remaining 25 per cent was put in a fund to defray the cost of the
indirect premium of the foremen, other supervisors, and maintenance men. Eighty points produced in an hour (an 80-point hour)
are considered an ideal amount of work. Machine speeds and
work assignments are adjusted in such a way that each operator
has a chance to make at least an 80-point hour. Where work is
not governed by machine capacity, there is no limit placed on
what an operator may earn. An excessively high point hour is regarded, however, as an indication that work is not being properly
performed, that, for example, time allowed for inspection is being
slighted in favor of getting out more production. In such a case

proper performance would be insisted upon, but no change would be made in the study. A 60-point hour is the equivalent of walking three miles per hour; an 80-point hour is a four-mile-per-hour gait.

The bases upon which changes will be made are cardinal principles, disregard for which, it is believed, can ruin the entire system by destroying employee confidence. Studies will be changed only for the following reasons: 1) If an employee believes a study is unfair he can ask for a restudy, and whatever changes are indicated by the restudy will be made. 2) If there are actual changes in equipment, methods, or materials, a restudy will be made to determine changes necessary. If a study is "too loose," that is, permits overly high production as compared with other jobs, the management accepts the responsibility for having made a mistake and for paying for it. Today complaints regarding the system are specifically controlled according to the union contract.

In order to make the system operate fairly, numerous rules govern special situations. What happens in case of machine breakdown? What happens if an employee has to wait for materials for a short or long time or if it is impossible to give a 100 per cent load—i.e., one which will permit 80-point-hour operation without requiring undue effort? Such considerations and many others tend to make the system much more complex than simple application of its basic principles would indicate. They are confusing both to employees and to executives who have not both studied and practiced application of the system. Questions, moreover, tend to arise where there is dissatisfaction or when a new job has upset an employee's routine. Hence the system is laden with possibilities for trouble, and only faith in its essential fairness and the fairness and ability of the man operating it—the time-study men in particular and the management in general—can prevent such troubles from becoming serious.

Impersonality is the essense of such systems. Concessions or adjustments must not be made on the basis of personalities. If a man is old or weak or needs money the system cannot be altered. It must operate like an impersonal machine. "What's fair for one is fair for another." Every job must present exactly the same opportunities as every other job. Who is doing the job does not matter.

Uneven application of the system would mean that those whose jobs were "tighter" would have a reasonable complaint that they were being discriminated against. Only stop watches, slide rules, calculating machines and the trained, impersonal skill of the time-study men are capable of making the system the smoothly operating machine that it is supposed to be. Mary may be on the job today, Jennie tomorrow. If Jennie can produce more, that is up to her. The job remains the same.

It will also be the same, as far as the effort required to make a point hour is concerned, as all other jobs "on the system." If the work is heavier, more monotonous, more skilled, more responsible, or requires more attention or training, then the base rate will be higher, and here again impersonality governs.

Base rates for various jobs are now set by the job evaluation committee. Previously rates had been set by rule of thumb, often with individual workers in mind. Length of service, loyalty to the company, personal needs, and other such factors frequently outweighed the requirements of the work assigned. It was constantly necessary when the first jobs were being rated to remind job evaluation committee members that they were evaluating jobs and not workers. Originally the committeemen were officers of the company assisted by members of the standards department. At present lesser executives, assisted by foremen, perform this task.

Even today this job evaluation system is not fully in operation. When it was installed it was determined not to cut rates on jobs which were being paid more than the new evaluation rate and not to cut the rates of individuals who were being paid more than the rate of their job called for. The idea was to adjust such rates when general wage changes were being made.[1] Today only a handful of workers in maintenance departments where the point system is not used receive so-called "personal rates," but a large

1. The most important move in this direction was made as part of a general raise in 1950. At the time management feared dissatisfaction because some employees received much larger increases than others. One of the important union officers discounted the possibility of trouble, since he believed the action, while not perfect, was about as good as could be done at the time.

proportion of the productive jobs has not yet been adjusted to the evaluation system. A specific clause permitting this situation is included in the union contract.

After the point system and job evaluation were adopted, it was no longer possible for an officer to listen to the requests of a worker, take the matter up with the other officials, and perhaps get the man a raise. The only exception to this rule is the merit rating which applies to machinists, carpenters, painters, and plumbers, whose jobs are not "on standard." These workers can be advanced or promoted through nine stages. Their advancement depends upon the deliberations of the merit-rating committee, which includes their foreman and members of the time-study and personnel departments. Meetings are supposed to be held once a year, and advancements are based on the man's ability to perform the relatively skilled tasks of his trade. In these trades, also, age and service bring small, automatic increases. Otherwise the rates are applied to jobs—not people.

Introduction of the point system is an excellent case of what anthropologists call "borrowing" or, as the executive who backed its installation said recently, of the effect of "ideas and fashions" which were spreading over the country. He and a younger executive became interested in the works of Frederick Taylor in 1926, read Taylor's and other books on incentives, and visited plants which had both Taylor and Bedaux systems. They were told that if they dared risk "turning their plant upside down" for a while, they would be more than pleased with the ultimate results. They chose the Bedaux system because, being less complicated than the Taylor system, it appeared to fit the company better and was easier to sell to their colleagues.

The firm they engaged made a preliminary study of work at the company and reported that some workers were producing as little as 25 per cent of what they should at an ideal rate, none as much as 100 per cent, and the average about 50 per cent. This was in 1928, long after the daily baseball games and other diversions had vanished.

As has been said, Murphy and the engineering firm's representative were given absolute disciplinary powers. In the manner of such things, however, they resorted to more subtle methods.[2] According to Murphy, the first worker actually put on the system was an unusually good operator. It was known that he was even then working at a speed which would have entitled him to premium payments. He was told that he was to go on the new system. He demurred and was told that he would either go on the system or take the janitor's job. He chose the janitor's job. The next day he was asked whether he wanted to go back to his machine. He shrugged. He was then told that he had been credited with working on the system the previous day and that his wages had been considerably higher than he had been getting at regular rates. Without a word he dropped his broom and went back to his machine. This, according to Murphy, was the opening wedge, and before long workers were asking for more haste in installing the system so that they could share in the larger earnings.

Ten years later, when a new product was going into production, certain workers were taken off the system for an extended period to assist in development. They were guaranteed substantially more than their previous base earnings, but nevertheless they frequently urged that their new jobs be studied and placed on the system so that they could earn premiums according to their own efforts. Moreover, in the course of the union negotiations in 1944 the employee representatives stated that they wanted the system left just as it was, except that they wanted guarantees which would enable them to force proper administration.

On the other hand many employees, including not only operators but foremen and some executives as well, believe that the system brought evil to the company. Some of their criticisms were mild, like that of an elderly Irishman who said in 1937, "There's no fun at all around here any more. Since they put that point system in everybody's working so hard they can't enjoy themselves." Others, including an officer of the union, believe that "the help have lost confidence in the management" and attribute the loss of confidence to the system. Such employees, some of them bitter, feel

2. Cf. F. W. Taylor, *The Principles of Scientific Management*, pp. 130–131, for an example of such methods in another setting.

that it forces people to work too hard, that it is too complicated to understand, and that, by design or otherwise, some of the studies are unfair. One particularly well-informed employee stated that he and others believed that the standards department had distorted the system, had unfairly tightened studies, and had destroyed the faith of the employees. He was inclined to believe that the employees still trusted the officials but not the time-study men, the foremen, or the lesser executives. He and other employees believe that this lack of confidence and lack of contact with the "top men" had a great deal to do with the success of the union in its organization campaign. Table I indicates that studies have not been generally tightened. Point hours have remained fairly constant.

Whether or not the system was favored by the employees, it comprised several factors which promoted the growing impersonality of relationships between the officials and the employees.

First, it was, as it was supposed to be, an impersonal device for measuring the work of the people and for causing them to work harder and more steadily by paying them according to the amount of work they produced.

Second, it tended to reduce visits by officials to the plant and to make such visits less significant. Some of the officials felt that one of their reasons for plant visits was to see if workers were on the job. With the system this was no longer necessary. The operators kept themselves on the job. In fact it even became necessary to lock department doors so that they would not spend their lunch hours at their machines. Some officials also did not understand the system in sufficient detail to be able to answer questions about it. In any event, questions regarding pay could only be settled after checking complex figures. In addition, officials hesitated to stop and chat with operators because time so spent might cost the operators money in lost production.

Third, it enlarged the growing hierarchy of functionaries between the operators and the officials. Time-study men were added to this group, and the duties of the foreman became more significant since he had to prepare the original cards from which pay was figured. It is interesting to note that the first regular foremen's meetings were held in 1929. By then it was realized that these men

TABLE I. DEPARTMENT POINT HOURS—HIGH AND LOW WEEKS, 1928–1945

Year	Department No. 1				Department No. 2				Textile Mill			
	High Week		Low Week		High Week		Low Week		High Week		Low Week	
	No. of Employees	Point Hour	No. of Employees	Point Hour	No. of Employees	Point Hour	No. of Employees	Point Hour	No. of Employees	Point Hour	No. of Employees	Point Hour
1928	8	106	5.7	58	6	90	8	60	61	78	62	57
1929	11.5	94	10.5	67	7	97	6.6	78	63.9	79	77.7	68
1930	11	101	11.2	78	6.5	94	6.6	70	61.2	85	65.1	81
1931	9.2	105	11.9	92	4.5	92	4.1	79	56.7	86	44.2	81
1932	14.6	96	11.3	85	2.5	91	5.2	83	42.9	85	62	75
1933	17.2	95	12.9	85	2.4	104	3.4	66	87.4	84	64.4	76
1934	17.6	95	12.5	87	1.9	102	2.7	75	80.4	94	79.2	83
1935	18	94	17.1	85	4.6	100	2.2	84	81.1	92	74	78
1936	16.7	95	16.6	86	6	99	2.5	93	71.5	83	66.6	79
1937	15.2	95	15.3	84	No figures available				71	85	67.6	77
1938	14.4	95	17.5	85	2	96	1.1	74	49.6	86	67.1	77
1939	16.1	92	12.5	86	6.1	90	10.7	78	73.9	81	66.6	75
1940	20.7	94	13.2	84	9.8	84	18.7	75	61	80	94.3	74
1941	17.7	93	18.9	87	17.7	92	15.5	87	101.1	79	94.3	75
1942	18.9	95	18.4	86	12.6	99	12.7	89	32	84	93	76
1943	17	88	13.7	83	96.4	107	64.9	95	49.4	86	52.6	78
1944	No figures available				47.7	107	74.4	99	57.7	90	48.1	82
1945	18.8	93	18.9	81	47.1	108	4.5	81	65.8	92	52.2	84

Note: The number of employees given is the average number working on productive jobs under the point system for the week listed. Figures for the textile mill are complete. Those for Department No. 2 are complete except for war years, for which representative shifts were chosen. The most representative division in Department No. 1 was selected, since many employees in this department are not "on the system."

needed training to fit them for jobs which were becoming more important.

Fourth, the system contained the seeds for many misunderstandings and grievances. As long as jobs remained relatively unchanged and as long as the feeling persisted that extra pay was being given for the extra work, grievances remained at a minimum. However, operators soon became accustomed to earning at or near an 80-point-hour rate and came to regard this as their regular rate of pay. The system ceased to be considered something which made pay rates higher. In fact, when operators did not make 80-point hours, the system was sometimes looked upon as the factor which made pay lower. Through the latter years of the 1930's, moreover, numerous revisions were made in jobs, especially in the textile mill, where changed machine speeds and other changes designed primarily to improve quality were introduced. The time-study department was not always able to keep up with these changes, and occasionally studies were well out of line. A recurrent point of friction was revision of such studies—especially when the change resulted in tightening the study. With the advent of World War II, the time-study department became entirely unable to keep up with changes. As a result numerous annoying or actually unfair conditions existed.

HIRE AND FIRE. Until 1942 when the new scheme of organization was adopted the officials jealously kept the power to employ and discharge workers. The single exception was the temporary delegation of the power of discharge to the men installing the point system in 1928.

As late as 1932 when the depression layoffs occurred this power was effectively handled by the officials, and during the remaining years of the 1930's turnover was so low that employment offered no serious problem. Officials interviewed every new employee, and the few discharges were subjects for discussion in executive committee meetings. So rare were discharges that the case of a man caught carrying matches in the plant was regarded as a major event.

As employment increased in 1940 and thereafter, however, attempts of the officials to approve each new employee hired created confusion, and it was not until 1942 that full power to employ was delegated to the manager of personnel, and the power to approve discharges was transferred to the chief of manufacturing.

The contrast between the layoffs in the depression and those after V-J Day is remarkable. Officials planned and participated in the depression layoff. Work of some kind was found for all old employees, and personal needs were the criteria for all decisions. After V-J Day, however, the personnel manager handled the matter without assistance and without referring even to the chief of manufacturing. Plans for the layoff were made on the basis of conversations with the union, in which general rather than personal criteria were agreed upon. This plan provided for laying off all employees who relied upon the company to furnish them transportation and all employees who were unable to perform work which the company had left to offer. An effort was made to determine which employees preferred to quit rather than take jobs the company had available after prewar employees had been given their prewar jobs. All others laid off were dismissed on the basis of length of service, tempered in some cases by a review of a recent special merit rating made by foremen.

Company officers did not know which employees were let go. In fact their principal interest was in reducing the force rapidly from 525 to less than 400 employees (including those employed at the Herford plant). Several women with many years of service were laid off—their advancing years and physical infirmities made it impossible to find work for them in the plant. The personnel manager tried to take the interests of employees into account wherever possible, but the people who, to the employees, are "the company" did not participate. In fact, during the three days when most of the decisions were made not one officer was present at the factory. For its part, the union found nothing to complain about in what was done, despite the fact that the union secretary, a young girl who refused a transfer, was let go.

ADMINISTRATIVE DUTIES. The reasons why the officers ceased to visit the plant are important. They stopped not because they wanted to but rather because other duties and interests demanded their time. These factors resulted both from internal growth and complexity and from changes in American culture as a whole. One of these factors was the steady increase in duties which kept officials in the office.

Growth of the business added to the volume of executive work. Not only was there an increasing number of orders to handle but the number of products and brands grew as well. Customers insisted on more exact specifications. Whereas early in the century one officer could handle the company's product testing by examining a few samples of Product No. 1 every day, by 1930 inspection covered a variety of characteristics of a dozen "regular" brands of Product No. 1 and many more special brands and of Product No. 3 and textiles. This multiplication of brands and the addition of new products complicated manufacturing schedules and purchasing problems. Although the tasks resulting from stricter specifications and new testing techniques were assigned to the research department, they actually added to the burden of officials, who felt they had to participate in all these controls.

Modern management techniques made for more administrative work. At the beginning of the century profit and loss were computed simply by adding up the company's assets in money and inventories at the end of the year, comparing them with those at the end of the preceding year, and crediting the difference to profit or surplus. Modern statements were required monthly by 1930, and each month they were studied and reviewed by all officers. Cost controls also became complex and exact. Some officials gave considerable time to the preparation of these figures, and all participated in periodic reviews of the costs of each brand and product. So complicated did the preparation of cost data become that they were seldom complete in time to be used as direct manufacturing controls. The annual sales forecast, begun about 1930, was another of the techniques which encroached upon the time of officials.

Investment reserves were kept large because of the hazardous nature of the business. Investments were accorded detailed study and lengthy discussion. Attempts were made to become familiar with stock-and-bond markets so that funds could be invested wisely. Some of the officers tried to establish an automatic investment schedule, but here the "partnership idea" of general participation by the officers remained especially strong. During the 1930's, moreover, the company acquired a number of foreign subsidiaries. While each of these was managed locally, the officers in Teasville found this another item requiring time and attention.

Mention has been made of the attention given by officers to reviewing time studies under the point system and to setting wage rates under the job evaluation plan. While these and the activities mentioned in preceding paragraphs were influenced by knowledge gained outside the company, they may be regarded to some extent as internal developments.

OTHER OUTSIDE INFLUENCES. More direct pressure from outside sources was exerted by such things as the growing burden of governmental controls upon business in general. While these had been increasing for a long time, the 1930's found them piling up in greater numbers and complexity. The National Recovery Act in addition to requiring detailed study produced rulings and regulations, any one of which, had it been overlooked, might have involved the company in difficulties with the government. The National Labor Relations Act, the public contracts act, the state unemployment act, Federal Social Security, the Wages and Hours Act, new tax laws, Interstate Commerce Commission regulations, and other legislation made the company subject to a veritable spider web of changing legal controls. As executives remarked, just reading the laws and regulations was a full-time job if one wanted to be sure of not getting into trouble. Wartime regulations after 1941 multiplied these controls tremendously.

An outside influence of a different nature was the growing fashion of suing companies of all kinds for damages, real, imagined, or false. During the 1930's a very large proportion of the time of one officer and a lesser proportion of the time of others were spent in defending the company in lawsuits in distant states. Officials believed it was necessary to maintain the company free of legal precedent upon which successful suits could be based.

A cultural influence of another kind was to be found in the changed working hours of officers. Early in the century it was customary for the officials to come to work early in the morning, to eat at the same hour as the employees, and to stay at the plant until late in the afternoon. It was even customary for all officers to report at the office on some holidays to open the mail and discuss matters of mutual interest. Vacations came once a year and were short. These customs meant that the officers were at the plant during the same hours as the employees. They also indicated to the employees that the officers had important and onerous work to do. By 1930 it was customary for officers to come to work after nine o'clock, to eat an hour later than the employees, to go home somewhat earlier in the afternoon, to take two vacations a year, and to take longer vacations than their fathers had. Naturally there was less time in which officers might visit the plant and less chance for employees to find officers when problems demanded attention.

The time spent by officers at the factory was also reduced by participation in such outside interests as directorships of banks, other companies, hospitals, and schools and attendance at meetings of trade or professional associations.

That the youngest officers built homes on the mountain, two miles from the plant (and from the majority of the employees' houses) is also significant, if only in an incipient manner.[3] It had

3. Through the first seven or eight decades of the company's history, it fitted well Le Play's description of the properous and happy community: "Chez les peuples prospères, les riches, tout en s'aquittant de leurs obligations envers la famille, se chargent de nombreux devoirs; et, pours les remplir, ils se croient tenus de résider en permanence sur l'atelier qui leur fournit les moyens de subsistence. Ils dirigent plus ou moins le travail de cet atelier. Ils président personnellement à la direction morale et à l'assistance matérielle des populations attachées à leur fortune. Enfin, ils s'appliquent à concilier ces devoirs privés avec l'exercise gratuit des fonctions publiques qui assurent à leur voisinage les bienfaits de la paix sociale." Le Play believed that local welfare is destroyed by degrees as the proprietor leaves his home and leaves the local duties which

long been a custom of employees to call at the homes of officers on
personal or even company matters. This custom continued in a
decreasing degree. Even when the union was in the process of
organization some old employees called on officers to ask for advice
about supporting the union. They were astonished and disappointed when this was refused.

With respect to the hours of the officials, one of them now believes that fashions in recreation had much to do with the changes.
He points out that his father, for example, had practically no
recreational activities. Golf was unknown, and dignified men did
not play the only outdoor game, baseball. The young men who
came to the company about 1900 played golf, and one of them
felt strong enough in his official position to get his younger colleagues to leave the factory in the latter part of the afternoon to
play with him. This annoyed one of the older partners so much
that he kept a record of all time lost in this way, but the practice
grew nevertheless. Doubtless the acquisition of automobiles and
the knowledge that businessmen of prestige elsewhere kept shorter
hours influenced the officials. As for the young men who built
homes on the mountain, they were getting away from what once
had been a quiet street but was now a busy main highway just
as many of their acquaintances in other towns were doing.

From the point of view of the employees certain "outside influences" were also at work. The Wagner Act may have helped
give courage to their leaders when they investigated unionization,
and of course they were aware of unionism as an available recourse.
Their procedure was to spend six months or more making inquiries and locating the proper national union with which to
affiliate. After that they had the benefit of direct advice from trained
organizers.

It was the thought of several officers at the time the union was
organized that the new employees who came from neighboring

---

were *professionnels* to his father. The change is the more dangerous because it
is at first disguised with the appearance of continuation of the ancient peace
and stability. Those whom the owner delegates to take his place cannot do so
adequately, Le Play believed, and misunderstanding soon ensues. (F. Le Play,
Les Ouvriers européens, VI, xxxix ff.)

towns during the war brought the idea of unionization with them. But the testimony of union officers and the fact that the old employees joined the union at least as readily as the new ones tend to refute this idea.

Workers, like officials, were also affected by social change outside the factory. As second-generation Italians and Poles point out, American education gradually erased the submissive attitude of those who came "from the old country" and certainly gave their children a more typically American point of view. The level of education in the town has also risen; whereas youngsters often went to work in their early teens 40 or so years ago, most of them complete high school today and some go on to college. To this relatively well-educated generation the prospect of unskilled work and slow, uncertain promotion at "the shop" is not attractive. Besides, opportunities for other local employment have multiplied considerably in recent years, and the automobile has made it relatively easy to seek work out of town. The effects of such influences are not clear. They are obscured by the long depression years which were followed so quickly by the feverish war years. They may well be reflected in the attitudes which led to the union, however, and in the difficulty the company has experienced in recruiting local young people and retaining them on the payroll since the war.

SUMMARY. The New Freedom Products Company was founded in 1836 as a small manufacturing concern in which the partners worked with and knew intimately all their employees. This intimacy, strengthened by the mores of the small town in which it was located, produced an institution which functioned as a primary group. By 1910 developments had appeared which tended to reduce the frequency and closeness of personal contacts between the workers and the men on the owner-management level. By 1942 these developments had transformed the company into a complex organization. Personal contacts between the officers and the workers had become negligible. Lesser executives and foremen had been delegated to discharge the functions formerly accom-

plished by direct personal relationships between the persons at
the top and those at the bottom of the organizational hierarchy.

This change was unpremeditated and was undesired by both
workers and officers until the older system had so far failed that
both parties sought relief, first by specific expedients and later by
more coordinated efforts at reorganization. Through the course
of these developments, changes first made themselves felt in the
altered roles of those on the top status level. As a result the people
on the lower status levels, whose roles had been adjusted to those
of their superiors, were forced to try to readjust their behavior.

The body of purposes, principles, and values which supplied the
incentives for cooperation was consolidated primarily by the face-
to-face conversations between the people at the top and those at
the bottom of its simple hierarchy. Antagonisms, also, were
minimized or resolved in the same way. There were few barriers
to intimate association between Drew and the other men who
managed the company and the workers. In the community, also,
they were closely associated.

In the course of the first 60 years of its history, the company
grew rather slowly. It numbered only 50 employees in 1866, 100
in 1887, and only about 200 in the early years of the present century. During this period the traditions of personal management
were passed down to Drew's sons-in-law and grandsons, and the
acceptance of the Drew family as the owning and managing group
strengthened the personal organization. The Drew family closely
resembled what Le Play calls "social authorities" [4] in that they

4. F. Le Play, *The Organization of Labor*, pp. 122 ff.: "Under a system of
government which secures individual liberty, the permanency of engagements
furnishes the highest expression of stability. It prevails, with its best characteristics, where the proprietors and workmen preserve a mutual attachment
through successive generations . . . Among the duties which the preservation
of these practices imposes upon the proprietor, the most important is the education of a successor penetrated with a sense of the obligations contracted by
his ancestors toward the workmen, guaranteed by Custom and transmitted
by local tradition with the ownership of the establishment." Elsewhere (pp.
37 ff.) Le Play includes among the social authorities employers who religiously
preserve the customs of their ancestors and transmit them to their descendants.
They are united with their workmen by ties of affection and respect. They

were the trusted superiors whose decisions eliminated or controlled interpersonal friction and who constantly strengthened common purposes, principles, and values. In fact, so well accepted was the family that the employees came to regard its management as constituting the upper status level of a proper hierarchy.

The advent of Irish immigrants during the last half of the nineteenth century apparently did not disturb the personal nature of relationships. Whatever friction these new arrivals may have occasioned has disappeared with the years, and the loyalty of some of the older Irish to the members of the Drew family is striking. The quick growth after 1900 and the arrival of non-English-speaking immigrants might have been expected to upset a system which depended upon close personal acquaintanceship between the company officials and all of the employees. But, although the seeds of disruption of this system were sown at this time, three factors prevented marked symptoms of disorganization from appearing.

The first of these was the fact that the newer immigrants—Poles, Lithuanians, and, after 1910, Italians—readily accepted the family authority as the image of what they believed was proper. Also, they were disposed to accept any authority without question. This group, until the children who went to American schools were old enough to assert themselves, was docile and content. Second, through the years, employees had come to place a higher value on security than on advancement or high income as a goal, and as a result ambitious young men avoided employment at the company, leaving the jobs to people who were satisfied as long as they were sure the company would always take care of them. Finally, general economic trends reduced problems which might have caused the weakened system to fall apart sooner than it did. There is little evidence of such problems during the prosperous years of the 1920's until the point system was established in 1928. This system, also, immediately increased the earnings of employees,

decide the questions which "in our day" give rise to endless discussion and, *by establishing harmony of opinion,* "present the most sure criteria of the reign of truth." They are found in large and small manufacturing establishments wherever the influence of family ties is maintained.

and before it produced disruptive repercussions the country was in the grip of the depression. At this point the old personal system reasserted itself most effectively, and the employees were again convinced that the officials knew them, had their interests at heart, and would take care of them. The depression also acted as a coercive force on the most dissatisfied employees; they dared not risk an open break with the company when they could see nothing but unemployment outside the safe factory walls.

Despite the apparent calm of the 1930's, however, dissatisfaction was growing. As has been noted, forces which finally destroyed the system of personal contacts were already in existence before World War I. The number of employees had reached about 300 when the war began; it never again went below that figure and at times far exceeded it. Also, before World War I, the officials were subject to influences which ultimately kept them out of the plant almost entirely. Increasing business and modern administrative methods required them to spend more time at their desks and less in visiting in the plant. The influence of modern recreational patterns and changing styles in working hours for executives had begun to decrease the hours they were available at the factory. It would be interesting to assess the relative importance of these factors—the increased size of the work force, the specialized demands of modern techniques of management, and the reduced hours spent by officials on the job—but the evidence available does not make this possible. For instance, it is obvious that even though the number of officials increased from three in the latter half of the nineteenth century to five in 1940 (seven for a short time in the early thirties) the increased number of employees probably made continuance of a really strong system of personal relationships impossible. But the point at which it became impossible is obscure, because the other factors complicated the situation. One of the older officials, after careful consideration of the problem, is inclined to believe that if the officials were willing to work hard enough and to spend enough time in the plant they could still manage the old system. In any event, they are not willing to and probably could not even if they were.

Although it was not clearly apparent at the time, the relationships between the company and the people of the town had subtly altered. For many years ambitious young men had seen that prospects for advancement were limited at the factory. Growth of the town made it possible for them to find other local employ-ment, while modern transportation made it easier to obtain out-of-town jobs. During the depression these factors did not matter, but during World War II and afterward it appeared that, at least in times of high employment, the company could not rely on Teasville and Herford for all the employees it needed.[5]

In 1940 business came on with a rush, and the strain on the weakened organization became acute. Even before then, however, the strain had been felt. The textile mill exhibited the most pronounced symptoms, notably in the form of the kangaroo court of workers and in an attempt by management to improve super-vision by delegating authority in order to build up a minor hierarchy. In 1940 the presence of personnel problems was recog-nized by the appointment of a superintendent of personnel, and in 1942 the complete reorganization of management took place. This showed a final recognition of the passing of close personal relationships between the officials and the workers and was marked by delegation of authority to chiefs, managers, and foremen. It also created the personnel department to formalize relationships which had previously been taken for granted.

The workers responded more slowly than did management, but eventually they sought advice from national unions. By the end of 1944, organization of the union was almost complete. It is difficult to make clear how radical a step this was for the workers to take. Many of them regarded it as treachery to a deep-seated set of loyalties—as did the officials—and they found their most effective rationalization in the idea that the union would restore direct relations with the officials. Like the reorganization of man-

5. The whole period from 1940 through 1946 was marked by a general shortage of labor. In 1946 about 10 per cent of the employees lived outside the two towns. Cf. Leonard Eskin, "The Labor Force in the First Year of Peace," *Monthly Labor Review*. In the spring of 1951 one of the personnel executives of the company claimed that employment was about as much of a problem as it was during World War II.

agement, the union was a recognition that the old system of personal relationships no longer existed, and at the same time it was an attempt to find a new system which would accomplish the same results.

The advent of the union also revealed the extent to which the views of management and those of the workers had come to diverge. There is evidence that 40 years ago workers and management were in fairly close agreement on important policies or at least that workers willingly accepted the views of the officials. Today there is still agreement on purposes, principles, and values, but it is clear that the workers do not always agree with management on which among these should be given first consideration. The officials almost always think first of the welfare of the company. The workers seem to take that for granted and to believe that the company could do more for them than it is doing.

In the face of these changes, it is remarkable that old traditions have shown such vitality. Despite the tensions created by organization of the union, both management and workers fell back on the principle of "friendly cooperation," and this principle continued to guide their dealings with each other. In the years which have passed since the first union contract was signed, there have been no serious quarrels and several examples of cooperation between company executives and union officers. Although a few employees still miss "the good old days," there is no concrete evidence for supposing that such arrangements as the personnel department and present relationships between the management and the union do not effectively replace the old system of personal contacts, at least as far as worker-management relations are concerned.

SECTION TWO

*Institutional Analysis
of the New Freedom
Products Company*

CHAPTER FOUR: *The Theory of Institutions*

In the preceding section the social structure of the New Freedom Products Company has been described in historical perspective, and it has been shown that in response to certain influences this structure changed considerably. On the whole it might be said that the company's career has not been a particularly exciting one. Its strategic position as the principal manufacturer of its main products has protected it from severe economic strains. Its labor relations have been marked neither by strife nor by the development of any remarkable innovations such as sharing management or profits with the employees. Since, however, this is not an adventure story, the absence of spectacular incidents may be an advantage. The subject of interest is social structure. The present chapter discusses the theoretical nature of this structure. Later chapters will show how the New Freedom Products Company can be analysed according to the theory and how dynamic elements operate within the structure and tend to alter it.

One of the functions of science is the development of methods for studying its subject matter. Thus any science sets a rough guide for itself when it defines its field. The chemist concerns himself with certain matters and avoids others. Such charting of subject matter, moreover, not only serves to limit inquiry to pertinent material but also attempts to outline all the pertinent elements within the field. It provides what amounts to a checklist for research.

In sociology such check lists are to be found among concepts

which have been constructed to describe social phenomena. The
selection of industry as a subject for sociological investigation implies that use will be made of the concepts of that science and that
these concepts will help to clarify the factors and relationships
inherent in industrial situations. This does not, of course, mean
that all concepts will be found useful or that any concept will be
found entirely adequate. It simply means that the appropriate concepts will obviate the wastefulness of undirected observation, will
bring to light unsuspected elements, and will put all factors into
their proper perspective. The practical advantages of this sort of
procedure are obvious. For the scientist the procedure has a different value in that it subjects the concepts to the test of application to an observed set of facts.

The structural analysis of the New Freedom Products Company
which follows in the next section is based on Malinowski's concept of institutions. This concept points the way to a useful classi-
fication of elements and opens the door to effective use of dynamic
and functional theories.

The choice of this conceptual tool rather than one of several
others concerned with organized social groups may, perhaps, need
explanation. The initial reason was simple. Before beginning formal work on the study, the writer became acquainted with Malinowski's idea and, despite its previous restriction to primitive
materials, was impressed by its apparent relevance to the factory
with which he was already familiar. Almost immediately the concept seemed to clarify certain problems, and later in the course
of the study this impression was dramatically confirmed. At that
point work already done indicated that social organization in the
company had been based on a system of rules and usages which
permitted close personal exchanges between the highest company
officials and all workers but that this system had broken down
during World War I, at least to the extent of greatly curtailing
customarily close contacts. At that time, the hypothesis being investigated was that the eventual formal reorganization of management and, more particularly, the formation of the union local
represented attempts to substitute a new kind of organizational

structure for the one which had failed. Nevertheless, there appeared to be no marked symptoms of disorganization during this period, although these might well have been expected. For this reason, the writer was almost completely discouraged and was tempted to abandon the concept as misleading. Still, the various categories set up by Malinowski made it clear that more work needed to be done, particularly in investigating the nature of various classes of personnel. Hence it was determined to carry through the inquiry, partly to give the concept the benefit of a thorough trial and, more importantly, because it seemed likely that the then new immigrants might never have experienced close associations with management. Therefore a number of additional visits to the plant and to homes of immigrant workers were made. It then became clear that to the immigrants the remaining opportunities for personal contact seemed generous and that they fitted nicely with a cultural predisposition to welcome what these new workers regarded as benevolent paternalism. Moreover, examination of old company payrolls showed that the new immigrants had become a numerical majority and that older Irish and American employees were beginning to advance into supervisory and office positions. Thus those of the latter who might have been most likely to furnish leadership for a rebellious clique were evidently relieved of the pressure inherent in the changed relationships. Finally, it was recalled that shortly after World War I there had been a walkout of ten or a dozen workers, almost all of them older workers who quite probably felt tensions which were unnoticed by the immigrants. To the writer these discoveries, coming at a point when failure seemed imminent, were a convincing demonstration that Malinowski's scheme was invaluable, especially because it had forced him to examine facts which he might otherwise have missed.

Examination of other concepts—some of them using the label "institution," others speaking of "associations"—also seemed to confirm the selection of Malinowski. Most of these appear to be aimed at the same problems Malinowski envisaged, and several of them identify approximately the same elements as the concept we have adopted, although none seems to be either so complete or so clearly stated.[1]

The term "institution" is used here in a quite specific and somewhat unusual definition: An institution includes six different but closely interrelated elements, but for the moment the important thing to note is that an institution consists of a group of people cooperating, knowingly or unknowingly, willingly or unwillingly, for some common goal or goals. This implies, of course, that the group is organized in the sense that the activities of the individuals in it depend upon and are integrated with each other. In this sense, any group other than ephemeral chance aggregations of people is organized and can be regarded as an institution. Even the crowd which gathers to watch a baseball game recognizes the common interest which draws it together and follows certain rules of conduct which prevent friction and permit satisfaction of the various urges of curiosity, desire for entertainment, and the like which the individual spectators and players experience. More permanent and formal groups possess more standardized aims and practices, but essentially any group and its culture can be analyzed in terms of the institutional theory.

This definition of the term "institution" differs markedly from other commonly used definitions. One of the latter, which can be dismissed at once, refers to such public or quasi-public establishments as hospitals, asylums, or prisons. A second meaning covers "recognized and established usages governing certain relations of men or a complex of such usages," while a third, similar to this one, calls an institution a "crystallization of mores around a core of interest." A fourth refers to the organization supporting a complex of usages.[2] Taken together, these definitions are similar to Malinowski's, except that they are generally used in a highly abstract manner. Thus a complex of usages can refer to typical practices which might be found in many organizations of a given kind. In this vein one can speak of the religious or industrial institution of a nation or even of the whole world. Or one can speak of the

1. For a further discussion of these concepts, see below, App.

2. Cf. L. T. Hobhouse, *Social Development*, pp. 49–50; W. G. Sumner and A. G. Keller, *The Science of Society*, I, 98–99.

economic institution of a tribe which has no separate organization for economic purposes since economic functions are performed by families. These comments are intended not as a criticism of other meanings for the word but simply to point up the definition used in this book. A description of religion in general is quite different from one of a particular congregation or cult, even though the abstraction—religion—may be based on knowledge of a great many congregations and cults. Some writers prefer such words as "association" or "organization" for the specific group. There is no great objection to such terms, provided the sense in which they are used is clear. The choice of "institution" for this book was dictated simply by the fact that Malinowski used it, and it is his conceptual development which is here employed.

The elements which are characteristic of an institution are *charter, norms and rules* (folkways, mores, laws, etc.), *material apparatus, personnel, activities,* and *functions.* Each of these requires elaboration, and it is important to remember that they are all interrelated and act in combination, rather than independently, to influence behavior.

Charter is one of the most complex of the elements. Roughly speaking, it refers to the philosophy which underlies group behavior, the beliefs, purposes, guiding principles, and values which the group holds in common. Each individual, of course, has his own conception of charter, which influences what he does, and to the extent that individual conceptions coincide, the concept of an institutional charter is valid. Like culture, charter refers to a consensus of numerous individuals which may not be precisely duplicated in any single person.

In some respects the word "charter" is not ideally suited to the use Malinowski makes of it. It all too readily suggests a written document or a formal compact, especially when one is discussing such an institution as a modern corporation. Nevertheless, even a written document has little significance until it is interpreted, absorbed into human minds, and translated into behavior. A written document may be a record of and a source of many of the ideas which make up charter in the sociological sense, but anyone familiar with written charters—the Constitution of the United

States, for example—would be naïve indeed to suppose that the printed words even approximate the fundamental notions which guide the activities of the government of this country. Perhaps another word—"rationale" has been suggested—would be better, but none comes to mind which seems wholly satisfactory. Possibly, like culture, charter will survive a period of ambiguity and attain an undisputed place in the vocabulary of social science.

→ For convenience, it has seemed desirable to divide charter into three main subelements, although this trio may not be exactly those which would be useful in analyzing another institution. They are purposes, principles, and standards. Purposes are the conceptions held in common by the members of an institution as to what it should do for society and for them. Principles are the members' ideas of basic means which serve as general guides for action directed at realizing the purposes. Standards are the limiting values which modify the manner in which activities are conducted and provide the bases for judgments concerning the propriety of various actions. To this list one might add a fourth subelement which can be called re-enforcements, although it is more logical to include these as a special variety of norms. Re-enforcements are the traditions, historical accounts, precepts, stories, myths, anecdotes, and symbols which convey morals based on the charter and express, make vivid, and strengthen the purposes, principles, and standards. Charter, then, consists of mutually, although often tacitly, agreed-upon goals, of principles or general means which are thought to realize these goals, and of subsidiary or modifying codes which are not precisely means to the ends sought but which, nevertheless, are regarded as standards of propriety. In addition, charter is conveyed by closely associated verbal and symbolical norms which strengthen and vivify it and which may be called re-enforcements.[3]

3. The word "re-enforcements" is not used by Malinowski, but it is a convenient one to carry the meanings to which he refers in various ways, and it has been used by other social scientists. E. Wight Bakke, for example, includes folklore, literature, art, symbols, slogans, and ritual under the term. The spelling is intended to differentiate "re-enforcements" from the psychological term "reinforcements" although the effect of a re-enforcement is probably that of a symbolical reinforcement. The reason for saying that re-enforcements

An example will, perhaps, make these points clearer. In many primitive tribes there have existed organizations known as ghost cults. The key purpose in the charter of such cults is to deal successfully with ghosts or spirits who are conceived of as beings which possess supernatural powers and which take an uncomfortable interest in the affairs of living people. In other words, the purpose of these cults is to control the ghosts. As means to this end, cults adopt one or more of a number of principles and follow a variety of norms and rules which implement these principles. One principle, for instance, is known as avoidance, which simply means keeping away from the ghosts—staying out of harm's way, so to speak, in the manner of individuals who give a wide berth to cemeteries and refuse to enter haunted houses. Another principle is propitiation, which means flattering or otherwise pleasing the ghosts so that they will not want to hurt the cult members. This may be done by singing praises, making sacrifices, or in a variety of other specific ways, all of which are based on the same principle. Still another principle for dealing with ghosts is to try to coerce them, that is, to force them to behave by bringing to bear powers which they are unable to resist. Finally, in dealing with ghosts, there are certain standards which have to be observed. In some cults, for instance, it is very important to be careful and precise. No matter what is done it must be done with care and precision. One must not be careless about avoidance or about propitiation. The charms which accomplish coercion have to be precisely correct, otherwise they may be very dangerous. Thus, these standards modify practices which are based on principle. They cannot stand alone in behavior, for it is impossible to be careful or precise unless one is doing something else. One can walk carefully or pray according to a precise formula, but he cannot practice care and precision in and of themselves. Or, to shift the example for a

---

should logically be included as norms is that in the shape of stories, proverbs, and the like they are actually verbal folkways or norms. Their content is so closely bound up with charter, however, that it seems simpler to discuss them with charter. (See E. Wight Bakke, *Principles of Adaptive Human Behavior.* It should be noted that Bakke uses the term "charter" in a much more limited sense than is here described.)

moment to industry, a worker, conscious of safety as a standard, can run his machine safely, or handle materials safely, or do other things safely, but he cannot go into the shop and perform safety as an independent kind of behavior.

This example introduces an element which is implied in charter, although it has not been made explicit in the above definition. This is the fabric of beliefs and knowledge which supports the purposes, principles, and value standards. Thus the purpose of controlling ghosts depends entirely on the belief that such supernaturals actually exist and upon further beliefs concerning the nature of these supposed beings. In the ensuing analysis of the New Freedom Products Company (and, by extension, in treating modern industry), this element has been largely omitted. This is done partly because it seems possible to assume familiarity with the typical knowledge and beliefs held by industrial personnel in our society, although the fact that some of these beliefs are not verifiable indicates that possibly they require more attention than is given them here. Generally speaking, the members of any institution hold certain truths to be self-evident, and generally speaking, some of these "truths" can be shown to be false. This is so even in industry, and any astute industrialist can recall convictions which, in the course of time, have proved ridiculous. Belief in the reality of economic man is such a conviction, and, although it is said that this ghost has been laid, its influence is still plainly evident in many industrial practices. Nevertheless, any systematic attempt to discuss the beliefs which pervade modern industry would very likely result merely in supererogation.

Two further points suggested by this example of the ghost cults concern the difference between charter principles and the norms and rules of an institution and the difference between charter and functions. These will be more evident when norms and rules and functions are discussed below. It is worth noting, however, that principles refer to broad means, whereas norms and rules define specific practices. Thus avoidance is a principle upon which a variety of norms and rules can be based. Keeping away from cemeteries, staying out of haunted houses, wearing disguises, and even moving away from a camp site where someone has died are all practices rooted in the principle of avoidance. On the second point, the difference between charter and function—this difference is exactly that which Sumner makes between purposes and consequences,[4] that is, between the results desired and the results actually ensuing from behavior. Thus the purpose of the ghost cult is to control the supernaturals, and this the members declare is what their activities accomplish. To the outsider, however, this is not a function. Indeed, it cannot be because there are no ghosts to control. Nevertheless, the scientific observer would argue that the activities of the cult actually do have functions—they produce results which satisfy needs, some of which are not recognized by the actors. Among other things these activities provide ways by which the need for a sense of security in an uncertain world is attained, a result not necessarily perceived by the cultists.

Part of the difficulty of presenting the institutional element of functions lies in the fact that all elements of culture are functional,[5] that is, are adapted, directly or indirectly, to the satisfaction of human needs. Thus charter itself has functions. By pursuing their purposes the members of the institution satisfy, more or less successfully, their needs. In so doing they employ principles of organization, value judgments as to the propriety of their actions, and re-enforcements which draw attention to the common purposes and sustain the principles and values. The major functions of a successful charter as a whole are to provide incentives for individuals and to hold the institution together. In like manner, other elements of an institution also have functions. But it is advisable to postpone further discussion of functions until these other elements have been described. They are personnel, norms, and rules, material apparatus, and activities.

Personnel means the members of the institution—"the group

4. W. G. Sumner, "Purposes and Consequences" in *Selected Essays of William Graham Sumner,* pp. 1–7.

5. In a sense it may be regarded as incorrect to say that some of these elements are functional—that is, that they produce results which satisfy needs. Strictly speaking, only activities produce results. However, since activities are performed in terms of a charter, norms, etc., to call these elements functional is a convenient shorthand.

organized on definite principles of authority, division of functions, and distribution of privileges and duties." [6] This definition itself suggests the close relationships between the various elements in the concept. The personnel create the charter, and it exists in their understanding. On the other hand, the charter is transmitted to members of the group and shapes their conceptions. Also, the charter tends to designate the kinds of people who may be members and to indicate the positions they may hold. Thus in the United States a family is conceived of as consisting of a husband, a wife, and their children, to each of whom are assigned duties, tasks, and privileges. The limiting effect of charter on the personnel of such an institution as a girls' school or a foundry is even more obvious.

Conversely, the character of the personnel which make up a group has definite influences on the formation of the charter, on reactions to rules and norms, on the sorts of material apparatus which may be used, and so on. Thus the fact that children are born helpless and pass through various stages of maturation is a primary condition of family ideology and activity. Similarly, it has been noted that the cultural conditioning of the family partners affects their values and the way they behave and may, in cases where husband and wife have been brought up in different cultural traditions, prevent the formation of a family charter strong enough to overcome the friction created by differing habits and beliefs. In a factory, the reciprocal effects of charter on personnel and of personnel on charter are particularly plain. Employment is directed toward procuring individuals who are physically and otherwise able to carry on activities which will accomplish charter purposes, while the skills and aspirations of employees are inevitably reflected in their conceptions of charter.

Norms and rules are the expected, customary patterns of behavior, the approved folkways, and the formal regulations. For convenience in this study the term "rules" can be used for patterns which have been expressly formulated, usually in writing, and "norms" can refer to those which have not. Thus in the family there may be a stated rule which requires children to go to bed

6. Malinowski, *A Scientific Theory of Culture*, p. 52.

at a certain hour, while the parents may follow an unformulated norm with equal regularity. The relationship between the charter and the norms and rules is important. The norms and rules derive their authority from the charter.[7] Those norms which are most closely based upon important charter elements have special significance. They correspond to mores as described by Sumner and Keller, while the charter provides the "welfare element" which attaches to them.[8] Rules and norms also provide patterns for negative sanctions. Thus in the prevailing conception of the American family, adultery is a breach of the rules for which penalties are provided.[9] The rules governing this are derived from the principle of fidelity in the marriage charter.

Material apparatus means in the broadest sense the physical environment, both natural and artificial, including wealth and instruments.[10] In the case of the factory this would mean "land, buildings, and equipment," materials, supplies, products, and money. The influence of charter upon the material apparatus is clear: the people use the objects which they believe will aid in realizing their purposes. Conversely, material apparatus influences charter. For example, the traditional emphasis on safety, a standard, at the New Freedom Products Company is related to the use of hazardous materials.

Activities are the actual behavior of the group members. "The distinction between activities and rules and norms is clear and precise. The activities depend upon the ability, power, honesty, and good will of the members. They deviate invariably from the

7. Norms and rules should not be confused with the principles which are in the charter. They are much more specific in that they designate patterns for activity. Principles, on the other hand, are general, and a number of norms may be derived from one or two principles.

8. See W. G. Sumner, *Folkways,* p. 30; and Sumner and Keller, *The Science of Society,* I, 33–34.

9. Thus, by law in most states, the innocent spouse is considered "the aggrieved party" and enabled to obtain redress by divorce. Traditionally, of course, the penalties for adultery are considerably more direct. It is interesting to note that in the legal view dissolution of the family institution is considered a penalty, at least for one of the parties.

10. Malinowski, *A Scientific Theory of Culture,* pp. 52–53.

rules which represent the ideal performance, not necessarily its reality." [11] The relationship between activities and the other elements of the institution is indicated by the following: "Organized on the charter, acting through their social and organized cooperation, following the rules of their specific occupation, using the material apparatus at their disposal, the group engages in the activities for which they have organized . . . [Function is] the integral result of organized activities, as distinguished from charter, that is, the purpose . . ." [12] In a dynamic situation, however, the correspondence between activities and norms is not necessarily close, and deviant activities tend both to inhibit old norms and to create new ones.[13]

Malinowski defines *function* as "the satisfaction of needs," and it is, perhaps, more precise to say, "results of activities in terms of the satisfaction of needs." [14] His meaning here depends, however, upon an understanding of his use of the word "needs." By needs he means both biological needs of human beings and what he calls "derived, secondary or instrumental needs or cultural imperatives." [15] The latter are derived from the former but, once they are established, become as essential or "deterministic" as the former. Thus the invention of a tool and its acceptance by workers create dependence upon the tool, and the same is true of all other cultural phenomena. To illustrate further, the need for fertilizer in a society which depends upon intensive agriculture is obvious. Feeding the soil satisfies no biological need of people directly, but

11. *Ibid.*, p. 53.

12. *Ibid.*

13. Cf. Bakke, *Principles of Adaptive Human Behavior*, especially discussion of routine behavior or folkways. See also Sumner, *Folkways*, pp. 2–6, in which he points out that folkways arise in individual acts, from among which those which satisfy needs with a minimum of pain are selected and become group customs, i.e., folkways. Sumner states that "so long as the adaptation [of means to ends] is so imperfect that pain is produced," the folkways are subject to "a strain of improvement." Presumably it would do no violence to Sumner's thought to say, "*Whenever* the adaptation of means to ends is so imperfect that pain is produced, the folkways are subject to a strain of improvement, and at such times the selection from experimental acts occurs."

14. Malinowski, *A Scientific Theory of Culture*, p. 111.

15. *Ibid.*

without fertilizer human needs would not be fully satisfied. Fertilizer may originally have been used simply to improve upon agricultural methods and may not have been a vital necessity. It is now so closely woven into the cultural complex which supports a larger population on a higher standard of living that it can easily be recognized as a "cultural imperative." Similarly in a factory practices which make for a faster working tempo are imperative in a system which also includes a shorter working week and more efficient machinery. Malinowski develops the idea of cultural imperatives as follows: "Since the collective and integral functioning of culture, high or low, supplies the means for the satisfaction of biological needs, every aspect of the collective production, in the widest sense of the word, is biologically as necessary as the full and adequate carrying out of all the vital sequences [i.e., satisfaction of all the biological needs]." [16] He further develops the relationship between the two kinds of needs by pointing out that the instruments which satisfy drives may, in a derived or secondary manner, become objects of desire themselves.[17] In other words, they acquire "drive value" of their own and become needs for the individual. This discussion is at the heart of Malinowski's functional theory, and the presentation here is necessarily brief. It indicates, however, that as far as the word "needs" and its synonyms are concerned it is not necessary to delve deeply into their biological derivation. It makes it possible to consider needs on the level upon which they are encountered, and it also makes it possible to speak of the needs of culture, or cultural imperatives, as Malinowski does. Functions may be related to the needs of individuals, more or less directly, and to the needs of the culture.

As is true of charter, functions are clearer when broken down into subelements or, rather, classified as being of different kinds. These are 1) extrainstitutional or outgoing functions; and 2) intrainstitutional or ingoing functions. The former are those which satisfy needs of society rather than those of the members of an institution per se. These include, usually, a principal or "integral" function and subsidiary functions. The ingoing or intrainstitu-

16. *Ibid.*, pp. 122–123.
17. *Ibid.*, p. 138.

tional functions are of two sorts: those which satisfy directly the
needs of the personnel and may be called consumatory functions,
in the sense that individuals "consume" them; those which meet
organizational or operational needs of the institution and may be
called instrumental functions.

Extrainstitutional functions are rather easily illustrated in the
case of a factory. The principal or integral function of such an
institution is the production of goods which society wants. A factory depends for its existence upon the successful discharge of this
function; society utilizes the products in the satisfaction of either
culturally derived needs or biological needs. Subsidiary external
functions include the payment of taxes, providing a market for
other institutions, and so on. Similarly, the integral function of a
family is the provision of new members for society, but it also has
other external functions which may be regarded as subsidiary.
"Society has automatically utilized the trunk-line and branchings
of the blood-kinship that follows upon propogation in order to
transfer along them, without disorder, both property and social
position . . ." [18] Even in the functions it performs for society, an
institution is likely to be a "comprehensive instrumentality,"
which, once it is established, can be used for more than one end.

Intrainstitutional functions in the factory are also rather easily
illustrated, although the distinctions between instrumental and
consumatory functions are not always clear cut. Thus messenger
service can be regarded as having an instrumental function. Ordinarily it serves as a means of communications to coordinate activities and thus to facilitate smooth operation of related departments.
On the other hand, distribution of pay envelopes satisfies, rather
directly, the needs of individual wage earners—a consumatory
function.

At this point, certainly for industrial analysis and probably for
other kinds of institutions, it is advisable to elaborate considerably
upon Malinowski's statements regarding functions. This may be
done very briefly for consumatory functions since they are treated
more fully elsewhere. Here it need only be pointed out that these
functions present a dilemma. On one hand, it can be assumed that

18. Sumner and Keller, *The Science of Society*, III, 1527.

any activity arises from a need of the individual performing it, and such needs can be described on a highly derived level. For instance, it could be said that the man who lights a cigarette has a need to smoke. However, to follow this rule is of no use in attempting to classify needs or to discover needs which are not being satisfied. Therefore, a list of more generalized needs (or drives) is desirable, especially in industrial research, since a limited, particularistic approach has so often led to incomplete views of motivation. The assumption that desire for money represents the only efficient motivation of industrial workers is a notorious example of the weaknesses of this approach. On the other hand, while the broad lists of drives which have been suggested by both psychologists and sociologists as universal in human societies are helpful, they are not specific enough. Thus one particularly satisfactory list of this kind states that the human organism has innate tissue drives (e.g., hunger, thirst, fatigue, and others), an innate sex drive (which is listed separately because it is much more modifiable than the others), and certain generalized drives which are inevitably acquired as a result of the ways in which human beings receive their most basic conditioning. These last include drives to avoid danger (fear, anxiety, aggression) and drives for such positive rewards as a sense of prestige, a sense of belonging, and the experience of aesthetic satisfactions.

To avoid this dilemma of overparticularity, on one hand, and overgenerality, on the other, a list of needs which seem to be universally felt by persons in industry is extremely helpful. This is especially true because not all of the "basic drives" are of prime importance in industrial situations. Sex, for instance, is ordinarily satisfied in institutions outside industry, and the industrial organization's concern with it is limited to such things as maintaining established community controls. A valuable list of this kind has been proposed by Bakke.[19] It includes needs for security, progress, justice, respect, understanding, creature comforts, and others abstracted from a broad body of empirical and other research. With some modifications this list is used in analyzing the functions of the New Freedom Products Company.

19. Bakke, *Principles of Adaptive Human Behavior*.

For the instrumental needs, no such ready-made list seems to be available, although Malinowski gave some attention to them before his death.[20] However, anthropological, sociological, and industrial literature are all suggestive in this connection, and the following functions can be listed at least tentatively as being those which are essential in any institution for maintaining and coordinating organization. They can therefore be designated "instrumental organizational functions" or, more succinctly, organizational requirements.

They include the following which seem to be found, at least in rudimentary form, in all human organizations:

Communications, which is a somewhat obvious requirement and which is almost necessarily woven into all social endeavor.

Recruitment, a requirement which can be taken to include placement, transferring of help, and the like in industrial establishments as well as the obvious function of maintaining the work force through employment.

Training (or education), which includes not only technical training but all activities which result in preparing individuals to participate in group activity.

Regulation (or control), which includes the entire system whereby behavior is sanctioned and channeled into approved patterns by formal rules and informal norms, as well as the entire system of authority and responsibility. Here it should be noted that regulation encompasses not only rules which are framed by officially recognized means and backed in an organized fashion but also folkways and mores which are supported by the various personal pressures of ridicule and avoidance ordinarily lumped under the term "public opinion."

Protection, which refers to activities that guard the personnel and property of an institution from harm by persons and forces outside the institution. In connection with protection, the interrelationships of institutions are particularly clear since, as in the case of industries, the government is relied upon largely to discharge this function through police protection and in other ways, although factories still install fences, locked gates, and guards.

20. See Malinowski, *A Scientific Theory of Culture.*

Technology, which includes the provision and maintenance of material equipment.

Welfare, which from the organizational point of view refers not to the satisfactions received by beneficiaries of welfare but rather to the maintenance of personnel for the benefit of the institution. Thus a welfare function of company hospitals is to maintain the health of employees so that they will work more steadily and efficiently.[21]

It may well be, of course, that this list is insufficient. No doubt in all institutions there are instrumental functions which cannot readily be classified under any of the headings above, and it may also be that functions which are necessary for the growth and survival of all institutions have been omitted. One of these may be research, that is, special activities devoted to the development of new products, methods, markets, and the like in industry and to new adjustments of various kinds in other kinds of institutions. However the apparent absence of this sort of activity in some institutions makes one hesitant to include it as a universal.

In the analysis of the New Freedom Products Company which follows, little attention is given to extrainstitutional functions (such as providing goods wanted by society), since changes in these bore only indirectly upon the relationships of the personnel of the institution. Their importance should not be overlooked, however. Suppose, for instance, demand for one of the company's major products had disappeared. Obviously the effect on internal operations would have been drastic. Conversely, greatly increased de-

21. The distinction between the consumatory functions of welfare activities and the organizational or instrumental functions is sometimes hard to grasp, especially since such activities generally have both sorts of functions. However, if one regards the United States as an institution and considers the welfare activities of the government in the 1930's, the distinction is clear enough. During World War I it was found that a large proportion of young men were ineligible for military service on account of physical deficiencies, some of which were due to malnutrition. Had the government not expanded its welfare functions greatly during the depression it is quite likely that this number would have been considerably larger and that the military strength of the nation would have suffered more seriously. In other words, welfare activities helped to maintain manpower for the benefit of the country as an organization.

mand would have had—actually did have—important effects. The factory grew because its markets expanded, and increased size was a fundamental factor in the changes described.

In recapitulation, the breakdown of institutional functions, which we regard as useful in analyzing a single institution, may be outlined as follows:

1) Outgoing functions: An institution performs functions in the whole society. These include a principal or integral function and subsidiary functions.

2) Ingoing functions, consumatory and instrumental—i.e., those which satisfy needs of the institution's personnel and those which answer needs of the institution.

In summary, an institution may be defined as a group of people organized to carry out certain purposes and performing certain functions for society, for their own group, and for themselves as individuals. Such a group has a charter which includes common purposes, principles governing the ways for achieving these purposes, and standards by which the members measure the propriety of activities and attempt to justify or rationalize their activities. Closely related to charter are re-enforcements which express and strengthen the standards, principles, and a sense of common purpose. Such a group develops a set of normal patterns for behavior, some of which may be explicitly formulated as rules and some of which may be informally accepted norms. It uses material objects, natural and artificial. Each of these elements—charter, personnel, rules and norms, and material apparatus—is influenced by all the others. In combination they produce activities, which differ from norms in that they are actual rather than ideal behavior. The functions of the institution are the product of the activities.

As an aid to visualizing these various elements the following synoptic chart prepared by Malinowski is helpful:

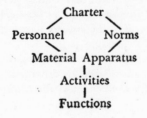

A useful elaboration of this chart might show the breakdown of the element of functions, thus:

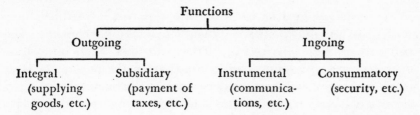

In approaching the analysis of an institution which has been changing, one further concept is useful, that of adjustment. As it is here used, adjustment has substantially the same meaning in which "equilibrium" is employed by many sociologists, except that it is related to the elements of an institution as described immediately above. It refers to a mutual adjustment of these elements in a way which provides optimum discharge of the institution's various functions. In other words, an effectively adjusted institution—that is, one in equilibrium—fulfills the demands which society in general places upon it, provides for the needs of its personnel in a way which seems to them satisfactory, and also operates to answer its own needs without friction. Such a perfectly operating institution may exist only in the realm of imagination, but it is obvious that if an institution were to function ideally incentives to change in it would be completely lacking, and its very perfection would inhibit such incentives. The religion of the Zuñi is a case in point. This tribe has adopted little from white culture, and its religious institution has not changed even under pressure of influences which might have been expected to alter it.[22] Zuñi religion, as described by Benedict, appears to exemplify perhaps as clear an approximation of an institution in perfect equilibrium as could be discovered or imagined.

Except for such rare cases of equilibrium, adjustment is always a relative matter. The elements of an institution may be more

22. Cf. Ruth Benedict, *Patterns of Culture*, chap. ii; and the writings of Sumner, Keller, Ogburn, and others who take the position that new objects of material culture ordinarily set in motion a chain of new adjustments in society.

or less perfectly adjusted to each other and to the world outside. In the case of relatively perfect adjustment, a change in any element will affect this adjustment. Any resultant maladjustment will be reflected in dissatisfaction of the personnel—which is, in terms of action, the essentially dynamic institutional element—and they will try new activities or neglect old ones. Such innovation or neglect in activities may affect the charter, the norms, the composition or organization of the personnel, or the material apparatus, or any combination of these elements, depending upon the specific situation. Essentially this is the position taken by Bakke [23] who approaches the subject from a somewhat different orientation. Where the original source of change is likely to occur is a question which need not be considered here. At the present stage of development of the social sciences it is perhaps not very fruitful to seek for original or ultimate sources when studying a limited situation. It is important, however, to be aware of proximate or immediate sources and to assess their effects.[24]

The ensuing chapters attempt to describe the elements of the New Freedom Products Company as an institution. Were this institution static—that is, in a continuing equilibrium—the problem of presenting its structure would be comparatively simple. The fact is that the institution has been changing for many years. The relationships of the personnel are the matters of central interest. The evidence points to the existence, early in the century,

23. Bakke, *Principles of Adaptive Human Behavior.*

24. Elsewhere note has been made of various sources of change in the New Freedom Products Company, some arising within the institution and some coming from outside. An example of a change arising within the institution was the advancing age of employees in the first two or three decades of the company's history. When the company was founded there was obviously no need to consider the needs of aged employees. When, however, employees became older and older in the company's service, the decision was made to assist them. This decision was, in part at least, the basis for incorporating the idea of security into the institutional charter. In this instance the source of change was in the character of the personnel, and its effects ramified to the charter and later returned to modify the composition of the personnel still further. The effect of changed recreational patterns for the upper classes upon the activities of officials has also been described and will serve as an example of change, the source of which was outside the institution.

of equilibrium in these relationships. Indeed, a superficial description of the present situation might also create an impression of
equilibrium, even though the forces of change may be strongly at
work.[25] In this section the focus of attention is not on change, but
the fact that change is present cannot be disregarded even while
our attention is directed specifically upon the elements of stability.

The analysis here presented involves a kind of artificial dissection which, although it seeks clarification, may be accompanied by
confusion. This is so because the people of the living institution
are not particularly interested in analysis and do not provide a neat,
definitive nomenclature for their various purposes, principles, and
values. Their minds are not files in which they methodically
pigeonhole their ideas. On the contrary, they are quite capable of
thinking of several things at once, of applying a number of values
to justify a single course of action, of treating principles as though
they were purposes, and even of regarding standards as though
they were goals in themselves. Thus the serving of milk during
long shifts at the New Freedom Products Company during World
War II was justified by executives on three counts. It was supposed
to promote safety, efficiency, and good feeling—three things here
classified as standards. These standards in turn modify at least two
principles. Principles, it will be recalled, are broad and basic ways
by which major purposes are supposed to be accomplished. Thus
manufacturing or, in the factory term, "production" is a principle,

25. This fact—the apparent equilibrium of an institution viewed at a
single point in time—may suggest that the functionalist position that every
detail of culture has its function is misleading. The argument that no action
would be performed unless it satisfied some kind of a need, true though it
may be, can obscure the fact that the action may not satisfy the need very well
and that the cutural element represented by the action may be retained only
because no better means for satisfaction are available. Any institution in process
of change is likely to abound in obsolete or obsolescent folkways, survivals
which while "functioning" may actually be of disservice to the institution in
the sense that they hinder performance of more important functions. Thus
the rural functionaries, sheriff and justice of the peace, who survive in the city
possess offices which certainly have consumatory functions as far as their in-
cumbents are concerned. Yet urban sociologists and criminologists alike are
agreed that these offices are a wasteful drain on the public treasury and stand
in the way of better adjustments.

but it is one which should be efficient and safe. A second principle is cooperation or "working together," and cooperation is supposed to be friendly and pleasant, that is, characterized by good feeling. The institutional purposes to be accomplished by production and cooperation are, of course, creation of products, current income, and long-run security. To this, upon reflection, most employees would agree. This fact does not, however, prevent individuals from losing sight of the major purposes in favor of what, to them, are more immediate goals. The safety engineer, for example, might consider safety an adequate end in itself, while the manager of production might be satisfied with the safety program only if he thought it increased efficiency.

What this means for the sociological analyst is that he must either brutally disregard the fluid, apparently inconsistent thinking of people in real life or accept the risk of bewildering his readers by sticking to the unconsidered vagaries of the people whom he is describing. The latter course seems preferable. The words used in the factory may be employed loosely, but they are the real words, and it would be unfair to deny the reader the opportunity of subjecting them to his own analysis and interpretation. A worker may not clearly differentiate between security, which is here taken to mean future satisfaction of personal needs and interests, and safety, which can be defined as elimination of current physical hazards. The worker nevertheless knows this difference, and the reader is entitled to know that the terms can, at times, be used interchangeably. Again, the employee may identify himself so closely with the company that he sees little difference between its continued success, which is described by the word "stability," and his own security. The two things are, however, not the same. Maintenance of company stability is a purposive principle aimed at obtaining security. Still, the fact that the terms are so closely associated is significant. Therefore, insofar as possible, factory phraseology will be used. This will mean that words may turn up with different meanings in different parts of the analytical framework. In each case an attempt will be made to eliminate the incidental confusion and to pursue the analytical "dissection" with a view to making clear the factors involved.

A presentation which offers the various parts of the institution for separate examination must somehow also make it clear that each part has meaning only in its relationship to other parts. Ideally, to describe the parts separately, to demonstrate their integration, and at the same time to show how each part, the integrated whole, and the method of integration are all changing would require a three-dimensional system of writing which does not exist.

CHAPTER FIVE: *Charter*

PURPOSES. The roots of the New Freedom Products Company's charter go back to the purpose of the inventor of the original product. James Freedom was inspired by pity for his neighbors to seek a means for preventing accidents in their physically dangerous calling. His motives were humanitarian.[1] His purpose was to provide safety for a large class of industrial workers. This consideration for the safety of human beings still exists in the charter of the institution.

By the time Freedom's invention was brought to America, however, another purpose had become paramount. The promoters of the American venture were interested in making money. The first American workers also regarded the company as a source of income. Still the original purpose was not wholly lost to sight. John Drew had absorbed it while working in the parent company, and he brought it with him when he was sent to oversee activities in this country. He was a religious man, possessed of a sense of duty and a feeling of obligation to his fellow man. As the leading figure in a very small company, he readily adopted the community tradition of neighborly responsibility; and within 20 years there were

1. Judging by the tradition as it has come down to the present, one would suppose that Freedom's motives were solely humanitarian. They may well have been so originally, but the fact that he carried his idea into a business enterprise indicates that they went beyond simple humanitarianism. The story is important, however, not for its accuracy but for its content.

112

clear indications that the tradition, later summed up in the phrase, "the Products family," was already in existence.[2]

Drew, moreover, was more interested in the long-term strength and stability of the company than in quick profits. It was over this point that he and the original American partner parted company. Also, as employees came to devote their entire time to factory work and to accumulate years of service, they depended upon the company not only for immediate income but for their future security as well. Here, of course, was the genesis of what was to become a dominating element in the company's charter. The desire for security is emphasized by employees and officials alike more than any other single purpose. But security is not the only reason assigned by the personnel for the existence of the company. Their ideas of purpose include all of the following:

1) *Product*—the manufacture of useful devices.

2) *Income*—including current wages, salaries, and profits for the personnel.

3) *Security*—including ideas regarding permanence of employment and care for the personnel in sickness or old age.

4) *Community responsibility*—including the idea that the company should provide employment for local people and should otherwise contribute to the town's welfare.[3]

These are the purposes upon which the charter is constructed. There is no reason to believe that they have changed greatly during the present century, although notions of what constitute adequate wages, salaries, or profits, or effective security have changed as have the products themselves.

Acceptance of the products as a major purpose is a recognition on the part of the personnel of the outgoing functions of the institution. They know that only by supplying products which people outside the institution are willing to purchase can they accom-

2. A letter written by Drew in 1850 expressed his belief that financial aid should be given to the widow of an old employee and that work should be found for one of her children.

3. Possibly the idea that the company should serve the nation in time of war is an extension of this idea. It may, however, simply represent a phase of a more general sense of patriotism.

plish their other, more personal purposes. In addition, the seemingly idealistic aspects of the products as safety devices and useful
tools have "practical" connotations as well. More or less clearly,
the products must be safe, reliable, efficient, and economical in
order to win and hold markets, that is, to produce current income
for themselves and to assure company stability and thus future
security for themselves. This close correspondence of the principal
function of the institution and one of the purposes of the personnel
is, perhaps, a characteristic to be expected of an economic institution. As Sumner and Keller [4] have pointed out, the folkways of
maintenance and, by inference, ideas regarding them are subjected
to a relatively stringent testing in the world of hard facts and are
least subject to "benumbing tradition."

Quite aside from this realistic view of the product as a step
toward attaining other ends, we find beliefs about it which even
more certainly mark it as a purpose. The story of James Freedom's
invention is still well known to most employees. It is an especially
striking example of the re-enforcements which—in the form of
stories, gossip, legends, and the like—convey and keep alive the
essentials of the charter. Hence the belief that the original product
provides safety for an important and numerous group of industrial
workers still persists. More recently developed products are by
their nature classed with the older one in this respect or can be
closely enough associated with it to make this belief appropriate
for practically all the things the factory makes. In addition, there
is a belief in the value of the products as elements in the entire
system of American industry.[5] During World War II the im-

4. Sumner and Keller, *The Science of Society,* I, 36, 37: "The mores that
have to do with self-maintenance, being closest to natural conditions, are
checked up more speedily and obviously upon the life-conditions than are the
rest of the mores. Causes of discomfort and failure are here more easily iden-
tifiable, impressing even the untrained mind. Hence the maintenance-mores
tend to follow the changing life-conditions pretty closely; that is they are least
insulated against selection, least subject to benumbing tradition, more sensitive."

5. This is made quite explicit in the company history and in the employee
manual, which has proved to be a particularly effective re-enforcement. A

portance of this belief was most pronounced. Indeed, "getting out" products to help win the war was almost the only reason some individuals had for working. Even before the company itself was engaged in war production, however, employees consoled themselves for not receiving the acclaim accorded aircraft workers by pointing out that "if those guys didn't have any materials, they wouldn't be able to make any planes. And without our products they wouldn't get any materials." Statements such as this, moreover, were not the result of war-induced propaganda. It was too early in the war for that. They were simply reassertions of beliefs of long standing. Years before the employee manual appeared, older employees were fond of stressing the far-reaching importance of the work they were doing. The absorbed interest with which employees greet stories of men "who have been in the field" and motion pictures of the product at work is further testimony to the reality of their faith in the value of the things they make.[6]

The second of the purposes listed above is income, that is, the

statement from the manual follows: "In the [company] history you can read how our products played a proud part in the growth of the United States. In the last hundred or so years [it has become essential in] the cornerstone of American industry. Highways and railroads were built. Harbors and waterways were deepened, subways were bored beneath rivers, foundations for skyscrapers were sunk to bedrock. On the farms [processes in which our products were used] became almost as useful as plowing and planting. In all these things [our product] was used. Somewhat later, when [industry called for even more effective equipment], the company introduced a new product to the country . . . then in 1936, after long experimentation came [Product No. 3] . . . an outstanding example of the way the company has kept up and sometimes even led the march of progress."

6. The importance of belief in a product's usefulness was stressed in the Job Instructor Training Program of Training Within Industry, War Manpower Commission, which was widely used by industrial plants during World War II. Part of the "first step" in this program is to get the learner interested. To do this the instructor explains as dramatically as possible what the product is for. Used at the New Freedom Products Company this technique proved to be one of the most effective parts of the program. Cf. War Manpower Commission, Training Within Industry, *Job Instructor Training; Training Sessions Outline and Reference Manual.*

current payments for which the personnel work—salaries, wages, and dividends insofar as they represent income for the personnel.[7] In saying that security is given greater emphasis than income as a purpose, it is not intended to indicate that income is not regarded as essential. Indeed it is conceivable that employees would work with no assurance of future security of employment, while they would certainly not work without receiving current payments from the company. On the other hand, employees believe that their income from the company is modest as compared with what they might receive elsewhere and that their prospects for advancement and higher income are slight. To this situation they reconcile themselves with the belief that their job tenure is secure and that even in old age the company will, as they say, "take care of them." In other words, they are willing to temper their desires for high income with considerations of future security. Most employees desire higher pay, but very few of those who have been with the company long enough to feel that they are fullfledged members of the personnel would insist upon higher pay if they thought it would endanger the ability of the company to provide them with security. Perhaps the emphasis upon security is the more obvious because income is taken for granted by the employees as an accompaniment of employment anywhere, while they believe that other employment would not provide them with as much security as they think the New Freedom Products Company does.[8]

7. The problem of how to treat dividends is a difficult one. To the officers and some others of the people who work at the plant, nearly all of them executives, they are, of course, income received from the company. Even to these individuals, however, they are not quite the same as salaries. While to the officials, at least, profits are of fundamental importance, they are to some extent regarded as a reflection of the company's success and of their success as company administrators. By the smaller stockholders among the executives this view of profits is held with varying degrees of intensity, while the dividends received are regarded much as are those which might come from other companies—as a more or less important supplement to salaries. In a sense, moreover, as will be shown later, dividends are regarded as a kind of necessary cost of doing business.

8. It should be noted here that this emphasis on security is not presented as typical of industry in general. As can be seen, the employees of the New

In any event, success, as measured by high pay and promotion, is not valued as highly in this particular company as is the desire for sure employment extending into old age and for income continuing even after retirement.

It seems unnecessary to labor the point that the personnel regard the provision of income for employees of whatever rank as a purpose of the institution. It is interesting to note, however, that no ritual is regarded as more immutable than the preparation and distribution of the pay envelopes. These must go out on Friday morning. It is inconceivable that they should not. Directors' meetings have been postponed; the date of the annual stockholders' meetings is set to suit the convenience of the larger stockholders; the factory whistle has failed to blow at noon; floods have blocked the paths to time clocks and machines—but the pay always goes out on Friday, even if ways have to be found to circumvent laws limiting the hours that women payroll clerks can work. The clerks themselves have been quick to assist in this on the rare occasions when it seemed necessary. Precisely what would happen if the pay did not go out on time nobody knows—and nobody wants to find out.

The third of the purposes in the charter is security. As has been noted, the emphasis placed on this purpose is very strong. The personnel look upon security as the special advantage of working for this particular company. They believe that they are not likely to make as much money at the New Freedom Products Company as they might elsewhere and that the opportunities for advancement are relatively slight. Nevertheless, those who stay with the company consider that these disadvantages are more than outweighed by the relative certainty of future employment and the prospect

---

Freedom Products Company themselves do not regard it as typical, although their opportunities for observing other companies are limited. Regard for high income can certainly outweigh desire for security in some instances. An executive of a large advertising firm has recently offered the information that in his company, and he believes in others, high income is the principal mark of prestige. Many employees keep their names on file at special employment agencies in the hope of obtaining higher paying jobs, and shifting employment for higher pay is common.

that even if they become disabled by age or illness they will probably still be employed or, if not, will receive pensions.

The goal of security extends from the top to the bottom of the
personnel hierarchy, and, as will be further noted in the chapter
on personnel in this section, its influence is felt at the time of
employment. Young men seeking executive positions are warned,
"You will never get rich here, but, if you do your work, you will
always be sure of an income." It is common to hear workers
remark, "This company will always take care of you." There have
been instances where parents employed by the company have put
great pressure on their children to work there because they regarded other employment as insecure. The lure of security induced
the first Italian workers who came to the company to abandon
their ambition to get rich quick and return to "the old country";
they decided to settle down and bring their families over to
America. The story of the company's care for employees during
the depression is cited over and over again as proof that workers
and their families can feel secure even in precarious times. Other
stories tell how officials have aided employees at critical times. In
1946 full-page advertisements were run in the local newspaper
each week. These were designed both to attract new employees
from the locality and to impress employees already on the payroll.
In them the steady refrain was security.[9] These advertisements
are cited to indicate that, in seeking to play up all possible ad-

9. Each of these advertisements included a large box which was the same from
week to week. The heading on this read: "Residents of the Teasville-Herford
Area can find SECURITY working at New Freedom Products." Under this title
26 advantages were listed. These included life, disability, and hospital insurance; workmen's compensation; "liberal retirement income plan"; hospital
and clinic facilities; and the fact that the company is old and strong. Nine of
the 26 items were concerned with such matters, while the rest mentioned such
things as the advantages of living in such towns as Teasville and Herford, the
beauty of the factory grounds, the suggestion system, good working conditions,
good safety record, the company houses, recreation building and activities,
the cafeteria, the ability of the foremen, apprenticeship training, educational
assistance plan, and the following three which are especially interesting: "Average earnings of NFP employees are as good or better than employees of
other companies in similar lines" (there are no similar lines within many miles
of Teasville or Herford, and employees are well aware of the qualified nature

vantages, the company could find nothing more important than security. The employee manual stresses security persistently, and the booklet dealing with the retirement plan commences with a discussion of all aspects of security at the company.

In the first union contract negotiation meetings, the insistence of the union committee was upon "getting the company to put in black and white that they will continue to do what they have been doing." Clauses concerning transfers, seniority, and benefits deal specifically with security, while others touch indirectly on this purpose.

The fourth purpose, community responsibility, is implicit in various policies and in certain beliefs but scarcely to be found in explicit statements. Occasionally a thoughtful employee, usually an executive or an official, will state that he believes the company "has a duty toward" the town. Such a remark is likely to be followed by an observation to the effect that the company is important in the town's economic life and hence must continue to be successful and to remain in the town. Workers are likely to phrase similar views more indirectly: "A lot of people here in Teasville depend on this company for jobs, even people who don't work here. It would be a heck of a thing if something went wrong with the company."

Such beliefs have their roots in the very small neighborhood in which the company started. They have become closely woven into the company's traditions and have resulted in a strong in-group

---

of this statement); "Responsible, co-operative Union Organization"; and "liberal, understanding management—open door policy."

One of these advertisements featured large pictures of a recently retired employee leisurely working in his garden. The caption, in large black type, read, "He worked for many years at New Freedom Products, and you can learn a lot from his story." The story includes the statement: "It sure is wonderful to know that now I've stopped working I can still be sure of enough to get by without being a burden on anybody." The rest of the copy emphasizes and re-emphasizes the security theme: "The day you lay down your tools and take off your overalls and punch out your time card for the last time will be a mighty important day in your life. . . . Will you face the future with dread and fear? Will you be forced to struggle along with a few dollars saved and know that when these are gone there will be no more?"

feeling. This expressed itself during World War II toward the so-called "outsiders" who came from the nearby city. This feeling was so marked that it is a fair question whether discriminatory attitudes against Negroes were not based upon it more than upon racial prejudice. Two local Negroes were regarded as exceptions to various generalizations about Negro inferiority.

In the phrase, "other things being equal," which is used to modify length of service as the principal factor to be considered in laying off or recalling employees, the first qualification suggested by management, and the one most readily accepted by the union representatives, was local residence. The basis for excluding watchmen and guards from union membership was that because a fire at one of the plants would endanger the community these men should think first and always of being on the job. In the event of a strike, they should not be influenced by loyalty to the union. Officials explicitly state that executives must live in Teasville. Employees are expected to participate in local affairs "according to their abilities," which means primarily that civic efforts are expected of executives. It is believed that "whenever possible" purchases of supplies should be made locally. A high officer has stated that he would never consent to the company's manufacturing "malodorous" products which would hurt the town.

During wartime the idea of community responsibility was extended to the nation, and war production became a paramount goal. It was believed that all interests should be subordinated to "getting out the products they need to win the war." Incidentally, when the first Army-Navy "E" Award was presented all residents of the area surrounding the two plants were invited to the ceremony, and a full-page advertisement was taken in the local newspaper to thank "our friends and neighbors" for helping to win the award.

In the employee manual the sense of identity with the locality is noted: "It can be said that the two towns where our plants are located are regarded as among the most beautiful in the country. They have fine schools, churches and stores, many opportunities for recreation, good homes and good people. They are good places to live." In the recent series of advertisements in the local newspaper also, emphasis is placed on the advantages of company employment to local residents.

This list of purposes does not, of course, exhaust the numerous other reasons which individuals may give for the company's existence or for their working there. It does, however, represent the common purposes upon which there is universal, if to some extent tacit, agreement. There is no reason to suppose that these have not been the main purposes for a long time. Definitions of them have, however, changed considerably. The products, as has been noted, have changed, although in their minds the employees seem to minimize the significance of the changes by attributing to newer products the characteristics and values associated with older ones. Income is no longer the dollar a day which was apparently satisfactory 40 years ago.[10] Security, perhaps, means pretty much what it has for years, although employees are no longer willing to rely upon the informal guarantees which were good enough 40 years earlier. The meaning of community responsibility has been expanded to include a larger area than it used to, and it is interesting to speculate upon the possible effects of the fact that a growing proportion of employees have no roots in the community.

PRINCIPLES. Implementing these purposes are the following principles or essential means by which it is believed by the personnel that the purposes are to be achieved:

1) Manufacturing
2) Selling
3) Carrying on research
4) Cooperating
5) Making money as an institution
6) Maintaining the stability of the company

The first three of these principles are technical in nature and are the obvious instruments which distinguish a factory from other institutions. This is particularly true of manufacturing or, to use the customary factory term, production. It goes almost without saying that goods must be produced. In like manner, the products must be sold, although, because of the peculiar position

10. It is interesting, also, that annual dividends are no longer the ten per cent or so which used to be considered proper.

enjoyed by the company and the usefulness of its products, the problem of sales is not evident to most of the personnel. Research is a newer and even less well-understood principle, although its associated value, science, has come to possess in the minds of employees almost mystical attributes.

The word "production" illustrates the difficulty of classifying the concepts of the personnel. Production is definitely regarded as a means for accomplishing the purposes of the organization. At the same time the word carries so much value in itself that it has to be included as both a principle and a standard. Many activities, including nonproductive jobs, are justified on the ground that they contribute to production. The notion that "we can't let anything interfere with production" is often accepted without critical analysis as a justification for anything. Thus the reason given and readily accepted for limiting union activities on plant property but not on other company property or during rest periods was that they might interfere with production. Even vacations are supposed to be used for "rest and relaxation" so that employees will be refreshed for their work. One of the rationalizations used in the often difficult task of tactfully persuading superannuated employees to retire is that they have completed their productive life and have earned a deserved rest. The point system is a means for rewarding high production, and workers with good production records gain the respect of their fellows. This was especially noticeable in the case of out-of-town Negroes. Those regarded as "good workers" escaped much of the discrimination aimed at the group as a whole, which was condemned as being "lazy and shiftless."

As has been noted, production is not an unlimited good. Excessive production by an individual is regarded with suspicion because it may endanger quality, safety, or the health of the worker (an aspect of safety). The reaction of management to personal overproduction is to caution workers and their immediate supervisors against neglecting rules governing quality and safety; workers sometimes comment that so-and-so is silly to work himself to death for a few extra dollars. The strength of the idea that high production is good in itself has increased in the last two or three decades and is probably connected with the production premiums available under the point system. It is notable that under the day rates of 40 years ago workers set themselves definite production goals well below their maximum capacity to produce. Even then, however, workers were glad to exert themselves "to get out orders," an attitude which seems to be associated rationally with the idea of manufacturing as a principle for realizing the principal purposes. The idea of stretching jobs by limiting production has made little, if any, headway in the company, although some workers support the notion that excessive production "may spoil the job for everyone else." This thought does not seem to carry much weight, however, and is probably an importation rather than of local origin. It is generally assumed that the fruits of production create the general income which supports the institution and all the interests of the personnel.

The principle of selling is recognized more in the values which are associated with it, such as quality and low cost, than in the idea of salesmanship. The fact that the word "orders" is commonly used instead of "sales" is indicative of this attitude. The personnel, even the highest officials, seem to believe that they have assured markets which can be held as long as quality is maintained and prices are low enough to offset competition from different devices made by other companies. The employee manual contains an effective summary of the characteristic point of view:

> Our products fit right into the foundations of basic industries—Therefore, as long as we do a good job—as long as we maintain the quality which is so important to the users of our products—we have a good prospect of staying in business, and as long as we stay in business there will be work to do.

The third principle—carrying on research—means, in the words of the employee manual, "the constant search for improvements which will strengthen the company for the future." Research is also directed at maintaining quality and promoting both safety and efficiency. Although the word "research" is of comparatively recent currency, respect for "the search for improvements" is not new. Drew is remembered for improvements he made, and the high regard felt for one of the present older officials rests to a considerable degree on his reputation for inventiveness. Many workers are constantly on the lookout for improvements, and this was true even before the system of paying rewards for suggestions was inaugurated in 1932. In fact, some workers still prefer to pass suggestions along to their superiors by word of mouth rather than fill out suggestion blanks. They even profess to believe that they should not be paid for trying to do something extra for the company. Members of the suggestion committee are convinced that it is usually more important to put a suggestion into effect promptly than it is to make prompt payment of the award. Employees have frequently shown keen interest in assisting research, even to the extent of sacrificing part of their earnings. When the most recent of the company's important products was in the developmental stage in 1937, workers were proud to "help iron out the bugs." Some years later, moreover, these same workers were considered by union officers as having first claim to preferred positions in the department which manufactured this product, even though certain others had superior seniority rights.

The last three of the principles listed above are less obvious than manufacturing, selling, and research. On the other hand, the meanings given by the personnel to "cooperating," "making money as an institution," and "maintaining the stability of the company" are critical in understanding this particular institution.

Cooperation is aptly, if redundantly, defined in the employee manual as "working together in a friendly, co-operative spirit." This principle has a long history in the company. It was noted in one of the earliest documents as the means of obtaining "a happy issue," and it is regarded as such in the present union contract.[11]

11. The preamble to this agreement reads in part: "Since the parties desire to enter into an Agreement relating to rates of pay, wages, hours and other conditions of employment, which will provide methods for harmonious cooperation between the Company and its employees, and to that end, accomplish fair and peaceful adjustment of any differences which may arise, without interruption of operations, the parties agree." A later section reads: "The Union agrees to cooperate with the Company and support the Company's efforts to assure a full day's work on the part of employees whom it represents, and to combat actively absenteeism and other practices which curtail production, to support the Company in its efforts to eliminate waste and inefficiency, to im-

There are, of course, differences of opinion as to how equitably the
burdens and rewards of cooperation are being shared, and as will
be shown in Chapter 8 antagonisms are present. Moreover, there is
a tendency to regard acquiescence by the other party as the most
suitable proof of cooperation. Nevertheless, the word "cooperation" and the standards, such as friendliness and harmony, which
are associated with it are charged with force, so much so that
cooperation is often regarded as a goal in itself. Individuals frequently subordinate personal interests simply "to keep peace in the
family," and groups evidently dread an open break in the friendly
atmosphere which is still supposed to characterize the entire institution. Indeed the strength of the feeling which led to union
organization may be measured by the fact that this move by employees deliberately risked such a break. The idea of cooperation
was useful to management in rationalizing its acceptance of the
union. Employees also rationalized their support of the union on
the basis that it would make possible better cooperation between
upper management and the workers. There is no doubt that the
values inherent in the idea of friendly cooperation deeply influenced the dealings of the union and the management with each
other. In accord with the expressed feeling that "if people will only
deal with each other in a real spirit of cooperation" they will automatically have pleasant relationships, meetings of management and
union representatives have sometimes been, in the words of one of
them, "regular love feasts." After a year and a half of official dealing
with the union, some members of management were even beginning to fear that the principal danger they faced from the union
was that union officers might not have a strong enough hold on
their members to receive real backing for their agreements. As
one of them put it, "The trouble is that the union may not be
strong enough!" On their part, however, the workers were well

---

prove the quality of workmanship, to prevent accidents, and to promote good
will between the Company and its employees." It is particularly interesting to
note the number of values referred to in these sentences, especially the emphasis on harmony and good will. "Union Agreement between The New Freedom Products Company and the Textile Workers Union of America, CIO
and Local No. ———."

satisfied with their leaders. All important officers were re-elected after their first year in office and were given what amounted to a vote of confidence by being sent to the annual meeting of the national union.

Cooperation also includes the idea of hierarchical organization with final authority lodged in the highest status level, that is to say, in the hands of the officials. No evidence has appeared that any employee questions this principle. What questions there are concern the propriety of the form of managerial organization rather than the necessity for authoritative coordination of institutional activities. Technically the organization chart is a graphic representation of the formally recognized management hierarchy, but it does not exactly correspond with the prestige system as it exists in the minds of the personnel. Some of the latter still retain the notion that membership in the Drew family is an esssential attribute of true authority. Today the officials themselves are inclined consciously to deny connection with the family as a necessary qualification for high executive status. Whereas Shields frankly declared 40 years ago that he believed firmly in the "principle of nepotism," relationship to Drew's descendants is now said merely to give a man an opportunity to "make good on his own merits." Nevertheless, with the exception of Kellogg, who became president in 1943 and who is identified with the family by intimate ties of friendship, every official is a relative. Moreover, in the eyes of the workers, Drew family membership is associated with official status. Older workers regard this qualification with approval, and no worker has been heard to question its propriety. Some chiefs and managers have expressed doubts as to its justice, but they appear to accept it as an unavoidable condition limiting their chances for promotion to the official circle. A complaint of minor executives is that workers do not accord them the respect they should expect from their position on the organization chart because they are not "one of the family." The company chauffeur, for example, will willingly accept orders from managers related to the family but not from other managers or even chiefs. This man represents an extreme insistence of the old "principle of nepotism," but other workers and foremen have confirmed the observation that his viewpoint is extreme rather than aberrant. While in a sense the persistence of this traditional idea may be something of a survival, it has a bearing on the difficulties involved in creating a system of intermediaries between the workers and the officials. It also strengthens the evidence pointing to an integrated system of personal contacts between the workers and the officials in the past.

Just as it is taken for granted that the company must manufacture and sell products, so also is it taken for granted that it must make money. In other words, it must not only meet its costs and provide income for the personnel, it must also make a profit. To some of the personnel, notably the older officials, profits represent the mainspring of the institution. Even among these men, however, the "profit motive" is not unqualified. One of them stated the matter recently as follows: "The profit motive is the thing which makes us go. There are higher considerations, of course, like our responsibility to our customers and to the employees. It's one of the great things of this company that in every generation management has kept these higher considerations foremost. But profits make the other things possible." To other levels of the hierarchy, profits represent simply a necessary condition, a kind of cost which must be met. Most of the workers, and other employees as well, believe that without profits "the company would fold up, and we'd all be out of a job." Employees also regard their own welfare as a reflection of the company's prosperity. If the company is making money it can afford higher wages and other benefits, and it can make provision for the future.

This last consideration, provision for the future, is perhaps properly to be regarded as an aspect of the final principle listed above, that of maintaining company stability. This principle is, of course, that which bears directly upon the goal of security. Reference has already been made to the belief in the company as a strong, permanent institution. The centennial celebration emphasized the first hundred years of existence as proof of the company's strength, and the slogan of a recent advertising campaign, addressed to present as well as prospective employees, was: "A good place to work for the next hundred years." Employees believe

that, once they have been with the company long enough to be
really a part of the personnel, they are almost certain of being
retained on the payroll. Hence they are inclined to interpret their
own security in terms of that of the company. This is so even of
aggressive employees. Asked whether he would favor pushing union
demands to a point where they might weaken the company, a
union officer said, "No. I want this company to stay in business just
as much as anybody does. I expect to educate my children on what
I make here." Many employees have expressed their feelings by
using the old cliché about not killing the goose that lays the golden
eggs. The effect of such a regard for company welfare upon the
activities of employees is obvious. It will be seen, however, in the
chapter on antagonistic cooperation that common purposes and
even commonly accepted principles for achieving purposes are
not enough to prevent an antagonistic alignment of different segments of the personnel. This is true because different levels in the
hierarchy do not possess the same facts and other criteria. Workers
do not see the factors which affect company stability from the same
point of view as officials do. Both parties may ardently desire to
maintain this stability and to achieve other purposes as well. Judgments on the extent of the concessions which must be made
in favor of stability and strength of the company can and do
vary.

This last point is well worth bearing in mind. It is a reservation
which has a bearing on the reading of any statement of charter.
Charter is, in a way, an ideal description of institution. It is the
purposes which the personnel cherish, the ways which they think
are right, and the values which they consider good. Charter ex-
presses how people think things ought to be, not how they are.

STANDARDS. The preceding paragraphs in this chapter have
summarized the purposes and principles in the charter of the New
Freedom Products Company. These elements are modified by
standards which are regarded by the personnel as amplifications
or limitations properly to be placed on their goals and their ways
of obtaining them. Thus the product must have quality, and co-

operation should be friendly and harmonious. A list of the more important standards follows:

Quality	Friendliness
Reliability	Neighborliness
Responsibility	Democracy
Safety	Harmony
Efficiency	Length of service (seniority)
Flexibility	Age
Science	Family
Profits	Local residence
Wages	Fair play ("decent treatment")
Salaries	Discrimination
Waste	"Equal pay for equal work"
Costs	Precedent
Overhead	

The fluid nature of charter appears most obviously when standards are under discussion. It will easily be seen that items on the above list overlap. In real life the situation is worse, at least from the observer's point of view. Where the personnel are concerned, however, there may be an advantage in being able to transfer values appropriate to one subject to another. For instance, quality is associated primarily with the products. Nevertheless, there is no strain in applying the word to workmanship or to the worker himself: "The quality of that man's work is poor.—His workmanship is of poor quality.—He lacks quality as a worker." In a more complex manner, standards may be applied to each other. Cooperation, for example, may be called efficient, or excessive efficiency may be condemned because it seems to negate the human considerations inherent in the idea of friendliness. Such difficulties are, perhaps, more apparent to the writer than to the reader. Everyone encounters such inconsistencies daily, indeed may perpetrate a few. Still, human beings do communicate with each other, and devices like simile and metaphor can be extremely effective.

As standards, quality, reliability, and responsibility are closely associated. Quality sums up beliefs concerning responsibility to the users of the products. Indirectly, also, these standards are thought of as essential components in maintaining the strength of the company. The employee manual states this view as follows: "Keeping the standard of quality is up to each one of us. If you or any other person departs even a little bit from the high manufacturing standards that have been set—if anyone lets down on careful workmanship—the principle of quality is endangered. And anybody who endangers quality is risking our jobs and our responsibility to the workers who use our products." The word "quality" carries so much weight that it can be invoked almost without qualifications as justification for disciplinary action or as incentive to more careful work. A new rule setting discharge as the penalty for a practice known to have deleterious effect on quality was unquestioned by anyone, even when it was applied with the full penalty a few days after it was announced.

In the employee manual responsibility is placed first among the attributes which make the company a good one. Having described a worker using the principal product, it says:

> That man trusts our product. He *trusts us*. He is one of hundreds of thousands who do dangerous work—regularly trusting their safety to our hands. *To be worthy of that trust has been our responsibility for more than a century.* You cannot beat this principle of gaining trust and keeping it by being responsible—and everyone here shares this trust and responsibility.

In the office there are almost ritualistic aspects of responsibility. The accounting department makes a great effort to pay invoices on the day they are received, and the traffic department regards it as essential to ship all but exceptional orders within 24 hours of receiving them. It is possible that acceptance of responsibility as a standard may lead to an overly high degree of trustfulness. This is so in the opinion of the professional auditors employed by the company; these men express both amazement and concern over practices which are apparently results of this attitude. In the plant, absenteeism is regarded as a sign of irresponsibility, and an employee with irregular attendance is regarded with suspicion by management and workers alike. In fact, regularity of attendance

on the part of some "outside" Negroes was an important factor
in breaking down the stereotype that all Negroes (except those
living in the community) were shiftless and unreliable. A few "outside" Negroes had attained almost in-group status after two years
in the company.

The high value placed upon safety is probably traceable to the
earliest days of the company, since the hazardous nature of the
materials used requires care. When Drew rebuilt the plant after
the disastrous explosion in the middle of the last century, he designed the buildings with safety in mind, and older officials have
always had safety admonitions at the tips of their tongues. Today
safety is further re-enforced by laws and by propaganda originating
outside the company. The officials regard membership in the National Safety Council as important. Minor executives and foremen
are sent to the annual meetings of this organization in Chicago,
and its posters are regularly displayed on plant bulletin boards.
Promotion of safety was one of the first duties assigned to the foremen as a group when regular meetings for them were inaugurated.
All employees seem to share this care for safety. Suggestions dealing with safety outnumber any other kind received by the suggestion committee, and appeals to this standard carry great weight.
The allegation that a practice is unsafe is often enough to condemn
it without further reference to its efficiency or other factors involved. The most dramatic rule in the institution is that which
prohibits smoking and carrying matches in the plant. The ostenta-
tious way in which employees search their pockets for matches
as they enter the plant gates amounts to a ritual, as does the handing of new packets of matches to employees when they leave the
plant. This rule is a definite symbol. It is drilled into new employees before they enter the plant; they are reminded of it the
first time they pass through the gates; and it is believed to set the
stage for the many other safety rules they have to learn.

Efficiency, like safety, is a standard which carries considerable
sanctioning force although it does not meet with such unqualified
acceptance. The mere statement that a procedure is inefficient may
remove discussion from personal or other grounds and leave its
justification to a determination of its relative efficiency. For some

employees efficiency becomes a goal in itself, and the results of
inefficiency, like rehandling of materials, become real sources of
irritation. The concept of efficiency, however, gains much of its
power from the general culture rather than from deep roots in
company tradition. Occasionally officials cite efficiency of a somewhat farfetched nature to justify activities which may be senti-
mentally inspired. The annual Long-Service Award party, for instance, is sometimes said to be good for morale, which is good for
efficiency.[12] Similar justification is found for vacations, for rest
periods, for the employee clinic, for the safety program, and even
for the pension plan ("workers will do better work if their minds
are at ease"). Such rationalizations are sometimes used "disingenuously by persons who realize more or less clearly that they have
other reasons but can frame their arguments more easily and with
less embarrassment in what they consider to be "hard-boiled"
terms. This is true both of executives and of workers. The president of the union offered the argument, for example, that a Christmas bonus would be good for the company because it would create
employee good will and would be economical because it might
offset demands for more costly wage increases. The most elaborate
party ever given for employees by the company, with the exception
of the centennial celebration, followed soon after a dance given by
the union. While the usual remarks about "morale" had helped
to obtain a modest budget allotment for this occasion, the hint that
the company ought to show that it could do as well as the union
made it easy to more than double the budget figure. The effectiveness of this hint was, of course, concealed by other, more acceptable

12. There is reason to believe that the tendency to rationalize activities on
the basis of efficiency was perhaps more characteristic of earlier decades of
the present century than it is today. Taylor, *The Principles of Scientific Management,* p. 93 states the matter quite simply: ". . . the final step—insures
them [the workers] what they most want, namely, high wages, and the employers what they most want, namely, the maximum output and best quality of
work, which means *a low labor cost.*" Taylor was the American apostle of
manufacturing efficiency, and it is significant that his book was read by New
Freedom Products Company officials ten years or so after it was published. It is
doubtful whether these officials or the workers would accept any such statement of goals today.

rationalizations, most of which were also sincere. Excessive emphasis on efficiency is suspected of endangering other, more human values. The terms, "efficiency expert" and "those efficiency fellers" (sometimes applied to the time-study men), carry more than a little antipathy.

Flexibility is an aspect of efficiency, but it is aimed at institutional stability rather than at immediate reduction in costs. It includes or justifies the policy of maintaining idle equipment and buildings and that of trying to train employees for a variety of jobs. Both of these policies are expensive. It is believed, however, that even though it should become impossible to operate any part of the plant or any machine keeping the extra equipment or buildings would provide insurance of production. It is also believed that a flexible work force serves the same end when demand shifts among the various products. The corollary of flexibility for the individual is versatility. This value is related to job security for individuals, and versatility is one of the qualifications applied to length of service in the event of transfers, layoffs, and recalls.

Science as a standard derives much of its strength from the general culture. It is often coupled with research, a less effective word, but it can lend prestige to other activities. For example, believing that new employees especially might distrust the job-evaluation system, management used the following wording in the employee manual: "jobs are scientifically rated under our Job Evaluation Plan." A more significant use of the word is in the union contract, where it is reasonable to suppose that it is employed with worker approval: "The Management has developed, and will maintain, properly trained time study personnel in order that job tasks shall be established by scientific methods." Words like "engineer," "technician," "chemist," and "laboratory" which are associated with science share some of its value. A test made by a 'technician" in the laboratory, for example, carries more weight than precisely the same test made by a practiced worker in the plant.

It is perhaps unnecessary to elaborate upon wages, salaries, and profits as standards. They have already been discussed as income earlier in this chapter. It is worth pointing out, however, that

salaries carry more prestige than do wages, even when they amount
to no more in money. This may be because salaried positions have
carried perquisites, such as vacations and holidays with pay, not
possessed by hourly-paid jobs. It is interesting to speculate upon
the possibility that the prestige of salaried jobs may vanish as these
differences disappear. It is, however, worth noting in this connection that salaries run into a much higher range than any wages
do and are associated with the highest positions in the organization.

"Profits" is a word so charged with meaning in the general
culture that it is extremely difficult to assess its full value in the
company. It has been pointed out that while some officials regard the "profit motive" as vital in industry most other employees
seem to lack interest in profits and merely take the attitude that
the company must make money enough to keep the owners from
"shutting up shop." Within the company the pressure for higher
pay seems to be not so much a matter of competing with the stockholders for the spoils as it is a feeling that wage rates should be at
least as good as those which prevail in industry, especially neighboring industry. Even here, moreover, employees are prepared
to sacrifice something in the belief that the security afforded by
the company offsets what they consider relatively low wages. The
amount of individual salaries is regarded as highly confidential information, although employees in the lower salary brackets usually
have a shrewd idea of what their fellows are paid. Wages, on the
other hand, are publicized on the daily posting sheets in order to
permit workers to detect errors promptly. This posting, incidentally, was not only approved but desired by the union negotiating committee.

The three standards of waste, costs, and overhead are associated
with the principles of making money and maintaining stability of
the institution. For most employees, waste is the most immediate
of these values and the one which is most clearly understood. Costs
and overhead, on the other hand, are in some ways more potent
ideas. Wasted materials and wasted time are definite things to be
avoided because they raise costs and, perhaps more significantly,
because they are felt to be intrinsically bad. This feeling is probably

a result of thrifty Yankee traditions and equally thrifty values of some of the immigrant groups, as well as of constantly reiterated traditions of the institution itself. Costs, however, are somewhat more subtle, and few of the personnel have more than a hazy notion of the items actually counted as cost in the mysterious ledgers of the accounting department. Nevertheless, costs beyond a necessary minimum are regarded as dangerous, and every employee, to a greater or lesser degree, is caught in the dilemma created by his desire for higher wages or other perquisites which the company might supply for him and the more or less clear conviction that costs ought not to be unduly increased. Moreover, the very wages which the worker holds as a primary purpose for working are a cost, and so also are the expenses of the pension plan which is a keystone in his security structure. As will be seen in the chapter on antagonistic cooperation, the conflicting viewpoints of various segments of the personnel concerning the ability of the company to withstand such costs are at the root of the crystallizing antagonism between upper management and the workers. Overhead is the most abstruse of the cost trio. In the minds of most of the personnel it means costs which are only indirectly applied to the manufacturing processes and which are likely to be of a continuing and ever accumulating nature. Vague though these concepts may be, they have considerable sanctioning power; indeed, their strength may lie in part in their very vagueness. To workers the assertion that a desired service, such as free hospital insurance, will build up overhead is a telling argument. Management and workers alike are troubled by the fact that the office force has increased so markedly in recent years. The personnel has an uneasy feeling that if hard times come again the burden of this overhead may endanger security. The effect of such feelings as a limiting factor upon the activities of both management and the union is obvious.

The standards of friendliness, neighborliness, and harmony are associated primarily with the principle of cooperation. Such phrases as the "friendly spirit of co-operation," "harmonious relationships," "our traditional spirit of neighborliness" appear frequently in the manual and other company publications, and they

are echoed in various ways by workers. At times, of course, these
values are used quite consciously by management and sometimes
by workers to gain their own ends. It is significant, however,
despite this occasional disingenuousness, that both management
and workers behave customarily as though they value these concepts highly. This was especially noticeable during the period of
union organization and the subsequent negotiation between the
union and the management. Initially, proponents of the union felt
that they were making a definite break with management, and
some pursued their activities militantly. Officials, executives, and
foremen (and many workers as well) felt keenly that the union was
driving a wedge of hostility into the heart of their beloved company and that employees who joined the union were despicable
traitors. Some of the officials tried to persuade themselves that new
employees—not their old friends in the plant—were responsible
for union activity, an opinion which proved to be false. Faced with
the necessity for dealing with the union, however, officials found
other rationalizations with which to ease the new situation. The
most effective of these was phrased by the president of the company, who said that, after all, it was traditional to deal with the
employees singly or in groups and that if the employees wanted to
deal through a union the company would continue its old policy.
This and similar ideas eased the tension greatly for management.
At the same time, union members spread the idea that the union
was simply a means for "talking to" the officials and higher executives and would be a good thing for the company. From this point
negotiations between the union and the management proceeded
with what at times amounted to almost ludicrous amicability. The
very fact that the erstwhile archtraitors, the union leaders, had
thereafter frequent personal contacts with several executives
seemed to lead to a degree of mutual respect and even to something
which at times resembled affection.

It should not be forgotten that the roots of these standards—
friendliness and neighborliness—go far back into the history of the
company and that the dissatisfaction which led ultimately to the
organization of the union commenced with the failure of the traditional norms for intimate, friendly contacts between workers

and officials. To be sure, these contacts had real functions both for the institution and for the personnel, functions which could not safely be sacrificed. More often than not, however, dissatisfaction was expressed or interpreted by employees as being caused by deterioration of the friendly, pleasant, harmonious atmosphere.

While the importance of friendliness and similar standards cannot be overstressed, they need some qualifications. First, it should not be supposed that they create an earthly paradise. Bickering and personal animosities, even interfamily animosities, exist and, as the history of Drew's relations with Trotter show, have existed for at least a hundred years. At times such animosities flare into disagreeable outbreaks. On the other hand, even though the company's interests may indirectly be involved, such bad feelings are regarded as personal matters. The institutional pattern remains, and ordinarily the appearance of conformity is maintained to a degree which often produces real conformity or, in any event, brings results which real conformity would produce. The individual who cannot disguise his aggression or dissipate it in impersonal ways is regarded as eccentric. There are jobs for a few such employees. It is often remarked of the most conspicuous of these that "that son of a bitch won't corporate [sic] with nobody." A further qualification is obvious from the history of the company. Friendliness can scarcely mean the same thing in the formalized, distant situation of today as it did 40 years ago when officials and workers knew each other personally and well. Today not all workers know each other. Nevertheless, this word and others like it have meanings which can be applied to present relationships, and the values remain powerful. Whether their strength can continue in the absence of the intimate situation which fostered them originally is a question which cannot now be answered.

A standard which corresponds in one of its meanings to those associated with cooperation is democracy. In this meaning the word refers to the manner in which a person of superior status, usually an official, behaves with workers or other inferiors. If he treats inferiors as equals, he is "democratic" and hence all right. While this value ostensibly favors equalitarianism, it actually includes an implicit recognition of status differences. There is no point in "democracy" between equals, although snobbishness would be wrong. By a curious kind of inversion, possibly reflecting an appreciation of *noblesse oblige,* democracy in a superior is a positive virtue. In another meaning, democracy refers to the force of majority opinion. Among executives this meaning is ordinarily discarded in favor of putting responsibility for decisions on regularly designated shoulders or, in the case of conferences, weighing opinions and reaching conclusions on the basis of evidence rather than by vote. To many workers, on the other hand, notably some of those who organized and now lead the union, democracy simply means majority rule. This was the case in the textile-mill kangaroo court, and it now poses a problem for union officers who are occasionally puzzled whether they should make executive decisions or should refer all matters to a vote of the membership. It is plain, of course, that the values described here by the word "democracy" are not peculiar to this institution but are derived from the general culture.

Length of service is a key standard associated with security for individuals in the company. It is an important requisite for full membership in the group and is also a basis for prestige. It is not believed that the company has the same obligations to new employees as to old ones. This position is stated in the employee manual as follows:

> The record shows that those who work at the New Freedom Products Company have always been surer of staying employed than they are in most industrial plants, and that the longer men and women work here, the surer they are of having work as long as they are able to work or up to the retirement age [when they are eligible for pensions]. . . . Length of service means more and more on the record of an employee as the years pile up, but the company also intends to recognize other valuable abilities and attributes so that each employee will be treated like a human individual with his own character—not like a file record which gets automatic treatment regardless of human personality.

This statement is accepted by both management and workers. In fact, union officials occasionally make use of it when arguing the seniority rights of individual employees since the clause in the union contract is more limited in scope. It is worth noting that, although the union contract sets six months' service as the preliminary for acquiring seniority rights, there is actually no precise period of employment which qualifies a person as a fully-accepted member of the institution. An employee with family connections, local residence, and characteristics leading to popularity or respect can become established in the group much more rapidly than one lacking some or all of these qualifications. During World War II five years of service was unofficially regarded as differentiating "temporary" from permanent workers. Since then, however, out-of-town workers have ceased to be regarded as "war workers," and some of the out-of-town Negroes with two or more years of service have moved a considerable distance toward in-group membership. Except, however, in the case of employees with some informal traditional rights, conferred usually through having relatives in the company, no such short period of employment as two years would qualify a person as a long-service employee. Indications of the length of time needed to acquire such qualifications are to be found in the fact that long-service awards are given for 25, 35, 40, and 50 years of service.[13] The Long-Service Award ceremony is the most important ritual in which all employees may participate. At this ceremonial, moreover, virtues of long service and other elements of the charter are consistently extolled and re-enforced. The badges awarded to employees for long service are the only talismans which employees can display, and they are worn with some pride. To become eligible for membership in the pension plan an employee must be at least twenty-five years old and have had at least three years of service in the company. Each year of service, after these eligibility requirements have been met, increases the amount of the eventual pension.

Age as a standard is connected with length of service. Except in one instance,[14] there is no expressed policy which favors age, but this standard carries weight nevertheless. Its operation can be seen,

13. Some downward changes were made in these periods during 1946.

14. Automatic wage increases are given annually to skilled service-department employees for each year of service above 20 and for each year of age above fifty-five.

for example, in hesitation about asking old employees to accept pensions, in admonitions to young employees not to complain about special concessions made to older people, and in the fact that the respectful titles, "Mr." and "Mrs.," tend to follow age across and even counter to the lines of institutional status.[15] Employees with 40 years of service are inducted into "The Over Forty Club," which has an annual banquet, and members of it, wearing white carnations, participate as ushers in the Long-Service Award ceremony.

The pattern of value placed upon family connections was, perhaps, set by the official family, but its influence carries through all employee ranks. Drew saw to it that all his children including his daughters worked for the company, however briefly, and official rank passed from him to his sons-in-law and eventually to their sons and so on to the fourth generation. At the same time the children of some employees followed them into the company. The Knowlton family, for example, is represented by a member of the fourth generation. Only lately and only very slightly has the influence of the official family as such been deprecated by higher executives. Occasional remarks of employees, especially among the older immigrants, express strong approval of this "principle of nepotism," in which T. J. Shields 40 years ago declared his belief. But no evidence has appeared that any of the factory workers disapprove of it. Even for minor executives connection with the official family carries some prestige. An elderly Pole expressed it thus, "It is good thing you be personnel manager—You in family. Help like that."

In practice, relatives of employees are favored for employment, and in the Long-Service Award ceremony a great deal is made of the number of relatives an award recipient has or has had in the company. On their part, employees are fond of recounting their genealogical integration in the institution. It is interesting also to note that family rivalries are not limited to that which exists be-

15. An amusing side light on this standard is the fact that when three men in their thirties were employed in 1937 for executive training, their immediate superiors were officials scarcely three years older than they were. The new men, however, were consistently referred to as "the boys," especially by the immediate superiors, and this appellation clung to them for several years.

tween the principal branches of the official family. When the first girl of Italian parentage was promoted to the office, a member of another Italian family immediately complained that consideration for clerical employment should have been given to one of his relatives.

Not far removed from this emphasis on family is that on local residence as a standard. This is officially recognized in company policy as follows: "A recommendation from a present employee is one of the best an applicant [for employment] can have. Preference is given to local residents and former employees with good records." This standard is also closely associated with the purpose described above as "community responsibility." It is believed that the company should provide employment for people in the communities where the plants are located. This belief is thoroughly shared by the employees, and local residence was the most readily accepted qualification on length of service in the union contract clause dealing with seniority.[16] It is interesting that since wartime expansion the company has been unable to recruit enough employees locally so that about ten per cent of the employees are "outsiders." The implications of this change are further discussed in the section of this chapter devoted to personnel. If this real situation continues, it may have strong effects upon the ideal situation visualized in the charter.

The standard of fair play—or to use more common factory terms, "decent treatment" or "an even break"—must be interpreted in the light of the entire charter. An action deemed "not right" or unfair is so judged according to the conception of the charter held by the individual or group making the allegation. Thus it is "not right"

16. This clause reads in part: "In event of decrease in production, and when it becomes necessary to decrease the size of the normal peacetime work force, the Company agrees to cushion the decline by sharing the available work in so far as conditions in the various operations permit. Length of service in the Company shall govern in cases of layoffs and recalls, provided other considerations are equal. Such other considerations shall include competence to perform the work, merit, and other reasonable factors." Local residence was the one "other reasonable factor" heartily agreed upon in discussions between management and union negotiating committees. In the post–V-J Day layoff, this principle was applied.

to place an old employee in a menial job unless his physical condition makes it evident that the assignment is a concession to his years of service. It is "not fair" to threaten the job security of an employee who believes he has been given a guarantee by an official, even though that guarantee was made by an officer who died nearly 30 years ago. What constitutes "decent treatment" in a given case may be a matter for dispute, but the arguments partake of the values in the charter. In fact, ideas of charter are so strongly held that they even seem to shape notions of what is practical. For example, if it were not for the charter, determination of merit simply by length of service would be the easiest method for management in most situations. Yet management cannot conceive that the adoption of "straight seniority" would not be disastrous—and unfair.

"Discrimination" is a relatively new word for special kinds of unfairness. It has been regarded as wrong for some time, but with the advent of the union and of a fairly large number of Negroes it has acquired added meaning. Management has used the word "discrimination" to gain the union's assistance in combating worker hostility to imported Negroes. In the same vein is the phrase "equal pay for equal work," a standard agreed upon in the union contract. This applies to nondiscrimination based on sex. Both workers and management give it lip service rather than complete adherence.

The final standard on the list, precedent, is closely allied to fair play. Its meaning can be readily seen in the phrase, "what's fair for one is fair for another." The word itself is used mostly by management, which has had experience with the precedent-building effect of seemingly isolated actions. Hence management tries to avoid hasty "precedents." On the other hand, although they are prone to deny the precedent-creating effect of actions which benefit themselves, employees are quick to take advantage of precedent in making requests.

RE-ENFORCEMENTS. Precepts, stories, legends, and gossip strengthen and transmit the standards, principles, and purposes.

Many of these re-enforcements like the story of James Freedom's humanitarian invention, the reference to cooperation in old documents, the reminiscences of long-service employees, and the assertions of the employee manual and other company publications have been illustrated in this chapter and in Chapter 2. Precepts such as the following exist in everyday speech rather than in writing. "There is no such thing as a safe explosive." [17] "There's a right way and a wrong way to do everything." "What's fair for one is fair for another." "Don't kill the goose that lays the golden egg." "These refer, respectively, to safety, efficiency, fair play, precedent, and company stability. Re-enforcements are often extemporaneous, as the word "gossip" suggests, but in such cases they are likely to be built around value words. A significant statement of charter is sometimes included in analyses of the character of individuals who have died or retired. Thus, within a few months of his death, one of the superintendents was being credited by workers with virtues which, though not pronounced in his character, reflected views of what ought to have been—and of what surviving members of management should be.

Much of the charter material presented here has been abstracted from such verbal forms. In addition, charter is observable in activities, especially at times when choices or decisions are necessary. At such times there are usually explicit references to charter, and the decisions are rationalized on the basis of the charter. Charter thus emerges as a pattern of vaguely formulated but strongly held beliefs. These vary somewhat from individual to individual in emphasis and value. The amount of variation was evidently small for a long period prior to World War I, a fact which probably accounts for the persistence of elements in existence then. Since then, however, at least two changes have had a strong bearing on the charter: the altered roles of officials, which have made it impossible to maintain personal relationships as they were a generation or so ago; and weakened intrainstitutional communications, which have threatened if not seriously damaged maintenance of a generally consistent view of charter throughout the institution. Otherwise, it does not appear that the charter has been greatly

17. A reference to certain ingredients used in some of the products.

modified, despite the subtle reinterpretations implicit in some rationalizations. To date the personnel still direct their efforts at keeping the charter unchanged. Whether they can succeed in developing norms and shaping the elements of the institution to fit the charter or whether the charter will also undergo thorough revision is, as yet, an unanswerable question.[18]

18. The fact that the union, an organization with a charter of its own, now supplements the older elements in the same area of activities can be expected to have an important effect in producing an answer to this question.

CHAPTER SIX: *Organizational Framework*

In the preceding chapter we have outlined at some length the charter of the New Freedom Products Company. Not all the ideas which would find wide acceptance in the company have been listed. Such a notion as industriousness, which is favorably regarded but which derives from the community ethos rather than peculiarly from the company charter, might have been included. Enough, however, to illustrate the importance of mental concepts have been described, and the significance of some of them will be made clearer in later chapters which deal with the dynamics of this institution. Vital though this idea structure is, however, it is meaningless by itself. The people, what they do, and what they have to do with are equally important, although in this case they do not require such lengthy description.

Four other institutional elements are treated in the present chapter. They are, in the language of the theory, personnel, norms and rules, activities, and material apparatus. They are presented in this order instead of that which may be more familiar to students of Malinowski simply to facilitate exposition. Personnel illustrates rather clearly the relationship between charter and other elements. Norms and rules are lumped with activities because the latter can be regarded as variations in the former, and the variations in the norms or traditional folkways which governed intercourse between officials and workers are central to an understanding of changes in the institution. In this case material apparatus, since it can be regarded almost as a constant, occupies a subsidiary position.

Despite the evidence that changes in equipment—so-called technological changes—have been at the roots of social change on a large scale in Western society, this element seems to have had relatively little effect upon the social relationships within this company. On the whole, changes in the *use* of machines, that is, in technological norms and rules, seem to have been more important than changes in the machines themselves.

PERSONNEL. The most obvious fact concerning the personnel of the New Freedom Products Company, if one is seeking factors which bear upon social change there, is the considerable increase in numbers. As compared with the early decades of the company's history when traditional beliefs and practices became established, the company became large during the past 40 years or so. Aside from this important development, however, one must look to the personnel as a factor which, generally speaking, modified and even retarded the ultimate effects of changes in other elements. The character of the company's personnel is important from a practical point of view, even though much of the discussion here is theoretical, in that it may be more directly significant in other institutions or in other circumstances than it is in interpreting the events under observation in this case. What people do is likely to be affected by the kind of people they are.

On the other hand, the character of the people is likely to be determined to a considerable degree by the character of the institution. Investigation in accordance with Malinowski's conceptual framework reveals the shrewd insight contained in his statement that, in a way, the personnel are "derived from and contingent upon the charter." To say that a manufacturing institution will seek employees strong or clever enough to handle its operations does more than underline a self-evident situation. It illustrates, in broad terms, the powerful influence of purposes and principles on eligibility for membership. A similar influence can be seen in the fact that emphasis upon safety as a standard reduces the eligibility of young, irresponsible people.[1] The influence of char-

1. It is not intended to suggest that the New Freedom Products Company is unique in its eligibility requirements. Federal and state regulations prohibit

ter upon the composition of the personnel, however, has more subtle and significant ramifications than those examples suggest. Acceptance or rejection of parts of the charter by various individuals may have a more important bearing on the kind of people in the institution than do the desires and specifications of the functionaries assigned the duty of recruiting and sifting applicants for membership.

Thus the fact that a higher value is placed on security than on advancement makes employment at the New Freedom Products Company more attractive to people as they grow older. For many years it has been hard to hold young workers; they have tended to leave the company and seek employment elsewhere, and sometimes, though not always, they have come back to "settle down." Local young people, familiar with this part of the charter, are likely to avoid the company in the first place.

Recent employment figures show the relative predominance of older workers:

Age	*New Freedom Products Company Employees, March 1946*		*National Work Force, 1940* [2]
	Number	*Per cent*	*Per cent*
65 years and over	27	7.1	2.7
55–64 years	72	18.8	8.7
45–54 "	76	20.0	17.6
35–44 "	91	23.8	23.1
25–34 "	69	18.0	30.0
24 years and under	48	12.5	17.6
Total	383 [3]	100.2	99.7

employment of youths as young as those who found jobs at the company 50 years ago. On the other hand, the company's minimum age requirements, except when relaxed for a limited number of jobs during World War II, are higher than those of the government.

2. Age of employed workers and of experienced workers seeking work, *Sixteenth Census of the United States: 1940; Population*, Vol. III, The Labor Force, Pt. I.

3. This figure is from company records as are those in the seniority list below. The fact that the totals differ reflects mainly fluctuations in the number of new employees, a considerable number of whom tended to remain at the company only a few days or weeks. Some of these may have quit because they

That the number of New Freedom Products employees less than twenty-five years old in this table is probably unusually high and includes a number of transients is shown by the fact that figures compiled a month before those above had only 35 instead of 48 in this bracket. Of these, 11 had been with the company six months or less, and three less than a month. Of the 35, 12 were office employees, and 11 were young women considered likely to leave sooner or later to "bring up a family." Two more were men employed during the war and carried on the payroll although they were still in military service, and an additional two had special handicaps for which the company was able to make concessions.

Additional positive evidence of the selective effect of emphasis on security in the charter and of the relative lack of opportunities for advancement in the company is the fact that from time to time capable and ambitious employees who have become well established in the company leave to go into business for themselves or to take other jobs which seem to offer more favorable opportunities for their talents.

That people tend to stay with the company once they have settled down is shown by the figures in the table on page 149. From these figures one may conclude, quite correctly, that the personnel of the New Freedom Products Company are, on the whole, mature and settled. This conclusion is even more evident if one recognizes that a considerable proportion of the employees with less than five years' service is, so to speak, in a trial period which will weed out many who do not fit into the general pattern.

A different set of interrelationships between the charter and the composition of the personnel is to be found in factors associated with local residence. Here it is necessary to look beyond the institution itself to determine all the influences at work. Tradition-

---

did not like the "atmosphere" of the company, i. e., factors which we have summarized in the charter. Probably some simply did not like traveling back and forth from the city where most of the recruits lived. The fluctuation in the number of new employees tends to emphasize rather than weaken the conclusion that, once established at the company, employees are likely to remain on the payroll a long time.

Length of Service
(taken from February, 1946, seniority list)

55	years	1
54	"	1
50	"	1
45–49	"	4
40–44	"	12
35–39	"	9
30–34	"	36
25–29	"	36
20–24	"	51
15–19	"	40
10–14	"	17
5–9	"	77
0–4	"	121[4]
		———
Total		406

ally the personnel has consisted of people living within ten miles of the plants. In March, 1946, however, some 44 workers (more than ten per cent) lived beyond this limit, and an additional number were individuals who had moved into town recently. Recruitment of local people has become more difficult. The town offers many more opportunities for employment than it did a generation or so ago, and transportation makes work in the nearby city practicable. Employment outside of Teasville no longer means moving away from home. Old residents recall the time when there were no more than ten or a dozen businesses in Teasville; in a recent program of an amateur play, 42 local establishments had advertisements.

Supplementing this extension of outside opportunity is the fact that today a high percentage of young people complete high school and expect to find better jobs than the unskilled ones available at the factory. Local girls will take clerical jobs in the office, but a high-school education does not in itself qualify a man for any of the higher status jobs the company has to offer.

4. See p. 147, n. 3.

It is difficult to estimate how long outside influences of this kind have been significant factors in employment. Even early in the century there was a feeling in the community that only easy-going young men who would never get ahead anyway took jobs at "the shop." Very likely the arrival of foreign-speaking immigrants, who regarded work at the factory as better than laboring jobs they could find elsewhere, saved the company from what might have been serious employment difficulties. Now that the people from the old country are retiring and their children have assimilated American education and American ambitions, the company may be affected by the discrepancy between the opportunities it has to offer and those which appeal to young Americans. This problem may be solved by technological developments, but it is unlikely that merely improving physical working conditions will be enough. In the meantime, one wonders whether Negroes, who comprise a majority of the out-of-town employees, will fill the places which used to be filled by newly arrived immigrants. This would be in line with developments in other industries as the growing Negro districts in many northern cities testify, and the fact that already some of the poorer jobs at the company are referred to as "nigger work" is indicative. As for the tradition of local residence, the company was forced to continue free transportation to and from the city after World War II ended, and three years after V-J Day it was still seeking workers from the wide labor market provided by the United States Employment Service.

While it is something of a digression, a comment on the Negroes at the company may be of interest. Of the 35 Negroes on the payroll in the first quarter of 1946, only three were local residents. Of this trio, one was treated as white, although it was known that she was "colored." One was respected as a "good worker" with a long record of service: he has since been made a union steward. The third was this man's wife. The rest were "outsiders." A few of these had been with the company more than a year, and worker resistance to them as individuals had considerably diminished. Many of the rest, however, had poor attendance records and were considered likely to quit without notice after a stay of a few days or weeks as had the great majority of their predecessors. Many of the Negroes have had jobs in the textile mill, and recently some white workers, including newly hired local people, have refused to take these jobs.

Today the Negroes are the only group which definitely feels the effects of prejudice on account of race or ethnic origin, although each succeeding group of immigrants—Irish, Slavic, and Italian—was considered inferior for some time after its arrival.

The last barrier in the way of general acceptance of Slavs and Italians was broken by admitting them to office employment. This came about almost as soon as they had acquired the necessary education and applied for office jobs. Officials do not believe that they would permit ethnic prejudice to influence them in promotions to executive levels. It is probable, however, that it would be difficult to persuade them that any of the local Italian or Slavic youths possessed the "background" considered necessary for executive status. This has been the case in the one instance where such promotion could have been made.

It is difficult to separate discussion of the organization of the personnel—that is, the division into status levels—from consideration of norms. The crystallizing standards concerning the education and training required for the various status levels have had the curious effect of creating a situation almost as static, as far as promotion is concerned, as that which existed when they were only two real status levels and membership in the official family was virtually a requisite for one of them.

On paper the organization chart looks like a simple promotional ladder, with workers at the bottom, foremen on the next step, assistants to managers on the next, and so on up. In practice this works only in exceptional cases. Membership in the Drew family, for example, is a qualification for official status which the chart does not show. Another is the difference in background needed for plant employment and that required for management, especially on executive levels where a college education is becoming almost indispensable. The worker who could start at the bottom and work up would be a remarkable exception. He might go as far as foreman but probably no farther, and there are intimations that even this modest rise is coming to require more than mere plant training and experience. Special in-plant training programs may provide ambitious workers with the desired qualifications for foremanship, but the jump from the plant to the office, where the ladder to executive positions begins, is a long one.

Only two foremen in the past 15 years have made this transition. Both of these men had special qualifications before they came to the company. One was hired to be a foreman during the expanded wartime operations and, partly because he had a college education, filled an office vacancy after V-J Day. The other was also brought in for foremanship training and was taken into the office when he demonstrated that his earlier experience would be valuable there. Probably no foreman now on the payroll will go higher. The qualifications for a foreman are not those needed for the jobs which lead to executive positions.

It is possible for other workers than foremen to move from the plant to the office, but only one male worker has done so in many years. Like his predecessors who took this step more than 15 years ago, he first became a time-study man. Later he was made an assistant in the personnel department. It was thought, however, that this was as far as he would go unless he improved his "background" and made himself "more the kind of a person you would want to introduce as an executive in this company." He has since gone back to the plant as a foreman.

Assistants in the office are approximately equal to the foremen in prestige, but the upward ladder to posts as managers and chiefs is definitely more promising for them. Here again there are qualifying factors. The top rung of the ladder—that occupied by the officials—is still held by the official family with the single exception which has already been mentioned. Moreover, other recently filled chief's positions have gone to men who were explicitly employed for them after they had proved their ability as managers for only about a year. Still other chief's positions are held by technical men, and for at least one of these there is no likely successor in the company.

Thus, although it is company policy to "promote from within whenever possible," it is seldom deemed possible. Six of the managers are men who were employed within the past ten years either directly for executive positions or with the idea that they would soon become executives. Nine of the 13 assistants were employed directly for these positions. Hence, in practice, the most promising line for promotion from worker status is strongly blocked at the foremanship level.

For women the only advance from worker status that has ever existed is from the plant to clerical positions in the office. This has always been regarded as a real improvement in status, despite the fact that the transition often entails a reduction in pay. Few plant employees, however, can qualify for office work, unless they have had so-called commercial courses in high school or other experience in office work. It is interesting to note that four of the eight clerks who have been with the company 20 or more years started as plant workers, but only three of the 23 who have been with the company less than ten years started in the plant. No woman has ever held an executive post although two have been assistants, and some others at the top of the clerical hierarchy are practically equal to assistants in status. As is true of men, plant experience does not assist women in obtaining promotion to office work.

It is too early to predict what effect the increasing practice of bringing in outsiders to fill preferred positions will have. It is noteworthy, however, that it is contrary to the in-group philosophy which animates the charter. In the old days, employment of members of the official family was a different matter. They had a sort of special in-group status, and also a pretense was made of having them "work their way up from the bottom." The employment of a chemist and an engineer was easily justified; they were scientists. Today, however, although departures from the charter are still excused on the ground that the institution has no qualified persons for each position as it is filled, it appears that this situation is becoming the rule rather than the exception.

In summary, the personnel of the New Freedom Products Company has been made up traditionally of local men and women. Over a period of time emphasis on security as a goal has made of them a relatively elderly, stable group. This emphasis on security and the related lack of opportunity for rapid advancement, however, combined with increasing opportunities for local young people to find work elsewhere have provided influences which threaten traditional attitudes. Local young people often shun employment at the company. Approximately ten per cent of the personnel is now nonlocal. Current trends within the company continue to block upward mobility. The qualifications suitable for workers and foremen are not those which lead to executive status, and specialized requirements for executives and technical positions have led the company to employ outsiders for several upper-status positions. It is a reasonable inference that continuation of these trends will have a marked effect upon an institution in which local loyalties have long played an extremely important part. The significance of these possible effects is heightened by the fact that a great majority of the workers have now affiliated themselves with the union, an organization essentially nonlocal in many respects.

NORMS AND RULES. To elaborate greatly upon the institutional element called norms and rules—that is, the customary practices or folkways and the formal regulations—at the New Freedom Products Company is unnecessary. First, changes in some of the norms, notably those which fostered personal relationships, have already been described and will enter into later analyses. Second, as any industrialist knows, to attempt to list, let alone explain in detail, all the multitudinous practices and prescriptions of even such a small factory as this one would be almost impossible and in a large degree irrelevant. Nevertheless, it seems advisable to devote a few more pages to outlining relationships of norms and rules to other institutional elements, especially with a view to showing their significance to this study. Occasionally one thinks of norms and rules as a formal complex of clearly stated patterns. This is true only to a limited extent. Both the management and the union promulgate formal rules and have united upon some of them in the union contract. The unformulated, customary modes of activity are at least equally important. They are the folkways of the institution.

Both norms and rules are related to the charter, and frequently the rules contain references to the charter which re-enforce their authority. Indeed, rules which do not appeal, explicitly or implicitly, to the charter are often resisted, as was the case when, without explanation, smoking was prohibited in a building where it had been temporarily allowed. Rewording of this rule to include reference to safety eliminated grumbling and resistance. The employee manual, which was the first codification of rules for employees, is full of references to charter. The rule prohibiting drinking, for example, reads, "For the safety of all here and for the maintenance of our high quality standard, the company will not permit drinking on the premises or even the suspicion of being intoxicated." Rules are also occasionally re-enforced by reference to the general community morality, which in a sense is incorporated in the institutional charter. Thus adherence to the standard procedure on jobs and the necessity for setting standards fair both to the employees and to the company are often amplified as follows: "Why, a wrong standard would be unfair to either the employees or the company. It would be just like reaching into their pockets and taking their money away from them."

Norms, lacking formal expression, are less explicitly referred to charter than are rules. They are, nevertheless, just as surely related to charter. One of the normal modes of behavior for officials, as described in Chapter 2, was the making of frequent plant visits. These had various charter rationalizations having to do with efficiency, safety, and quality. They also made possible friendly chats with employees, in line with the ideas of friendly cooperation contained in the charter. Officials also performed numerous duties within the office. These had to do with sales, purchasing, and other matters deemed necessary for the institution. In the course of time these duties absorbed increasing amounts of the officials' time, and other activities also led officials to neglect their plant visits. This failure to continue old norms was critical in the evolution of this institution. Employees customarily used their personal contacts with officials for various satisfactions, and maintenance of close, friendly relationships was considered right. The significance of this change is discussed elsewhere in this study. What is important to note here is that in deserting these norms, officials felt it necessary to excuse themselves in several ways. They refused to admit that they were no longer "close" to the employees. They failed to realize how seldom they were seeing and talking to employees. They repeatedly resolved to "get out and see how things are getting along." And they justified themselves with such clichés as "After all, we've all got to put first things first," which is an indirect appeal to efficiency.

Present rules reflect recognition of the complex, hierarchical nature of the institution today as contrasted with the relatively simple primary group of the past. The organization chart in itself comprises a set of rules governing relationships between different statuses. One of the most important points in these relationships, moreover, is bolstered at length in the employee manual, where a whole section is devoted to emphasizing the idea that workers should make all their contacts with persons of higher status through the foremen. Similarly, the union contract supplements these intermediaries with others designated by the union and details the manner in which grievances shall work their way up through a double hierarchy of company and union functionaries. There are, however, activities expressive of incipient norms which run counter to these rules, though not to the charter. In many instances employees by-pass the foremen, and occasionally the stewards, and go directly to the personnel department. If the union agreement is not concerned, both personnel executives and foremen tend to encourage this practice, the foremen because it saves them trouble and the executives because they believe it increases the prestige of their department. To date the practice consists in more or less isolated activities and does not constitute a definite folkway. It represents attempts of employees to establish something like the former relatively full and frequent interstatus contacts. If it should become a generally accepted norm, however, it would probably have disastrous effects on the official norms prescribed by management and the union contract. Incidentally, this set of deviations clearly illustrates the difference between activities and norms and rules. It also indicates the way in which activities,

in the form of deviations of individuals from norms, provide variations which may be "selected in" and become new norms.[5]

Looked at from another point of view, norms and rules are
the substance of roles assigned to individuals, and social organization depends upon the way in which interdependent roles correspond to one another. In this case there was a separation between
the roles of officials and workers. Subsequent activities attempted
to bridge the gap between these two interdependent roles, and to
some extent such experimental activities still persist. In the meantime two sets of rules, those of the management's reorganization
and those of the union contract, have been established. These
rules are intended to replace entirely the old norms and, in the
hopes of their proponents at least, to improve upon them. This
development and the fact that the shift has been from norms of
personal interchange to impersonal rules are, in substance, principal theses of this study.

ACTIVITIES. Activities differ from the other parts of the institution in the sense that instead of being capable of separation from
the rest for examination they are the behavioral expression of other
elements. They are, so to speak, the glass through which the others
may be inspected. This is true even when the behavior is verbal.
Hence, every other element, with the exception of some functions,
is observed in the activities which express it, and its description is
an abstraction from these observations.

On the other hand, a few comments upon the nature of certain
activities as minor or major deviations from established patterns
seem to be in order. Rules and norms represent sanctioned or
customary modes established by fiat, by agreement, or simply by
habit. In a static institution an account of such folkways or culture

5. Cf. Sumner and Keller, *The Science of Society*, I, 31–32, 35–36, 40. Here
the processes of social change or evolution of the folkways and mores are
described as being variation, selection, and transmission. "The first originates
in the individual, who throws out tentatives in response to need felt personally."

traits may be a sufficient description. Many ethnographic reports have limited themselves to such accounts. It is well to bear in mind, however, that human beings seldom conform exactly to norms or rules and sometimes depart from them radically. Although rules and norms provide roles for individuals, each individual, through his activities, may be said to interpret his roles. Ordinarily he is motivated by his own interests and guided by his own conception of the institutional charter. Usually he follows the norms, which are patterns selected over time as successful, and the rules, which have been formally proposed as successful patterns and which are generally sanctioned by authority. There is a permissible degree of latitude, as suggested by the aphorism, "You've got to make allowances for human nature." Changes, however, create situations not provided for by rules or norms. In such cases, needs and interests do not cease to prod their possessors, and individuals are forced into activities for which no norms are available.[6]

This is, of course, what happened at the New Freedom Products Company. During the nineteenth century, norms developed and reflected an integrated set of intrainstitutional adjustments. The elements of the institution balanced each other. When, however, the officials commenced to reinterpret their roles, to cease making frequent plant visits, and thus to make themselves less available to workers, this equilibrium was disturbed. The roles of workers and officials no longer met at points where they were interdependent. Experimental activities ensued, and ultimately two major, coordinated efforts to restore equilibrium, the union and management reorganization, resulted.[7]

MATERIAL APPARATUS. With a few exceptions, changes in material apparatus have not been particularly significant in the developments which have marked the past 40 years at the New

6. It is interesting that Durkheim's term, *anomie*, although used to describe profound disorganization, can be translated literally as "normlessness."

7. This paragraph is intended to be no more than illustrative. Fuller treatment of the changes at the New Freedom Products Company will be found in a later chapter.

Freedom Products Company. Both plants have occupied the same sites since long before this period started, and the buildings and machinery are similar to or the same as those which were in use before 1900. As was noted in the section on personnel above, the processes do not require highly skilled labor, and much of the equipment can be operated by women. These facts are important in the history of the company and remain important for its future, but they need little discussion here because they are only indirectly related to the changes in personal relationships which have occurred.

An exception to this statement is the office. In 1900 this was a small, three-room building in which the officials and a few other office employees worked practically shoulder to shoulder. Twenty rooms have been added to the original three in this building, and there are offices in two other buildings. Thus the proliferation of administrative duties which first began to be felt by officials early in the century has gone on and on until the very size of the office may be contributing to a depersonalization of relationships not unlike that which marked relationships between the officials and plant workers. Coincidental with this growth of office space has been the introduction of office machinery. This appears to have been in response to administrative demands, however, rather than a precipitant of change. Logically such equipment might have been expected to free officials from such time-consuming duties as writing and copying letters by hand, but, if it had any such effect, it was more than counterbalanced by other influences.

The original product of the company is made of highly inflammable materials combined with textiles. It is intended to operate in a uniform way under normal conditions and to resist rapid deterioration caused by some of the conditions it is likely to encounter. It discharges a function for which dangerous, haphazard methods had previously been employed. For many years it was the only reliable device for this purpose, but for half a century competition from a device based on different principles has been steadily increasing. It is likely that Product No. 1 will retain an important position in certain basic industries but that it will never regain the dominance it once had.

Early machinery for manufacturing this product looks somewhat crude today, but 50 years ago it incorporated all of the
essentials of modern machinery. Much of the modern machinery
has been in operation for 30 or more years, and some older machines are occasionally used. Improvements in the past half-
century have been in the nature of refinements which do not
materially affect the operation of the machines. The principal
change in machine operation has been speeding up to match the
increased pace of operators after installation of the point system.
In some cases this increased work load has been accomplished
by assigning more machines to each operator. Such assignments
have not varied greatly since 1928, according to the time-study men
and outside industrial engineers who have checked several of the
jobs. The attempt is to give each operator a theoretical "100 per
cent load." On some jobs energetic operators prefer heavier loads
in order to earn more money. On some jobs operators complain
that the load is too heavy to permit them consistently to "make
their premium," that is, an 80-point hour. On some jobs machinery
is so incidental that operators set their own pace, and on these
point hours are frequently much higher than they are when
machine assignments limit production.

Manufacture of Product No. 2 commenced just before World
War I. It also incorporated inflammable and hence dangerous
materials. Its principle of operation differed radically from that
of Product No. 1, although it was used by the same industries.
Its manufacture differed in some respects, but operators familiar
with processes for No. 1 could easily learn Product No. 2 jobs.
Product No. 3, a more efficient device for the same purposes, super-
seded Product No. 2 completely just before World War II, and
it proved to be the company's most spectacular contribution to the
war effort. The manufacture of Product No. 3 is even more like
that of No. 1 than that of No. 2.

The other products—textiles—are also of long standing in the
company, and the processes of their manufacture, while different
from those of Products 2 and 3, have not changed radically in this
century. Like Nos. 2 and 3, textiles are a development from the
manufacture of the original product, and for many years the tex-

tile mill was operated solely to provide materials for the other products. Today at least half of the potential production could be sold to other industries, but potential production has not been realized since World War II because workers cannot be obtained and held in sufficient numbers. Because the odor of some processes pervades the mill, many workers dislike work there, although mill operatives declare that they do not notice the odor at all. It has been customary to employ new workers for mill jobs and to treat other jobs as a kind of reward for long service. Moreover, for the skill and labor required, mill jobs are less well paid than others because they carry no premium for hazardous conditions—conditions which are weighted more heavily by management than by the workers. One of the mill jobs is more difficult to learn than any other in the company and can be regarded as the most skilled job for machine operators.

None of the company jobs, with the exception of that just mentioned and some of those in the maintenance departments, requires much skill. Practically all of them can be learned within a month, and the majority can be learned within a week or ten days. Most of the jobs are light, although some are strenuous.

While agreement is by no means universal, there is a somewhat vague preference scale for jobs. Machinists' and some inspectors' jobs rate at the top of this, followed by the other skilled trades. Jobs in Department No. 1 are preferred to those in the textile mill, and Department No. 2 is preferred to Department No. 1. Operators believe that the difference in prestige of jobs is matched by differences in pay, but this is not entirely true, despite the fact that rates outside the textile mill are built up on account of the hazard factor. Mill jobs for women tend to be more fatiguing than those in other departments.

The general lack of skill required and the fact that many jobs do not demand great strength or endurance are factors in maintaining ideals of security, especially for older and physically handicapped employees. Within limits it is usually possible to find work which such persons can do. Employees are encouraged to learn as many different jobs as possible, not only because a flexible work force is supposed to make for efficiency but also because they can thus guard against layoffs should their jobs become temporarily or even permanently unnecessary.

A few minor exceptions to the statement that changing technology has not greatly affected work at the company indicate how seriously major changes could alter the stability of employment and the adjustment of workers. For example, shifting from horse-drawn wagons to automobile trucks for distributing materials made it necessary to find new jobs for teamsters. This was done for all of them; but one of them at least had great difficulty in reconciling himself to the loss of his horses. He made frequent trips to the stables of the new owners to take the animals chewing tobacco, a delicacy he believed they required. This pilgrimage, he felt, was especially important on Christmas Day.

Just as the nature of the products and the processes have influenced the charter, elements of the charter limit the selection of new products. The company is looking for a product which will make it possible to support the present organizational structure, will continue the company as an important element in the town's economic structure, and will make it possible to go on making money despite the loss of sales for Product No. 1. Considerations in the selection of a product include stability of markets, utilization of the knowledge of the present technical force, processes suitable to the same sort of workers the company now has, processes which will not create a public nuisance (such as smoke or odor), and processes which can be handled in existing company buildings. In the search for new products there is a tendency to emphasize the disadvantages of each prospect rather than the opportunities it presents. Some progress has been made, but there is a chance that emphasis on stability, security, and the other conservative elements in the charter will inhibit enterprise to an extent which may cause the institution to become weak through inertia. Such considerations are by no means new. When the product which is now the principal competitor of Product No. 1 was in its infancy, the New Freedom Products Company could have purchased it. It was judged too dangerous, however, and while present executives look ruefully upon the lost markets they still concur in the judgment of their predecessors.

CHAPTER SEVEN: *Functions*

Taken together, the elements described above—charter, rules and norms, personnel, material apparatus, and activities—constitute the working parts of the institution: the people, the purposes, the ways by which they pursue their purposes, the equipment and materials they use, and the behavior they exhibit. To the personnel these elements represent what the institution is and what it accomplishes. Some, if not all, of the personnel have reservations as to its success in producing the ends they hold desirable; and most of them realize that it also does things which are incidental to the main purposes. Many question the efficacy of this or that rule or machine. Many are not satisfied that everything is as it ought to be. But, except in moments of philosophical detachment, all think of the institution in the more or less ideal terms provided for them in the institution's charter.

The social scientist has a different point of view which might be characterized as one which strives for detached omniscience. While he must see and understand what the personnel think and believe, he can also observe group factors beyond their immediate field of vision. The results actually produced by the interaction of purposes, principles, standards, rules, norms, material equipment, and activities may differ from those which the personnel conceive to be the results. Just as the truly religious person is convinced that his church glorifies the deity and wins him remission for his sins, so the factory employee may have ideas about the workings of his institution which the scientist cannot accept as realities. Both in the long perspective of societal evolution and in the view of the scientist, any institution has functions which more or less successfully contribute to the survival of the society, to the satisfaction of individual needs, and to the survival of the institution itself. The ideal functions, as expressed in the charter, may differ considerably from the actual functions although they may, as is often the case in the factory, coincide at various points.

In order to systematize the treatment of the rather complex subject of institutional functions, I have classified them in the following manner, as explained earlier in this book:

> Extrainstitutional functions
> a) integral
> b) subsidiary
> Intrainstitutional functions
> a) instrumental
> b) consumatory

The integral, or main, or summary function of the New Freedom Products Company—the principal function of the institution in the whole society—coincides fairly closely with one of the charter purposes. The company does produce goods which society finds useful. The company's products implement certain basic economic undertakings, and thus the institution is integrated with the "total culture." While this book is concerned primarily with internal adjustments, and hence with intrainstitutional functions, it is worth noting that the company has discharged its main integral function so successfully throughout its history that the personnel's faith in its stability has never been severely shaken. The company has grown with American industry in general, and its fortunes have reflected those of the national economy. Hard times have been blamed not on weakness or bad management within the institution but on extrainstitutional "economic conditions." Nevertheless, the company's products do not now constitute so firm a foundation for continuing stability as the history of its first hundred years would seem to indicate, and some of the personnel realize this. Product No. 1 has long been losing important markets, and a continuation of this trend could become disastrous. Product No. 3 (successor to Product No. 2) is relatively new and seems to have bright prospects. Alone, however, it will never be able to support more than a small fraction of the present company personnel. The textile department employs about a third of the workers, but the volume of production is small and the company has not been able consistently to compete with larger textile factories elsewhere. Half of the textile mill's production and thus half of its personnel and overhead are supported by "interdepartment sales" to Product No. 1. At present the company's overhead including administrative and executive salaries and expenses, among them the cost of pensions and tenement maintenance, is adjusted to a scale of operations which a return to production at the prewar level could hardly support. The search for new products which would enable the company to maintain its organizational structure and provide employment for at least as many people as are now on the payroll has been slow and rather unproductive to date. Thus cold facts challenge the brave slogan in recent company advertisements: "A safe place to work for the next hundred years." Cold facts, also, are not unrelated to dealings between the union and management and may, in time, force modification of charter, personnel, and other elements.

Indeed, although our attention is focused upon intrainstitutional relationships, it should not be forgotten that these have always been influenced by the integral function—that is, by the relationship of the company's production to the needs of society for its products. Growth of the company, for example, has followed increasing demands for the products, and concentration of the officials on administration has been influenced by competition or the threat of competition. Both of these developments are behind the decrease in personal contacts between the workers and the officials. Moreover, while this observation may be speculative, it seems probable that the company could not have remained strong and stable if it had not kept pace with demand and outdistanced competition. Thus internal changes have been, in part at least, in adjustment to the requirements of the integral external function.

Pleasant though the days of free personal interchange may seem to those who look fondly back at them, a return to them would be impossible.

Subsidiary external functions of the company include payment of local, state, and federal taxes, purchase of goods and services from other institutions and individuals, and, indirectly, provision of income for many persons in the community who are not on the factory rolls: storekeepers, professionals, and others. Except insofar as they relate to the belief that the company is a part of the community and should contribute to its support, these functions are not reflected in the institutional charter. They illustrate admirably, however, the way in which society may seize upon "a comprehensive instrumentality" and utilize it for ends other than that which provides its principle reason for being.[1]

The intrainstitutional or internal functions, it will be recalled, fall into two categories: consumatory functions, that is, those which are more or less directly associated with the needs of the personnel; and instrumental functions, that is, those which exist primarily to keep the institution going.

Needs differ from purposes in that they exist as basic or primary drives of the human organism or as acquired drives or needs derived from primary drives. They may or may not be consciously recognized and expressed as purposes. Thus, in the factory, such a thing as providing prestige or recognition would not be listed as a purpose of the institution, but this does not mean that it is not a need of the individual members of the personnel. We need not here attempt a precise differentiation between primary and acquired drives; this is a matter of concern mainly to the psychologist. In terms of social function, needs in general can be regarded as acquired drives, and they can be expressed in terms of the rewards which satisfy or reduce them, as is quite clear when one speaks of the need for money.[2]

1. Cf. Malinowski, *A Scientific Theory of Culture*, p. 112.
2. Cf. N. Miller and J. Dollard, *Social Learning and Imitation*, pp. 18–20: "A drive is a strong stimulus which impels action . . . certain special classes of stimuli seem to be the primary basis for the greater proportion of motivation. These might be called the primary or innate drives [such as thirst, extreme hun-

The problem of establishing a list of needs which are characteristic of industrial workers and which industry might be expected to
satisfy is a difficult one. It has engaged the attention of many students of industry. The most satisfactory list of such needs known
to the writer is that drawn up by E. Wight Bakke in his *Principles
of Adaptive Human Behavior*,[3] and even this is offered tentatively
by its author. It has, however, the advantages of sociological
orientation, of being based on comprehensive studies of industry,
and, at least for our purposes, of matching fairly closely observations at the New Freedom Products Company. The first six of

---

ger, pain, fatigue, sex]." These are obscured by the fact that social organization
usually protects its members from them by providing satisfactions before they
mount to agonizing heights and by imposing inhibitions which prevent frank
statements about them. "The conditions of society tend, besides obscuring
the role of certain primary drives, to emphasize certain secondary or acquired
drives. These secondary drives are acquired on the basis of the primary drives,
represent elaborations of them, and serve as a façade behind which the functions of the underlying innate drives are hidden. . . . Some of the stronger
of the acquired drives or social needs are not based on any single drive, but
rather on a number of more primary drives. Indeed, it is probably from this
fact that they derive their strength and persistence. Thus the desire for money
is the focus of many needs." See also *ibid.*, 29: "Though it is convenient to
think of rewards as events producing reduction in the strength of drive stimulus,
it is not necessary to be able to identify the drive which is reduced and the
manner in which it is reduced in order to determine empirically that certain
events are rewards under certain circumstances and to make practical use of
this information."

Cf. also Clyde Kluckhohn and W. H. Kelly, "The Concept of Culture,"
The Science of Man in the World Crisis, ed. Ralph Linton, pp. 103–104.

3. Bakke, *Principles of Adaptive Human Behavior*, p. 10. It should be noted
that Bakke has revised this list, notably in a processed publication of the Yale
Labor and Management Center in 1950. In this he lists the "goals" as "security, progress and justice" with respect to the first six noted above. This
was done because such aspirations can exist only in terms of other goals. We
have retained the original with the addition of "security" and "pleasant working conditions" for three reasons. The first of these is that some of the other
goals are also interdependent. Second, "justice" seems to be comprehended
by "integrity and wholeness," and finally the writer is still uncertain about
how to interpret "progress," especially since many workers do not seem to
desire advancement in the conventional sense of that term.

the following are Bakke's "goals." The last two have been added because they seem necessary in the case of this company:

1. *Respect of fellows*

   The desire to play a socially respected role and to be treated justly, i.e., in accordance with one's conception of his own worth.

2. *Creature sufficiency*

   The desire to have that degree of creature sufficiency (food, clothes, shelter, health, etc., and the means to provide them) enjoyed by the most favored of one's customary associates.

3. *Increasing control over one's own affairs*

   The desire to have one's own decisions and actions effective in shaping the course of his own life . . .

4. *Understanding*

   The desire to comprehend the forces and factors which operate in one's own world, "to know the score."

5. *Capacity performance*

   The desire to utilize in living the full range of capacities possessed, both actual and potential.

6. *Integrity or wholeness*

   The desire to experience consistency within one's self, among the parts of one's world, and a significant relationship to that world.

7. *Security*

   The desire for assurance of future creature sufficiency and for continued satisfaction of other needs.

8. *Satisfactory working conditions*

   The desire for safe and pleasant physical surroundings and for comfortable relationships with other people.

These eight needs appear to exist in the majority of people in industry whether they are "workers" or "management" and whether or not they are in this particular institution. To say that they are characteristic of all people everywhere, however, would be to draw too long a bow and one which would miss its target. Even to say that they are characteristic of all groups in American society would probably be incorrect. Anthropologists have often noted that the motivations of primitive peoples do not correspond to those commonly regarded by twentieth-century Americans as springing from "human nature." [4] Sociologists also have pointed out that some groups within our own society seem to possess motivations which do not correspond closely to those of others. Southern Negroes, for example, often do not press for greater and greater material possessions, although these, especially in the form of money, represent the key to satisfying many of the above needs for most northern industrial workers.[5] Hence this list is presented

4. Cf. such works as Margaret Mead's "Sex and Temperament" or Ruth Benedict's *Patterns of Culture*. Both these authors point out that different cultures emphasize different potentialities within the normal range of human capacities and that the highest desiderata of some peoples are incomprehensible to normal members of other tribes. In other words, they assert that acquired drives, whatever their primary basis may be, are so shaped by culture that a list of needs applicable to any single cultural unit may be grossly misleading in the case of another. Such assertions do not necessarily deny the existence of cultural universals, that is, of acquired drives or needs shared by all cultures. It is worth noting, however, that even such universals can be interpreted by most individuals only in the terms provided for them by their own culture or subculture.

Thus the competitiveness implied by the phrase, "enjoyed by the most favored of one's customary associates," in the second of the above goals may well remove it from universal application. Thus also the need for security implies foresight, which, as Lippert has pointed out, is a product of culture existing in various degrees and in various forms in different cultures (Julius Lippert, *The Evolution of Culture*, pp. 21–22). Still as the universality of religious institutions indicates, this need probably exists in some degree in all of them.

5. Cf. Kimball Young, *Sociology*, pp. 263–264: "Our schools reflect the American emphasis on rivalry, competition, and speed, and mental tests given to pupils may easily arouse in them the desire to 'shine' and to make the best possible records. With American Indians, with Negroes, or with children of immigrant backgrounds, it may be difficult to secure their interest. It is hard to measure this matter, but it is highly important to recognize it."

Cf. also Ruth D. Tuck, *Not with the Fist*, pp. 135–136. In this discussion of a Mexican community in a city in southern California, Miss Tuck points out that the drive to accumulate money is not strong among even second-generation Mexican immigrants and that the possession of much money may be considered dangerous: "Money is appreciated in the *colonia*, but merely neither as a new compilation of universal drives nor even as a complete summary of the needs of people in American industry. As a quick résumé of the New Freedom Products Company's charter will reveal, the people there have purposes, principles, and standards which stand as goals for them and thus represent acquired drives or needs. Nevertheless, this list of needs includes those which must be satisfied if the functions of the institution are to be accomplished successfully. It is important to note that while some of them are reflected in the charter others are not. Creature sufficiency includes the charter purpose of making money, but rare indeed is the worker who would say that the institution should provide "respect of fellows." One must be on guard against confusing charter and function, especially when needs are under discussion. This is because the personnel themselves define their needs, insofar as they consciously recognize them, in terms of the charter. Thus, in many respects at least, the need for "integrity or wholeness" may be expressed by the personnel as "fair play," which can refer not only to overtly recognized values but also to dissatisfactions which are not formulated in words. An employee may not be able to put his finger on the reasons why he feels lost, but the impersonal interviewer must try to get at the truth.

Although employees do not mention recognition, prestige, or "the desire to play a socially respected role" as reasons for working at the company or for the company's existence, provision of respect of fellows is actually one of the functions of the institution. Supervisors who deal directly with workers know that the admonition, "Give credit where credit is due," is worth following.[6] Especially high value is placed on praise from persons in authority. Some of the older employees are fond of recalling occasions "in the old

---

because it provides a more satisfactory way of life. Sights are seldom raised to include the amassing of money for the sake of power and prestige. The possession of a great deal of money is thought of as being dangerous. . . . It is true that opportunity has been so limited that ambition may not have had soil in which to grow. However, an instance or two can be cited in which an able man actually saw a path to big money-making and turned aside from it."

6. This phrase was a slogan in the Training Within Industry program. It was offered as a method for gaining cooperation and confidence.

days" when officials complimented them personally upon their work, and one or two immigrants are emotional about such recollections.[7] Simple recognition was greatly appreciated by immigrants in their early years at the company, as their stories about being called by their "own names" show. Loss of the personal contacts between officials and the workers naturally reduced the possibility of this sort of satisfaction for the workers. Moreover, since officials came to the plant very seldom their praise was robbed of authenticity. Conversely, the officials also miss this kind of recognition. The fact that they are no longer able to establish genuinely personal contacts with the employees is a real source of embarrassment to them.[8]

The desire for just treatment in accordance with one's conception of his own worth corresponds to part of the charter, although it is not regarded as a purpose of the institution or as a reason for membership in the personnel. Justice, fair play, or "decent treatment" is measured in terms of the charter. Thus, while prestige is not in the charter, friendliness is. An official or lesser executive walking through the plant would not be regarded as satisfying a desire for respect if he spoke to a worker, but he would be criticized if he did not greet everyone he met,[9] and traditionally such greeting should have some kind of personal overtone. Similarly, the two 50-year employees who complained that it was "not right" arbitrarily to shift "old-timers" to menial work were disturbed because

7. Shortly before his retirement a Polish worker said, "I always remember when I get my 40-year pin. Mr. Perkins put his hand on my shoulder and say, 'F——, you always done good work.' I carry these words in my heart until I die."

8. Early in 1946 the president of the company, on the ground that "we need more of the old personal touch," spent over a day going through the Teasville and Herford plants. His satisfaction because he had had a "nice chat" with every single worker was manifest, but five years later when he retired he had not repeated the venture.

9. The writer learned this forcefully. A worker, during a period of intoxication, made his way even into the officials' inner sanctum where the writer was conferring with one of his superiors. Tearfully this man listed his troubles, but the worst of them all, the thing that really started his grief, as he declared over and over again, was, "You didn't speak to me when you was walking through the department the other day. That hurt."

they believed they were not being treated justly, i.e., in accordance with their own conception of their worth. Even the man who cleans out the ashpits at the power plant insists that his job is essential and that no one does it as conscientiously as he does.

To a considerable degree, wages (and salaries) can be regarded as a principal component of creative sufficiency. On the basis of the evidence at the New Freedom Products Company, the need for creature sufficiency as a desire for satisfactions *equal to those enjoyed by the most favored of one's customary associates* requires some modification. Extensive interviews and field work among employees might show that every member of the New Freedom Products Company has such a desire, and some would no doubt like to excel the most fortunate of their acquaintances. On the other hand, New Freedom Products people have, on the whole, set their goals at levels realizable in their own statuses or in statuses to which they can reasonably aspire within the institution. Reluctantly or otherwise, they have modified their goals in an effort to build balanced structures of living for themselves. Many seem to prefer comfortable jobs to changes which might bring levels of remuneration nearer to those of more favored associates. Some seem to place other satisfactions ahead of food, clothes, shelter, health, and others which one might expect to find in the category of creature sufficiency. A few spend their money for such things as liquor or entertainment, even to the extent in some cases of slighting food, clothes, and health. That all members of the personnel would like more immediate income is not to be doubted, but to obtain this most of them would not make certain sacrifices, important among which would be sacrifice of security.

Practically, however, most of the personnel measure adequate income by their notion of what persons of corresponding status receive in other factories.[10] Throughout the organization it is believed that New Freedom employees are not so well paid as they would be elsewhere, although precise bases for comparisons are not available to the personnel. Such bases would have to take into account similarity of skills and trades and other factors. Actually,

10. This statement refers to the general standard. Any individual might compare his own earnings with those of other employees.

on the worker level wages are not much lower than those prevailing in the county, as shown by comparative figures of industrial workers' earnings. In fact, wages of women workers at New Freedom Products, judging by those figures, exceed the county average:

Males	Average Hourly Earnings	Average Weekly Earnings	Average Hours Per Week
New Freedom Products Company	$1.08	$47.	43.5
County [11]	1.11	51.	45.
Females			
New Freedom Products Company	.85	35.	40.5
County [11]	.77	32.	41.

In view of the fact that there are several large metal-trades industries in the county which employ highly skilled workers, while most New Freedom jobs are not highly skilled, these figures do not bear out the belief commonly held at the New Freedom Products Company. Although it is possible that the average employee could qualify in another company for wages better than those he receives at the New Freedom Products Company, it is also safe to say that where comparisons with other factories can be used as a yardstick the company fulfills its function of providing adequate creature sufficiency, at least as far as this relates to pay. In this connection it is significant that the union has not strongly pressed demands for higher wages.[12] Nevertheless, the fact that workers think they get less than they might elsewhere and are generally content to offset this supposed inadequacy by considering other advantages is significant.

11. Figures prepared by the County Manufacturers' Association, Nov., 1945.

12. In its first bargaining sessions with the company in the spring of 1945, the union asked for minimum wage rates about nine cents an hour higher than existing minimum rates. This demand was quickly dropped in favor of getting the company to agree to "keep on doing what it has been doing." In 1946 the union requested a 15-cent hourly-wage increase, less than what might have been expected in view of the well-publicized requests throughout the nation for 30 per cent and the many 18 per cent increases actually gained. The union settled for somewhat less than 15 per cent with apparent satisfaction. More recent increases have reflected but not exceeded national trends.

Comparison with such figures as are available indicate that salaries paid New Freedom office workers—clerks, stenographers, etc.—are about the same as those paid in other industrial offices in the same area. Going rates published by the government during World War II matched New Freedom rates closely. Comparisons with a survey made by a large utility company also give evidence that pay for clerical work is approximately the same as that of other companies. Thus, although a good many New Freedom office workers would not believe it, it is fair to say that in comparison with other companies this institution fulfills the "creature sufficiency" function adequately for clerks, stenographers, bookkeepers, and other office workers.

The rates of assistants to executives, time-study men, professionals, and similar employees below executive status are difficult to compare, both because such jobs tend to be individualized rather than standardized and because pay is often determined by factors which have little to do with the work performed. Thus one assistant received $360 per month in 1945, not counting overtime, mainly because of the length of his service and the nature of posts he had previously held, while rates for some assistants were as low as $150 per month. Such employees could discover what they might earn elsewhere only by seeking new jobs. The fact that no one of them has done so indicates that the combination of income and other satisfactions gained at the company can be considered adequate.

The same factors which make comparison of assistants' salaries with those elsewhere difficult are even more confusing in the case of executives. It is traditional that New Freedom executives must weigh security, the advantages of living in a pleasant community, and similar considerations against the possibility of higher income. No executives have left the company for higher salaries, while in the ten years from 1937 through 1946 six men from outside took executive positions with the company.

Foremen's salaries are equally difficult to evaluate. The content of the foreman's job varies markedly from company to company, and the title itself is often misleading. In one company the foreman may be a relatively high supervisor while in another he may be little more than a lead man. In general the New Freedom Products Company attempts to maintain what is supposed to be an adequate differential between foremen's pay and that of the hourly-paid workers whom they supervise.

In summary, it can be said that while facts may not warrant it employees below the official level, and probably even those on that level, believe that earnings for comparable jobs elsewhere are higher than those at the New Freedom Products Company. This undoubtedly has a bearing on the fact that on the worker level younger persons frequently leave the company and that recruitment of local youths is difficult. It also supports the inference that throughout the institution other goals outweigh income in value.

Before leaving pay as a measure of "creature comfort," it is well to recall that money is more in our culture than simply a means to buy food, clothing, shelter, or even future security. It is also an important measure of prestige. The case of an employee in another company who complained that her pay was inadequate is pertinent. This girl said she was underpaid and pointed out that another girl whose work, she claimed, was no more difficult received $5 more per week. Plainly the first girl thought that money was all she wanted, for she said a $5 raise would satisfy her. She declared, however, that a $5 raise for both herself and the other girl would not improve the situation at all. Obviously what she wanted was not creature comfort but recognition. Satisfaction of this need, also, may be tied to things other than money—to washrooms, for instance, to the character of company houses. The facility with which employees obtained attention for housing requests was an important factor in the transition from the system of easy personal contacts with officials.

While money may well be treated as an essential phase of creature sufficiency in a factory, it should be remembered that more primary needs of the human organism must be taken into account. Human comfort demands food, facilities for elimination, air, water, protection from pain, relief from fatigue, and shelter from heat and cold. These physical requirements are, of course, of varying relevance for industrial personnel. For some factory workers food may be of no concern while on the job, although for others the provision of restaurant or cafeteria facilities may be of first importance. As it happens, most of these requirements played a minor role in determining worker satisfaction at the New Freedom Products Company, although several of them presented petty sources of irritation. Maintaining a comfortable temperature in the office, for example, was a constant problem for the office manager, who was tempted to conclude that no two women employees could be satisfied with any given setting of the thermostats. More important was the comfort of textile-mill workers who had to accustom themselves to the odor of the materials they processed. This odor unquestionably played a part in the low prestige accorded mill jobs, although mill workers claimed they soon became used to it and did not find it objectionable. Some progress has been made in eliminating the odor, and mill workers approve this heartily. It still remains, however, as a possible crystallization point for irritation, although it cannot be said that it played an important role in the developments with which this study is concerned. In other companies such considerations of creature comfort assume a much more significant place in any assessment of social and other relationships.

The need for a sense of control is rather easily susceptible of misunderstanding since control is readily associated with formally recognized authority and also because a *sense* of control is a subjective matter. Thus, in industry the worker who stands at the bottom of the formally recognized system of organization may appear to lack control altogether. If, however, he thinks his own abilities and intentions are important in shaping his own activities and their reception by others, this need is satisfied. It has been argued, for example, that the weakness of even beneficent paternalism is that it puts the worker in a position of absolute dependence. Nevertheless, it is notable that during their first years in this country the immigrants at the New Freedom Products Company were content, indeed pleased, with their lot, whereas American workers and, later, the children of immigrants were not. This was due, in part, to the fact that paternalism was consistent with the expectations of the immigrants. To them the system was more free than that which they had known "in the old country," and the fact that they could speak to the officials gave them a degree of influence greater than any with which they had been familiar. To others this sort of control might have seemed illusory, but as far as the immigrants were concerned it was effective enough. In other words, for this particular group paternalism worked because it was congruent with their standards and aspirations and hence did not diminish their sense of control. Similarly, while it has been argued that the individual member in a large union may have very little to say in union affairs, he still may regard the union as his protection against the power of his employers and thus, although he may not verbalize his sentiments, as a means of control for him.

While some writers, including Bakke, regard the desire for control "over the factors which influence one's own life" as being a desire for increasing control, it is debatable, at least on the findings at the New Freedom Products Company, whether this is literally so.[13] Certainly individuals resist any decrease in the amount of control they believe they possess, and when they feel a loss of control they attempt to regain it. Some, of course, do press for more control, but others seem to be content to hold their ground.

During the period of relative equilibrium at this company before World War I, a principal means of control was found by officers and workers in the intimate personal contacts which existed between these two status levels. Through these contacts officials were able to keep closely in touch with practices related to production, quality, and safety and to pass along charter re-enforcements which served to bring the points of view of upper and lower status levels together. Workers, on the other hand, used these contacts to advance their own goals and to bring their problems to the attention of the officials. Just as officials sensed a loss of control when those contacts disappeared, so workers became dissatisfied. They did not believe that such intermediaries as foremen could present their cases as effectively as they could them-

13. In conversation Bakke has explained that he does not mean increase necessarily in the sense of obtaining more and more power but rather in the sense of developing control consistent with advancing age and other statuses.

selves, and they found that red tape interfered with satisfaction of their desires. It is worth noting that satisfaction in the shape of a denial accompanied by an authoritative explanation seemed, in practice, to produce as much or nearly as much satisfaction as did the granting of a request. Employees felt that at least they "knew the score."

"Capacity performance" means more than advancement or "getting ahead," although, particularly to young and ambitious employees, advancement may be the most important reward for the drive to use one's abilities fully. In the case of some employees at least, capacity performance cannot be construed as full utilization of potential abilities on a given job or even within the institution. They find and perhaps prefer other outlets for their abilities.

For many employees, advancement is a less important goal than security. Indeed, as is indicated in the section of the last chapter devoted to personnel, there was a marked selection in favor of persons willing to sacrifice chances for promotion for assurances that they need have few fears for the future. In a few employees this feeling goes to extremes; they are comfortable in the jobs they know and do not want to risk learning new ones.[14]

Nevertheless, the failure of the company to satisfy this need for capacity performance has affected some individuals strongly. Two, at least, of the men who assumed leadership in bringing the union into the company had been frustrated in their desire for advancement. One of these men, the first president of the union, had proven leadership ability which was not utilized by the company but which revealed itself first in his presidency of a large social organization and later in his union activity. Another reflection of the company's inadequacy in satisfying this need is found in the reluctance of younger men in the community to work at the company. As has been pointed out, the spread of high-school

14. This was strikingly illustrated in the case of a textile-mill employee who dodged training courses which might have led to promotion for him. This man even resisted the urging of fellow workers who thought he was missing an opportunity. In his case there was evidence of extreme shyness, possibly of a slightly neurotic disinclination to accept responsibility. Less striking instances are frequent. In the opinion of some employees, several of the men who volunteered for a so-called foremanship course were "wacky."

education, increased choice of occupations within the community, and modern transportation which has made working outside the community easier have all contributed to this difficulty. Other indications are the frequent resignations of young men to go into business for themselves or to take more promising jobs and the scarcity of men in the lower status levels who could qualify for promotion to executive positions.[15]

Like the need for control, the need for understanding the forces and factors which affect one's life is closely related to the methods of communication between the higher and lower status levels of the institution. Workers formerly received from officials what they assumed to be thoroughly reliable information regarding the business and their part in it. Conversely, officials were informed directly about affairs in the plant, including the problems and morale of the workers. The personal contacts fulfilled the charter ideals of neighborliness and friendly cooperation, and they performed the function of satisfying the need for understanding.

With the diminution and loss of these personal contacts, both workers and officials lost a sense of mutual understanding. Neither thoroughly trusted intermediaries to inform them correctly, though it is probable that the workers felt more distance than did the officials. Under the old equilibrium each employee was satisfied that he had adequate access to the information he needed in shaping his life within the institution. Written communications, letters to employees, and bulletin-board notices have not approximated in effectiveness personal conversation as media for transmitting ideas. Nor have the intermediaries proved satisfactory channels for inter-status communications. Even words carefully chosen to convey specific messages have lost force and meaning when unaccompanied by the gestures, expressions, and intonations which enhance conversation. An extreme example of this occurred during the period when the union was being organized. Legal restrictions

15. It is interesting that among the plans now being considered by personnel executives are some which propose to utilize employees' capacities more fully. Two of these are a tentative recreation program, which it is hoped will engage employee loyalties during nonworking hours, and the possibility of some kind of "management sharing."

were then added to the difficulties already created by the separation of officials from workers. The best management could do in trying to present its views to the workers was to write guarded letters and bulletin-board notices. One of these was so careful to stay within the restrictions of the Wagner Act that it was actually interpreted by some workers as advice to join the union! On the other hand, one of the strongest arguments presented by the group backing the union was that through the union the members would gain direct access to the officials.

Within the office there is a similar contrast. The officers, behind the little door which shuts off their suite from the rest of the company, do not rub elbows with each other as they did when they shared three adjoining rooms and always kept their doors open. The rest of the office people are scattered on the three floors of the main office building and in other buildings. A symptom of the growing sense of social distance inside the office is the fact that officials are no longer invited to the informal parties of the office personnel.

Satisfaction of the sixth need listed above, the need for a sense of integrity or wholeness, is also closely related to ease of communication among the personnel and to the charter of the institution. This need corresponds rather closely both to the charter value of fair play and to the principle of friendly cooperation. It goes somewhat further than these expressed ideals, however, and includes the need for a sense of belonging.

The integrating effect of a common sense of charter and of free communications is indicated by the relative institutional equilibrium reached before World War I. At that time it was possible for people on the various status levels to know each other's points of view and to feel that they belonged to a group united by common purposes, principles, and values. As individuals they could see that their relationship to the group was significant. They knew where their own jobs fitted into the scheme of production, and from time to time they heard firsthand reports from officials of what the products were doing in the field. Older workers as well passed along stories and anecdotes which strengthened the sense of identification with the institution. In the view of some observers the development of a vertical hierarchy in industry has placed labor and management in two hostile camps.[16] No such situation has as yet fully developed at the New Freedom Products Company. Antagonisms do not outweigh recognized common interests. But there is evidence that workers do not always interpret the charter in the same way as management does and that weakness in the present system of communications and indoctrination is responsible, at least in part, for the divergence of viewpoints.[17]

More than any other factor, the threat to security, which came to be felt as contacts with officials became fewer, created the tensions and anxieties which set in motion what Bakke calls adaptive behavior.[18] So many satisfactions were implemented by personal contacts with officials that loss of these contacts destroyed the employees' assurance that their other needs would continue to be

16. Cf. W. Lloyd Warner and J. O. Low, *The Social System of a Modern Factory*, p. 37. In this book the authors describe the development of vertical hierarchy to a point where absentee ownership and management took the top levels not only outside the factory but far outside the local community. They also describe horizontal extensions of organization carrying outside the factories in "Yankee City" through trade associations and unions. The emphasis which these authors put on the split between labor and management can be seen in their reference to unions as, among other things, "weapons for the workers to defend themselves and attack their enemies." It is interesting to note that, as the authors quote him, the union president, in this case the leading outside organizer, expressed quite a different viewpoint. He stated the objects of the union as "to do good for the workers and to stabilize the industry so that the employers could do right by their workers and also make money."

17. This problem is further discussed in Chapter 8.

18. Bakke presents several propositions which incorporate his conclusions regarding adaptive behavior, that is, efforts by individuals to restore equilibrium in their "structures of living." In summary, his argument is that disequilibrium creates tensions and anxieties which lead to experimental actions, and, from among these, those which tend to greater equilibrium are continued while others are discarded. As a supplement to this, the present study endeavors to show that the institution must be regarded as more than merely the arithmetical sum of individual adjustments. The institution provides much of the material from which "structures of living" within the institution are built. In the case of the New Freedom Products Company, changes in institutional norms played a leading part in disturbing the equilibrium of individual structures of living. Cf. Bakke, *Principles of Adaptive Human Behavior*, pp. 5–24.

satisfied. The uneasiness and rancor which characterized these feelings of insecurity have already been described at some length as have the various, more positive efforts to restore equilibrium. The manner in which the union sought to strengthen job security and security of employment is worth reviewing. The first union bargaining committee concentrated on obtaining guarantees from the company that it would not reduce wages, would continue the point system unchanged, and would continue benefits then in effect. Through the contract seniority clause, the union sought to establish a pattern for security. This clause was particularly difficult for the union committee; it could not find a formula which covered all the points it wanted covered. Although the committee members first asked to have length of service be the sole measure of whether an employee should be laid off or recalled after layoffs, they readily agreed that such qualifications as ability to do the work required and local residence were pertinent. In the end they accepted a clause which simply confirmed existing company policy on layoffs and recalls. The membership was disappointed when it discovered that transfers and promotions were not covered. Similarly, the grievance procedure, with its provisions for checking studies under the point system and for calling in outside arbitrators, was intended to increase worker security.

It is perhaps significant that the union placed so little stress on the so-called company benefits, many of which are designed to promote worker security. Possibly these were taken for granted or were thought to be adequately covered by the contract clause which simply guaranteed that they would not be changed. They include the pension plan, group life insurance policies ranging from $500 for new employees to $1,000 for employees who have five years or more of service, hospital and disability insurance, workmen's compensation,[19] medical care,[20] and an irregular system

19. The company guarantees a larger return to workers injured on the job than the law requires.

20. In addition to hospital facilities for employees injured at work, the company maintains a free clinic for workers and their families. The service of this clinic is officially limited to diagnosis and minor care in order to avoid condemnation by the American Medical Association, but the company doctors, in their discretion, are inclined to offer more elaborate care in some

of lending money to employees temporarily in need. The cost of all of these, except the hospital and disability insurance plans, is borne by the company. Employees pay premiums through payroll deductions for hospital and disability insurance if they elect to take either or both of these services. During World War II, the company retained on the payroll all men who went into the armed forces or the merchant marine and paid them a proportion of the difference between their regular company pay and their base military pay.[21]

cases. This the company feels it cannot control because cases are regarded as confidential matters between the doctor and his patients. Usually the matter of competing with private practitioners is an academic consideration, as the company doctor would ordinarily be the private physician of the patients anyway.

21. The hospital insurance plan is that of the Blue Cross. This was introduced soon after it became available in the state. After a slow start it became popular with the workers, although a few still are not covered by it. The disability insurance plan is carried by a commercial insurance company. At the time the contract was written, it paid approximately $7 per week to female employees and $10 a week to male employees during the period they were certified as being unable to work by their doctor. Premiums fluctuate slightly with the company's record of liabilities. Maximum premiums are 90 cents a month for men and 60 cents a month for women. Benefits are limited to 13 weeks, commencing the second week of an illness. This insurance is not nearly so popular as the hospital plan.

During the depression, financial aid for employees was administrated by a committee under the direction of the president of the company. Actual records of the work of this committee are unavailable, but benefits in some cases were substantial and were probably supplemented from the pockets of Shields and other officials. The present lending of money is a hang-over from the days of the welfare committee. It is in the hands of the personnel manager, who seldom advances more money to a worker than he has already earned. Tenants in company houses are permitted to be delinquent in their rents during illness, and occasionally delinquent rents run for several months. Collection of rents from employees while they are working is automatic through payroll deduction.

The pension plan is operated on the basis of need in individual cases, tempered by consideration of the basic earnings of the employee in question. This plan was formalized in 1944. The entire cost is borne by a trust fund to which the company is the sole contributor. Benefits include pensions for employees who are permanently disabled regardless of their age, pensions for

Except for the pension plan, it is difficult to assess the effectiveness of these benefits in contributing to the employees' sense of
security. The workers count on the pension plan. It is part of
what they mean when they say, "This company will always take
care of you." Moreover, the plan was formerly closely bound up
with the personal relationships between workers and officials.
Workers regarded the pensions as proof of the officials' interest
in their welfare, as a symbol of friendliness and neighborliness.
While the new plan has not been in operation long enough to make
substantial observations possible, there is a question whether its
impersonality will reduce the sense of integration which the older
system gave. The other benefits seem to be either taken for granted
or forgotten. There is reason to believe that they add something to

---

employees who retire after reaching the age of sixty-five, reduced pensions for
employees who, by agreement with the company, retire before they reach
sixty-five years of age, and severance benefits for employees who have been
with the company 20 years and are at least forty-five years old. Employees are
eligible for the plan after they are twenty-five years old and after they have
three years of service. Disability and retirement pensions amount to one per
cent of an employee's earnings after he becomes eligible for membership (one
per cent of his average annual earnings multiplied by the number of years
he has been a member of the plan). To offset the fact that for older employees
the early years of their service produced relatively small earnings, earnings for
years previous to the inauguration of the plan were calculated as having been
the same as those for the year the plan began. Benefits for disabled employees
are increased approximately 15 per cent until they reach the age of sixty-five
to offset the fact that they do not receive social security benefits from the
government until they reach that age.

The military service benefits amounted to one-quarter of the difference
between average company earnings and base military pay for men and
women with a year's service in the company plus $20 per month for each
dependent for a maximum period of 14 months. Some workers received nearly
$100 per month under this plan. Payments were made to the local savings
bank for men without dependents, to the dependents for other men. In addition, the company offered to pay for government life insurance up to the
amount that would have been paid for any person for group life insurance at
the company. Very few men took advantage of this offer. It is interesting that
this plan of military service benefits was not publicized very much, and one
of its beneficiaries did not know about it until he returned to the company
and was handed a savings bankbook with credits amounting to about $400.

a general sense of security but little evidence that most employees attach much immediate importance to them.[22]

Despite the ever-present hazard of the inflammable materials used in Departments 1 and 2, the final need on the list above— that for pleasant and safe working conditions—seems to be best satisfied in these departments, in the office, and in some of the maintenance departments. In these departments the physical surroundings are regarded as pleasant. Relationships among the people in the departments give little evidence of friction or strain aside from the stresses associated with maladjustments accompanying the progressive depersonalization of interstatus contacts. The risk of a flash fire, which could kill or maim people, has been minimized by rules and by the value placed by the personnel on safety practices. Most of the workers seem to forget the inherent danger. Pay for jobs in hazardous areas is somewhat higher than for comparable work in other parts of the plants, and in the most dangerous areas the amount of productive work expected is decreased to permit attention to safety factors. Most of the rooms are clean and airy. Most employees consider these departments better places to work in than the textile mill.

We have already noted physical working conditions in the textile mill in connection with creature comforts, and it is apparent that this sort of need tends to overlap the need for pleasant working conditions. The more important aspect of these conditions, however, is to be found in personal associations of individuals with other people.[23]

The textile mill has suffered not only on account of its physical discomforts but also from the fact that for at least ten years the

22. One of the few times when employees gave evidence of being keenly aware of the group life insurance benefit was during an organization rally of the union. At this meeting the union speaker declared that the union would obtain a $500 death benefit for the workers. It was reported that many workers were amused at this offer since they knew they already had $1,000. Union officers have spoken of "demanding" that the company pay the hospital-plan premiums, but so far they have not done so.

23. Cf. L. G. Reynolds and J. Shister, *Job Horizons*, in which the importance of pleasant relations with co-workers, foremen, and others on the job is made clear.

employees there have found their relationships with supervisors less comfortable than those in most other departments. Historically the mill foreman has had more authority than the others. Ten years ago the man who held this post was autocratic, and his disposition was made even more uncongenial by persistent illness. This situation was relieved somewhat when he was pensioned in 1938, but his successor was also unable to establish harmonious relationships with some of his subordinates. To complicate matters further, the mill manager was a technical expert, who improved the quality of the commercial output but was inclined to disregard the foreman in giving and canceling orders to the workers. The result was friction and uncertainty. Below these two men in the mill were a number of maintenance men who were given limited supervisory authority, and they too were often at odds with their superiors.

Whether matters will improve as a result of recent efforts to iron out these supervisory difficulties remains to be seen. The mill has suffered from the crosscurrents and animosities produced by years of supervisory friction. It has been a center of discontent. Moreover there is a question whether it can ever be fully manned with people who have gone through American schools and have visions of better jobs not too distantly available. Further amelioration of physical disadvantages may improve the mill's prospects. Improvement in the personal relationships might make more difference than improvement in the physical surroundings. Studies made in other plants indicate that this would be likely.[24]

Further insight into the effect of personal relationships may be derived from the following cases. During World War II a cer-

24. Cf. T. N. Whitehead, *The Industrial Worker*, p. 97: "In the previous part we arrived at the general conclusion that usual changes in the details of physical environment did not greatly affect the style of the operators' work activity. To be more precise: the habitual variations in the speed of assembling relays could not be understood as resulting from changes in the physical circumstances. The direct effects produced by the latter were too small to account for the former." According to this writer, "social activities" have important effects. These are defined as "any form of human activity which is significantly guided, or modified, by the performer's sentiments, emotions, beliefs, or understandings, with respect to any other person or persons."

tain job in Department No. 1 proved extremely difficult to fill
with any but a few old operators who had been on it for many years.
Learners complained that the work was unpleasant and that they
could never achieve high earnings. They pointed out that the
older men had been on the job "thirty-five" years and hence could
make high point hours. Direct evidence that the older men were
discouraging the learners was not forthcoming, although this could
be inferred. It was remarkable that a son-in-law of one of the older
men learned the work quickly and expressed no dissatisfaction.
An almost identical situation existed on another job where learning
was admittedly more difficult. Here the type of work and the weight
of materials handled indicated that women could replace men.
Close scrutiny disclosed that the older operators on this job were
discouraging the women learners, and no women succeeded in
thoroughly learning the work. There is some reason to believe that
these old operators did not deliberately discourage the learners.
They may have been unconsciously protecting themselves, or the
discouragement may have been incidental to their pride in their
long years on this job.

That a fine network of personal relationships exists is undoubted.
Some of them are pleasant, some unpleasant. Sometimes they are
complicated by family connections, by ethnic backgrounds, and
more recently by racial distinctions. But the consensus of the persons interviewed in making this study, the testimony of many
conversations with operators and foremen over a period of years,
and personal observation all lead to the conclusion that the New
Freedom Products Company is generally regarded as "a good place
to work" as far as association with people is concerned. This is less
true of the textile mill, but on the whole employees are inclined
to blame physical conditions rather than the personal relationships
which are possibly more important. It will be recalled that friendliness and neighborliness are charter values. It may be that they
are believed in to an extent which tends to obscure the existence
of interpersonal friction. Insofar as such friction exists, the institution is deficient in meeting this need. Nevertheless, outside of the
textile mill, it may be said that failure to satisfy the need for satisfactory working conditions has contributed little to the disturbed

equilibrium which precipitated the organization of the union and the reorganization of management.

In summary, it will be noted that perfect achievement of consumatory functions does not exist at the New Freedom Products Company. The contrast with the ideal picture drawn from the discussion of charter is marked, even though, as compared to some other factories, the company satisfies the needs of its personnel relatively well. There is also a contrast with the equilibrium of pre-World War I days, when these needs were more adequately satisfied. Indeed, changes which have occurred during the present century largely account for the relative inadequacy of present satisfactions. The significant changes can be classified under two headings: those which followed the altered roles of the officials; and those which are traceable directly to modification in the community, that is, changes in the general culture.

Thus, improved education for the workers and increased opportunities for employment outside the factory, which are provided both by the growth of the town and by modern transportation, have modified the needs for respect of fellows, for creature sufficiency, and for capacity performance. In the days when the alternatives to factory jobs were farm work, domestic service, or leaving town altogether the satisfactions offered by the factory came much closer to being adequate for a much larger percentage of local people. This was particularly true of immigrants, whose aspirations were modest. Today unskilled work, at what are supposed to be relatively low wages and without much prospect of advancement, does not appeal to young high-school graduates who believe that they can easily find other jobs which promise them more. Already the influence of this change is evident in the composition of the personnel: ten per cent of the employees are non-local, and there is some evidence that Negroes are taking the place formerly occupied by immigrants in the least desirable jobs. This change, moreover, may have the effect of further increasing the social distance between upper and lower status levels, for common residence in the town was one of the ties which tended to keep this distance from widening, and racial barriers in American society are too serious to be lightly dismissed.

Up to the present, however, the other change, that which eliminated the personal contacts between workers and officials, has been much more significant. Employment of out-of-town workers is new; its effects are still mostly in the future. The shift from the old primary group, with its informal organization, to the present impersonally organized structure, with its managerial hierarchy and its union, followed upon the changed norms of the officials. Workers depended to a great extent upon their friendship with officials for recognition, for control, for the information which led to understanding, for a sense of integration, and for a sense of security; and these contacts were part of the system of pleasant relationships with other people. Management also depended upon these contacts for similar satisfactions. As the contacts disappeared, uneasiness and frustration grew, and finally both management and the workers adopted what, in their minds at least, were radical measures to establish a new basis for satisfactions.

The dissatisfactions which led to these changes were centered mostly on the needs for control, for understanding, for integrity, and for security. As far as the established personnel of the company are concerned, these needs still seem to be imperfectly gratified. For the established personnel, there is also some question about the fulfillment of the need for respect of fellows and for capacity performance, although the results of dissatisfaction of these needs have been reflected mostly in the activities of a few employees, notably some of those who became union leaders. On the basis of such comparisons as are available the need for creature sufficiency seems to be adequately met, but on the basis of employee beliefs there is some discontent here also. Working conditions are satisfactory, except in the textile mill. In general, for the established personnel the new adjustments could conceivably prove capable of providing enough satisfaction to restore some kind of equilibrium. Recruitment, however, remains a problem, and the degree of gratification of the needs for prestige, advancement, and satisfactory working conditions seems almost certainly to presage a shift from employment of local people to employment of less ambitious outsiders. Unless conditions in the community change, it is unlikely that enough Teasville and Herford people will be attracted by the guarantees of security which have played such an important part in determining the character of the personnel in the past.

For our purposes, it is unnecessary to dwell at length upon the instrumental functions, that is, those which serve primarily to keep an institution operating in an organized fashion but provide only indirectly for the consumatory needs of personnel. Some of these functions are of first concern for management and industrial engineers. The organization chart, for instance, has an instrumental function in that it constitutes a set of rules which regulates the flow of authority and responsibility and defines the roles of various specialists in ways which are supposed to increase efficiency and minimize friction. Similarly the technological functions, such as maintenance or design of equipment, purchasing of supplies, and the like, have perhaps been concentrated upon at the expense of consumatory needs. And for this reason at least, it is necessary to re-emphasize their *instrumental* nature. The success of the activities devoted to such functions rests ultimately upon satisfactions received by individual human beings; they are inevitably geared to people. The engineer, a technological expert, all too often interprets his problems in mechanical terms alone. He forgets that people must operate his machines and that the success or failure of these operations may well lie within the range of human rather than mechanical reactions, that is, in the degree to which the machines satisfy or frustrate consumatory needs.

This connection between the requirements of individuals and instrumental activities is, perhaps, most clearly seen in such functions as communications, recruitment, training, and welfare, although in some of these it is easy enough to overlook purely human factors which can obscure organizational logic. For functions such as regulation and material technology these human factors are even more difficult to bear in mind. A conveyor belt, for instance, may seem so well planned for production that its effect in reducing the workers' sense of control may be completely lost to sight. Even protective activities, which ordinarily appear completely neutral, can irritate or frighten workers if they do not understand or trust them.

Of all these instrumental functions, none has been given more attention lately by persons who are interested in human relations than communications. And certainly in the case of the New Freedom Products Company, the breakdown in communications which accompanied diminution of personal contacts between workers and officials was crucial in the developments which marked the recent history of the company. Nevertheless, the tendency to regard communications as a panacea for all industrial ills is a mistake. While communications is, perhaps, the "integrative function" par excellence, no organization can hope to operate smoothly unless all other functions are discharged at an adequate level. People who are physically, intellectually, and emotionally capable and willing to carry out activities must be recruited and trained. They must be guided and controlled by rules which coordinate activities and which are sufficiently sanctioned to guarantee predictable behavior. Persons and property must be protected from hostile elements, human or natural. Material apparatus must be kept available and in usable condition. Trained and hence valuable personnel must be maintained through activities which we have described by the term "welfare." And finally these activities must be adjusted to each other, to the outgoing functions of the institution (to production, in the case of industry), and to the needs of the people in the institution. This, of course, suggests that institutional elements at all levels (charter, rules and norms, and the rest) must be taken into account, a point which has already been stressed and which will be further developed in the succeeding chapters.

SECTION THREE

Dynamic Aspects

CHAPTER EIGHT: *Antagonistic Cooperation*

There is an aura of paradox about such a phrase as "antagonistic cooperation," a kind of quizzical, epigrammatic quality which tends to obscure the deep insight which underlies it. Cooperation means "working together." [1] In general usage, however, the word carries an overtone of harmony and friendliness which hides an element usually if not always present in cooperative endeavors. That is the fact that cooperation, working with others, entails self-sacrifice and self-abnegation, sometimes to an extent which may reduce friendliness to a minimum or even eliminate it. So important are the conflicting elements that Sumner coined the phrase to describe combinations of persons or groups which suppress "minor antagonisms to satisfy great common interests." [2] The New Freedom Products Company is such a "combination."

Impressed both by the fact that cooperation is a universal characteristic of human societies and by a recognition, tacit or open, of the factors which work against cooperation, other writers have sought to explain why men work together by suggesting instincts of "mutual aid" or gregariousness. Still others have offered explanations based on more modern psychological knowledge. The most satisfactory of these hold that the need to associate and co-

1. Cf. *The Shorter Oxford English Dictionary*, p. 390: "Co-operate . . . 1. *intr.* To work together, act in conjunction (*with* another person or thing, *to* an end, or *in* a work). 2. *intr.* to practice economic co-operation . . ."; also "Co-operation . . . 1. The action of co-operating; joint operation . . ."
2. Sumner, *Folkways*, pp. 17–18.

operate with others is inevitably learned in infancy when practically all rewards are gained from other people. Moreover, cooperative behavior is reinforced throughout childhood. Hence the principle of cooperation may easily be generalized to adult situations; as the individual grows older he does not need to be directly rewarded each time be cooperates. He has learned that cooperativeness is worth while; it has acquired reward value of its own. Independent and aggressive behavior is similarly learned, and, although this fact may worry people who want things to be either black or white, every individual is ambivalent in the sense that he possesses both kinds of drives—an acquired drive to cooperate and another to strike out on his own.

The point of such theorizing is, of course, that it removes the basis for cooperation and aggression, in part at least, from the realm of conscious, rational motivation. People respond more or less automatically to both kinds of impulse. Nevertheless, reason, whether based on correct or mistaken premises, plays a part. People can recognize certain activities and choose them deliberately. Or they may fall into somewhat unreasoning habits based on more or less specific acquired drives and cues, as New Freedom Products employees do when they respond to the desire to get along with one another whenever the word "cooperation" is mentioned. Thus culture, in the shape of charter ideals and customary norms, becomes incorporated into the individual personality and, in an institution, comes to characterize the entire personnel. Naturally, the effect of cultural conditioning varies from individual to individual, but, since most individuals in a given culture are subjected to similar conditioning from infancy, the majority of the personnel of a given institution is likely to respond similarly to the same stereotypes. There is enough variation so that some individuals will adjust more easily than others to a given institution. Some institutions may, in fact, satisfy only a limited number of people. It is plain that not everybody fits readily into the expectations of the New Freedom Products Company. Indeed there seems to be enough automatic selection in favor of individuals who prefer peace and security to struggle and ambition so that interpretation of this particular institution would be incomplete without taking this factor into account.

Having noted this psychological factor, however, it is well to point out that the concept of antagonistic cooperation derives from a different point of view. Regardless of the individual personality, cooperative activity is a means for satisfying needs, and antagonistic elements are usually, perhaps always, present in the joint endeavors of human beings. There is no necessary reason to suppose that antagonism implies hostility or animosity, although these may accompany or result from antagonisms. Antagonistic cooperation simply means the suppression of some interests in order to pursue others through cooperation. Cooperation is a matter of expediency rather than the product of instinct, and it may occur in the face of hostile feelings. It is forced by circumstances. In a going institution, moreover, antagonisms may be suppressed and cooperation enforced by formally sanctioned rules or by the power of public opinion behind customary folkways. Also, the sense of antagonism may be blurred or concealed by the fact that an individual may come to accept the goals of the institution as his own, while the rules and customs may be borne in upon him so subtly that he is scarcely aware of them. There are positive as well as negative sanctions—punishments for not getting along with people and rewards for cooperating.

Simply to state that antagonistic cooperation is a fact, however, is not a sufficient reason for using the concept in analysis. It is necessary to distinguish the incentives to cooperation, the kinds of antagonisms present, and the norms and rules which facilitate cooperation or solve the problems created by antagonisms.

INCENTIVES TO COOPERATION. It has been pointed out that people work at the New Freedom Products Company to "make a living" and stay there because they believe that the institution guarantees them security. In other words, they are willing to exchange their time and energy for wages, and their chances for high wages or advancement for security. These choices sound like ra-

tional ones, but it should be remembered that the community believes that working is not only a necessary but a desirable way of
life. Teasville has maintained practically unimpaired the American traditions of the virtues of work and the evils of leisure. Even
the wealthy man in retirement is likely to have some apparently
and overtly useful occupation, while tradition holds that the retired worker is likely, in idleness, to fade away to an early death.
Such beliefs minimize the sense of sacrifice. Men in their late sixties
and in their seventies often resist retirement, even in the face of
the telling argument that they have worked hard and earned their
rest. The same standard is applied to younger people. In the factory and outside of it, a man who says he would like to "quit and
just loaf" is almost always answered by the question, "What would
you do if you didn't have some work to do? You'd go nuts. You'd
be looking for a job inside of a month."

Once a person enters the company, his incentives are intensified
and re-enforced by the institutional charter. Among these incentives, the desire for security is emphasized over and over, until
employees acquire great faith in the company's ability and willingness to take care of them in the future, and they evince considerable pride in working for a company which "looks after its
help." Employees in the armed forces during World War II wrote
home that they boasted about the company policy of allowing
them pay and retaining them on the payroll. Such evidences of
care for the welfare of employees enlist loyalty to the company
itself. A case in point is that of the man who, after a fit of irritation,
said, "Quit? You know goddamn well I wouldn't quit. Why, after
what this company has done for me, I'd kiss their ass in front of the
town post." [3]

Membership in the institution becomes an interest in itself. An
extreme example of this was the statement of an elderly Pole who
spent most of a year, after a heart attack, trying to decide whether
to retire on a pension or to go on working. Even after he was
frightened by a similar attack suffered by another employee, he

3. The principle of generalization is plainly evident here. The man visualized the company in the persons of certain officials, as the rest of his story
showed. Cf. Miller and Dollard, *Social Learning and Imitation*, pp. 74–78.

went to the personnel office six times to say that he would accept the pension and five times to say he had changed his mind and wanted to continue working. Since he is the owner of a small store and all members of his family are employed, it is unlikely that financial considerations were of paramount importance to him.

Italian immigrants were first attracted to the company because they wanted to settle down to steady employment, bring their families to live with them, and give up roaming about in search of the highest paying jobs. Later some of this group brought pressure on their children to work for the company or to stay with it when there were prospects of higher pay elsewhere. As late as 1941, a son of one of this group obtained a higher paying job but came back a few days later because, he said, his father made him, telling him not to be a "damn fool" and leave a company where he would always be taken care of. On another occasion an Irish father lamented when his son went into business for himself. "He's always been stubborn," this man said, "I could never do anything with him. I couldn't budge him with a one-inch rope, while somebody else would lead him around with a rotten t'read."

These cases indicate that the desire for security is not so important to younger employees as are chances to get jobs which they believe offer more money or which are vested with more prestige. Here the antagonism of interests often results in a decision not to come to the company in the first place and frequently leads young men to leave the company. Incidentally, a similar antagonism is that which impels young women to quit either for the purpose of getting married or, if already married, to have children. In such cases the choice is inevitable.

Within the company it is realized that possibilities for advancement are limited and that it is unwise to keep aggressively ambitious young men against their will. Occasionally executives remark that they will "never stand in the way of a man bettering himself. If he can really do better elsewhere, all we can do is let him go and wish him luck." In such a statement there is an implicit realization of the lack of opportunities for promotion which has caused aggressive young men to leave the company and kept others from applying for employment. A group of half a dozen

high-school students, including two whose fathers were foremen
at the company, declared in 1938 that they did not want to work
for the company because they would never "get anywhere" there.
Perhaps the fact that today the union leaders and the likely candi-
dates for foremanship training are largely second-generation immigrants is an indication that this group entered the company
before they were affected by such ideas. Nowadays many of the
children of immigrant employees are receiving professional education and thus are lost to the company.

Among the ideas in this company's charter which are strongly
approved as being "right" is that of cooperation itself: "the
friendly spirit of cooperation." The influence of this manifests
itself in various ways. Members of the personnel sometimes break
off arguments because they "don't want to start anything," to
"keep peace in the family," or because "fighting doesn't get you
anyplace." Union officers readily agree that they desire to cooperate with management and once reprimanded a steward for an
apparently uncooperative attitude. Executives are plainly pleased
with themselves when they cooperate with the union.[4] A man who
"puts his shoulder to the wheel" (with everyone else) is all right.
A man who "drags his feet" is not. The failure of the officials to
keep up their plant visits, when it was noted, was regarded as a
violation of the principle of cooperation. The "friendly spirit" as
a motive for becoming and remaining members of the cooperating
group was attested by out-of-town workers during World War II.
Despite the fact that they were regarded as outsiders, several of
them declared that they sensed a feeling of consideration and
friendliness which they thought was lacking at previous places of
employment: "You feel like you was a human being here." Negroes were among those who made such assertions, and they seemed
to prove their sincerity by getting friends and relatives to work at
the company.

Frequently a number of ideas and precepts from the charter are
woven together to enforce a point. For example, the chief of pro-

4. One executive boasted about this as follows: "So far we've gotten along
fine with the union. It's because we know how to cooperate. If you're willing
to work with somebody and go half way, they'll usually come along."

duction has spoken substantially as follows at a number of foremen's meetings: "You fellows have got to *cooperate*. Now if Henry
[the foreman of the trucking department] falls down on his job
and doesn't get supplies to you, he's not cooperating. But you
production foremen have got to cooperate too. Let him know
when you need supplies and when you have stuff to move well in
advance. Then he can schedule his trucks and you'll all be taken
care of. Otherwise machines will be down, and we'll lose *production,* and the help will lose their *premiums*. That don't make for
good feelings. Don't forget downtime costs you *money*. It's just
plain *inefficient*. It's just like *waste*. That's all it is." In this speech
there are references to at least five different charter elements, some
of them invoked a number of times.

To summarize then, the charter of an institution provides the
incentives to cooperation, the goals and values which are recognized by the personnel, which more or less successfully command
their loyalty, and which they use in persuading each other to work
together with at least a reasonable degree of harmony. For this
reason, if for no other, the concept of charter assumes crucial
importance as a key to understanding organization. Whereas rules
and norms can provide habitual patterns for cooperation and
coercion may force individuals into cooperative behavior, coordination based on such blind adherence to ill-understood rules
or on unwilling adherence to coercive prescriptions will almost
inevitably fall short of producing the goals which the people in
both industry and society desire. One reason for this is that mere
habit is inflexible. If rules could be designed to meet every possible contingency they might suffice, but in industry conditions
constantly shift and even the lowliest employees need to make
decisions. Only when they can do this logically on the basis of
commonly accepted purposes and principles, which are provided
by charter, are their decisions likely to be intelligent as judged
by their fellows and by organizational requirements and goals. A
second reason for the failure of mere rules and coercion is that
by themselves they cannot achieve the degree of morale which
characterizes highly successful human relationships. Indeed,
morale could well be defined as full acceptance and understanding

of a common charter—a shared set of values which enables individuals to understand each other and to subordinate their private interests in favor of the interests of the group as a whole.

The implications of this conclusion for industrial training programs and communications systems should be obvious. It is not enough to teach techniques or to communicate orders and operating information. The successful training program includes indoctrination in charter as, perhaps, its prime function, and the successful communications program provides constantly for the dissemination of charter and of knowledge which re-enforces charter. Here, then, is a clue to a deficiency which marks many discussions of communications; these discussions stress communications as a vital function, but they fall short in answering the question of what should be communicated. They mention orders, technical information, and the like, and they frequently dwell on communication of grievances and incipient sore spots in human relations. But, because they are seldom tied to any notion of charter, they omit a most important factor, the conveying and strengthening of grounds for agreement and incentives for mutual endeavor.

The discussion of the New Freedom Products Company earlier in this chapter tends to create a picture of almost ineffable harmony—something too good to be true. This impression is, of course, false. The effort here has been merely to illustrate the positive effects of fully shared charter values. That these effects are ever fully achieved is doubtful. It appears that the New Freedom Products Company came fairly close at one point in its history, but even in the happy days of yore this company never reached utopia, and the history of other companies makes it all too clear that there are other than positive elements at work in all human groups. It is with these that the following paragraphs are concerned.

ANTAGONISMS. Antagonism, as the word is used in this study, means the mutual resistance of two opposing forces, physical or mental. So used, it can refer to rivalry or hostility between individuals or groups, to differences between individual interests and the opportunities presented by an institution, and to conflicting ideas existing in the mind of a single individual or held with differing degrees of intensity by various individuals. Thus the following types of antagonisms are to be found at the New Freedom Products Company:

1) Interpersonal friction, appearing in hostility or rivalry between individuals or groups. This type of antagonism does not arise from situations, other than proximity, which are created by the structure or organization of the institution.

2) Conflict between individual interests and the institutional demands in which the individual interests are at variance with generally approved opportunities or other conditions presented by the institution. In such cases, according to the prevailing views of the personnel, the institution is not at fault; adjustments are the responsibility of the individual.

3) Friction arising as a result of conflicting rules and norms or badly defined principles of organization.

4) Conflict arising from significant differences in charter interpretation, in which the structure of the institution is brought into serious question. Differences are backed by enough weight of authority or numbers so that solutions go well beyond those of adjustment by individuals. This class includes the antagonisms which have marked the widening gap between the upper and lower status levels of the organization and have aligned management and workers in two different camps.

This last class is of especial interest because the differences of opinion may exist to a greater or lesser degree within the mind of the same individual. Hence the stereotype of well-drawn battle lines in which groups animated by inimical interests fly a flag of truce but regard each other with suspicious eyes is deceiving. Individuals do not as a rule carefully assess their interests. Instead they follow the institutional patterns and are motivated by the charter. The purposes in the charter are not, however, altogether consistent; they leave open such questions as the degree of security or income which may be considered satisfactory. The meaning of words like "security" or "decent pay" changes from time to time, as do norms for conduct. Hence any individual may find himself confronted with dilemmas which old symbols do not help to solve and for which new symbols are not immediately available. The advent of the union has tended to clarify this situation by drawing more sharply the lines of difference. The reorganization of management has had a similar effect. But it cannot be said that either is yet well enough understood to provide a substantial basis for a new equilibrium. Even the president of the union sometimes casts a sentimental glance backward to the old days when officials and workers dealt with each other on a strictly personal basis, when there were no demands and no thought of arbitration. But neither he nor anyone else who has given the subject careful thought believes that those days can be recalled.

Examples of interpersonal antagonism between individuals are to be found in cases where two operators want a job which is open to only one of them or where two executives desire the same vacation period but only one can be absent at the same time. Interpersonal antagonisms also exist between groups of employees. During World War II there was hostility to the out-of-town Negroes. White employees not only complained that Negroes were poor and unreliable workers but also believed that they were dirty, diseased, and "buggy," that is, had lice. They disliked working with Negroes, and some of them made elaborate efforts to avoid using the toilets Negroes used. Similarly there has been hostility between various ethnic groups. Even today there is a tradition that Poles and Lithuanians do not get along with each other, and during the period of union organization some suspicion was expressed that one or another of the ethnic groups was trying to gain ascendancy through the union. It is interesting to note that the union organizing committee included members from all important ethnic groups, just as do political slates, and that the four union officers have different ethnic backgrounds. Personal animosities exist between individuals on each of the status levels and between persons on different status levels. There is enough hostility between the two principal branches of the official family to cause others to refer occasionally to the "family feud."

Interpersonal friction is covered in the union contract, which makes the following subject to the official grievance procedure: "differences not specifically covered by this agreement which have to do with working conditions and which are of a minor, personal and detailed nature not involving fundamental principles or relationships, or any substantial economic advantage or disadvantage to the parties."

Antagonisms between individual interests and the institution itself include those in which an employee believes he should have a promotion or an increase in pay when none is available. They arise when young men find that the institution does not satisfy their desires for income (creature sufficiency), prestige (respect of fellows), or advancement (capacity performance). This kind of antagonism is in the nature of a conflict between individual needs or desires and charter, since the charter puts a higher value on security than on high income, prestige, or full utilization of the capacities which young high-school graduates often believe they possess. Such antagonism was noted before World War I when young men left to find better work. It has been intensified by the multiplied opportunities for work outside the company in the town and in the nearby city and by the fact that a much higher percentage of young people go through high school than did 40 or more years ago. Employees who leave the company on account of physical disability or to "go home and raise a family" can also be classed with those whose personal interests are in conflict with the institution.[5]

The third type of antagonisms—those arising from conflicting rules or principles of organization—hardly needs much discussion here. This is the sort which management engineers typically tackle

5. Two specific examples may clarify this kind of antagonism. One concerns a young woman who was so anxious to maintain her earnings that she lied about the date when her child was due to be born. She was finally sent home in tears only a few days before the baby actually arrived. Another involved an employee who suffered a stroke which impaired his mental faculties. The company was afraid to give this man a job because it was thought he might wander into a hazardous area. He was pensioned but continued to beg for work because "he wanted something to do." In both cases it was impossible for the employees to remain in the industrial environment; their desires were in conflict with the industrial situation.

when they draw up organization charts and create careful job descriptions to prevent "overlapping of functions," crisscrossing of authority, and so on. The nature of such conflicts and the fact that they can engender interpersonal hostility are emphatically illustrated in the history of the New Freedom Products Company, especially in the period which preceded the reorganization of management in 1942.

In approaching the fourth class of antagonisms—those arising from differences in interpretation of the charter—it should be recalled that the purposes in the charter are held in common by nearly all, if not all, members of the personnel. It is agreed that the institution should produce goods, provide income for the personnel, give security to the personnel, and contribute to the welfare of the community. There is also agreement on the principles by which these purposes are attained. The company manufactures its products, sells them, and carries on research to strengthen itself for the future and to guard against inferior quality or other defects. On a slightly different level, the personnel cooperate to attain their purposes, essential to which are the principles of making money and maintaining the stability of the company. These purposes and principles plainly limit each other. For instance, manufacturing more products than could be sold profitably would result in losing money and would threaten the stability of the institution and have serious repercussions on the purposes.

In a sense, two of the purposes can be said to compete with each other. There is an inevitable conflict between the desire for high immediate income and the desire for security, especially because the personnel visualize their security in terms of long-range job tenure in the company and pensions to be received from the company. Since maintaining the stability of the company is the key to security and since security is a more highly valued goal than high income, the antagonisms in this fourth class frequently revolve around the question of how much the company can afford in the way of higher wages or other benefits to the personnel. Simply stated, the most deep-seated antagonism is that between the interests of the institution itself and the personal interests of the employees.

This fundamental opposition results in a conflict which exists, at least potentially, in every employee's mind. Thus the president of the company may desire longer vacations, shorter hours, or a higher salary. On the other hand, he is aware that he must weigh his personal satisfactions against the welfare of the company. The same multiplicity of interests exists on all status levels of the institutional hierarchy.

If the charter meant exactly the same thing to all members of the personnel, this conflict would not reveal itself in a split between different status levels. As it is, however, knowledge about the financial capacities of the company is not equally available to people on the lower and upper status levels, and the breakdown of the system of interstatus personal contacts has intensified the difference between the points of view. Officials, at the top of the hierarchy, are directly aware of the conditions which affect the welfare of the institution, while workers lack firsthand information to re-enforce them in restraining their personal interests. No sharp line divides the personnel in these differences. There is, instead, what might be called an interest scale, with company officials at one extreme and the least informed workers at the other. Between these extremes emphasis shades from that placed on institutional prosperity by the higher executives and officials to that placed on individual welfare by the lower ranks of employees.

Of all the personnel, the officials are those most familiar with market conditions as they relate to products and supplies and also to the costs of production. Hence it is relatively easy for them to weigh problems in terms of costs and sales. They are aware of the fact that Product No. 1 has been losing markets steadily for some 25 years and that it does not enjoy a secure sales position as it did early in the century. They also know that lawsuits for damages allegedly due to imperfections in the product have been brought many times. They believe that if one of these suits against the company should ever be won it would establish a precedent which might wreck the institution's financial structure. They are fully cognizant of the disaster which fire can bring to the company. They see costs as large lump sums. Materials costing only a few cents per pound amount to expenditures of hundreds of thousands of dollars a year. Pensions have in the past involved an annual expenditure of many thousands of dollars, and the reserves for the new formal pension plan will total several hundred thousand dollars.

The force of precedent is also strong in official minds. They see a favor granted to an employee not as an isolated act but as one which may give rise to the argument, "If you did it for him, why can't you do it for me? What's fair for one is fair for another." This reasoning is particularly noticeable with respect to the company's houses. On the company's books these usually show a loss of about ten thousand dollars a year. Hence officials resist granting requests for new kinds of improvements for fear that what one tenant receives others will want.

Experience and training have taught officials to look for costs in small, recurrent figures. An extra week's vacation for the employees means not a single week's pay but ten or fifteen thousand dollars. Serving milk during rest periods costs not five cents a bottle but ten thousand dollars a year.

Being stockholders themselves and friends or relatives of most of the other stockholders, the officials put a high valuation on profits, both as a measure of their own success as administrators and as a reason why the owners continue to support the institution with their capital. They are aware that dividend rates have declined in the past generation from ten or twelve per cent of the par value of the stock to six per cent. Moreover, they realize that this six per cent figure is somewhat fictitious. It is barely four per cent of a conservative book valuation of the stock and perhaps not much more than two per cent of what the stock might sell for on the open market.

For all of these reasons, officials emphasize policies and activities which are thought to contribute to the strength of the institution as distinct from those which increase the returns to individuals in the institution.

In a general way, lesser executives take the same point of view, although as one goes down the institutional hierarchy the factors which draw attention to costs and efficiency are less and less familiar to the personnel. Specific facts are replaced by generalized concepts. Words like "efficiency," "cost," and "waste" are more important for their own value in terms of the charter than because they refer to factual situations. Thus chiefs of functions are relatively well informed on current business and future prospects. Managers receive some information, although it is usually related to their own departments. Efforts are made to inform foremen, but at this point the specific information received is slight and is usually couched in general terms. Foremen are told that "business is slow," that the cost of pensions is "tremendous," that "waste is running high." Moreover, what foremen learn comes to them entirely on the authority of others. They do not have access to firsthand information. The employees below the foremen receive only irregular trickles of knowledge, and most of this is from persons who are thought not to be "on the inside," that is, from foremen or managers.

Thus the kind of knowledge which gives institutional perspective and re-enforces the desire to make the institution prosper is shared in diminishing degrees by members of the various statuses below the officials. Chiefs of divisions are presumably as well informed on many aspects as are the officials, but they tend to concentrate on their own departments, and only those involved in compiling profit-and-loss statements are directly aware of the company's current business success. Managers have even less direct access to firsthand information, while assistants and foremen have still less, and workers have the least of all.

The extreme in the worker point of view is that represented by the belief that the company is a permanently strong and rich institution. It has existed for more than a century and has grown and prospered. Some workers analyze the matter no further. The company is strong and rich; that is all there is to it. Other workers, perhaps most other workers, realize, when they think about it, that this extreme point of view needs qualification. Nevertheless, they have firsthand evidence of strength and stability and at best only secondhand information about costs, markets, and other adverse factors. The worker is inclined to see many expenses, certainly those with which he is most familiar, as isolated sums: a ten-cent raise, a 50-dollar pension for someone "who has given the best years of his life to the company," a new coat of paint on one house, a nickle bottle of milk—amounts which the company ought to be able to afford easily. Workers take safety for granted. There have been no fires for more than 30 years, and the last one was under peculiar wartime conditions. Quality is highly valued for its own sake and for the sake of other workers who will someday use the product and not because defects could cost the company a great deal of money.

Another difference between the upper and lower statuses supplements the divergence in information. This is the difference in the value attached to immediate returns from the company. Every official has sources of income outside the company, and salaries of people on the upper status levels are high enough so that they are not so completely dependent on the company, on a day-to-day basis, as are the workers. Besides, officials and executives feel more secure in their positions than do most workers. Finally, the worker is more keenly aware of what it means to sacrifice his interests to the company welfare. In slack times the worker's income suffers immediately through shortened hours of work, but executive and office salaries are reduced only under the most extraordinary circumstances.

Basically, then, this fundamental antagonism is not one between persons supporting conflicting interests and ideas, although it is expressed as though it were. Nor is it precisely a battle between the company and the workers, despite the fact that the union contract names the company as one of the parties. It is an antagonism between two points of view on how common purposes shared by both management and workers should be accomplished and which purposes should be emphasized at the expense of others. Both management and workers desire income and other rewards from the company. Neither group appears to begrudge the other as great rewards as their sense of proportion leads them to consider just, provided that the cost of these rewards does not endanger the institution's capacity to provide them. This "sense of proportion," moreover, leads neither group to demand unlimited rewards. Proper rewards are determined in ways which have been described in the chapter on "functions." The difference lies in the conception of the institution's ability to provide these rewards over a period of time. The focal point for the expression of this difference is currently the rewards designated for workers. The union presses for increasing pay and other benefits for the workers. Management is convinced that the company's capacity to provide these rewards has been reached or nearly reached. Therefore, although agreements on pay, vacations, overtime, and "benefits" have been accomplished amicably, they are now points for open discussion. In the spring of 1946, officials stated that an increase in prices would be necessary to meet the increased costs occasioned by the 1946 union contract. They were worried, moreover, about whether the market would pay the higher prices for New Freedom products or would turn to competing products. This concern of management evidently carried weight with the union. The increases agreed upon amounted to 12 per cent of wages rather than higher amounts which, according to the published reports reaching the personnel, workers generally were getting elsewhere.[6]

While wages constitute the most conspicuous symbol in this pattern of antagonism, they are not the only issue. The conflict between the management and the union is also one over control, although it is not defined as such. To management, control means unhampered administration of the company's affairs and determination of policy—to quote the union contract, "the rights, powers and authority customarily exercised by management." To this, union leaders have no objection: they state that they want no share in managerial responsibilities. Obviously, however, they want the power to resist actions which infringe upon the rights of the workers. As the representative of the national union said, "You go ahead and manage, and we'll tell you if there's anything we think is wrong." Many workers take an even less positive point of view than this. They do not believe that their fellows are capable of

6. Cf. Frances M. Jones and E. K. Buschman, "Postwar Increases in Basic Wage Rates," *Monthly Labor Review* (Sept., 1946), p. 343: "Hourly wage rates advanced by at least 18½ cents—the pattern set in the steel case—in plants employing about one-fourth of all manufacturing workers . . . although the largest number of workers had rates increased 18½ cents, the average increase was about 14½ cents . . . including those not affected by general wage changes, the average gain amounted to about 11½ cents."

management, and while each one may believe that he could give management some good advice, he is willing to concede that, on the whole, the executives know how to run the company better than he does.[7] Nevertheless, the individual worker also believes that he has rights and wants to be able to "stand up for them." Organization of the union did more than emphasize the gap between management and the workers. It also made explicit the workers' need for some measure of control over the forces influencing their lives.

REDUCTION OF ANTAGONISM. Antagonisms at the New Freedom Products Company are subordinated, kept under control, or reduced in three different ways: by norms which facilitate harmonious relationships between people, by rules which carry sanctions, and by appeals to the charter. The charter strongly influences norms and rules and the sanctions attached to them. The charter, moreover, is in itself a cohesive force, and the fact that the charter has come to be interpreted differently by upper and lower statuses of the personnel is one of the most significant developments in the history of this institution.

Norms and rules governing interpersonal contacts and tending to eliminate friction range from the custom of exchanging personal greetings all the way to the application of severe penalties, such as discharge for carrying matches or fighting. Care is taken to maintain appearances of acquaintanceship and friendliness. These are supposed to go beyond mere greetings and to include, whenever possible, personal inquiries or remarks or, if no better subject is available, some comment on the weather. Traditionally, in these interchanges, first names are preferred, except where differences in age are great, although in recent years differences in status have be-

7. This sort of remark is not uncommon: "If they're so goddamn smart, why ain't they up there in the office? Of course there's some things I don't think are just right. Take the way they shoved Joe Brooks out of the boiler room. But it seems to me the management of this company's done pretty good for over a hundred years, and they got their headaches, too. Sure they make mistakes. Who don't? But there ain't any of us here in the shop could do any better. Hell, we couldn't even start in on their jobs."

gun to elicit use of the respectful title "Mr." Even so, employees occasionally object to the use of such titles, especially when applied to themselves. Some care is taken to prevent employees who are known to dislike each other from coming into any more contact than necessary. The foreman of the textile mill, for example, sometimes complains that one of his "headaches" is keeping certain women on jobs where they will not quarrel with one another. The practice of assigning houses in special neighborhoods to different ethnic groups was justified on the grounds that it would prevent fights.

Safety rules are often designed to prevent employees from causing injury to others. As the employee manual points out: "The rules are mainly commonsense rules which only the thoughtless person would disregard. For your sake and the sake of other workers who might be endangered by thoughtlessness, we urge you to learn and follow these rules." Fighting is a grave offense, and in the one case which has occurred in recent years both participants were dismissed.[8] Absenteeism is also regarded as inimical to the interests of all workers, whose production records may be interrupted if some are not on the job. Repeated absenteeism is recognized by both management and the union as just cause for discharging or laying off an employee.

For the employee who cannot reconcile his own interests with those of the company, the only means of reducing the antagonism is to show him that his interests will be better served in the institution than they would be elsewhere. As has been noted, this method is sparingly employed as far as executives are concerned. They hesitate to "put pressure" on anybody who thinks "he can better himself" by leaving the company. Special concessions are seldom made to such employees. Individual concessions would be barred by the union contract in the case of workers represented by the union, and the management strongly resists pressure by other employees. Favoritism, indeed, is considered a form of discrimination.

In the language of the factory, antagonisms which have crystal-

8. This fight occurred not on company property but at the door of the bus bringing employees from the city. Both participants were women, one of them a Negro. Workers as well as executives approved the decision to discharge both.

lized into overt expression are called "grievances," and there are formal procedures for handling them. Until the union was organized, the procedure for all employees, including those in the office, followed the pattern described in the employee manual: [9]

> We sometimes get on each others' nerves, or think we have a raw deal—and sometimes things really are not the way they should be. When things do seem wrong—whether they really are or not—it is important to get them straightened out as quickly as possible. A grievance which is allowed to grow old can get worse and worse until it creates real unhappiness.
>
> . . . If you have any difficulty with any part of your job (your machine, your material or anything else) or if you feel you have been treated unfairly in any way (your hours, your pay, your work assignment, no matter what), *tell your foreman about it at once.* . . .[10]
>
> If you are not satisfied after you have talked with your foreman, you may take the matter up with his superior [or any executive] . . .
>
> The "open door" policy is one of the oldest the company has. It means that right up to the top officers, everyone is anxious to be helpful when something goes wrong and to try to help get a fair decision. No employee need ever hesitate to go as high as he likes with a problem—*the doors are always open.*

For employees represented by the union, this procedure has been modified by the presence of union stewards, by other union assistance, and by preventing employees from going beyond the foreman to present their own grievances until the matter has been placed in the hands of the proper union functionaries. Under both procedures, however, channels for eliminating or reducing antagonisms are indicated, and both the union and the management believe that all grievances should be brought into the open and handled promptly.

9. Less formal means were also used by foremen, as appears in this statement: "Why that was no grievance. I straightened that out in no time at all, and she's perfectly happy now."

10. In the office the employee is directed to tell his immediate superior, usually the manager of the department in which he works.

While the function of rules and norms in controlling antagonisms is not to be overlooked, it is more obvious, though probably no more important, than that of the charter. The charter is almost certain to be invoked in cases of interpersonal antagonism, whether the matter is considered a grievance or not. When two persons desire the same job, for example, length of service together with merit are used as a basis for justifying the selection made. Merit consists of an analysis of efficiency as measured by training and productivity, quality of work, reliability as measured by attendance, willingness to cooperate ("help out" or "do more than is actually required"), and adherence to rules, especially safety rules. Employees stress length of service in such cases, while management often spends considerable time seeking justifications for disregarding this factor in favor of "merit." It is likely that employees prefer length of service because it is easier to measure and because it is a symbol of security. Management, on the other hand, insists upon other considerations because they provide more flexibility of control and may affect the welfare of the institution.

Even in such cases, although the rules and norms are fairly clear, it is difficult to distinguish between the function of charter as a basis for set patterns and as a guide for activities for which clear patterns have not been developed. This latter function is more clearly evident in the following cases.

The ideas of production and patriotism were invoked on behalf of the outside Negroes during World War II. Foremen and local workers were reminded that "after all, we've got to get workers wherever we can. The army needs our products. We may be scraping the bottom of the barrel, but we've got to make a go of it somehow." Later, individual Negro workers who were doing well were cited as proof that not all Negroes were lazy and shiftless, and the local workers were urged to look at the Negroes as individuals and not as a type. Discrimination was one of the effective values in this case.[11] The Negroes who remained with the company—a handful

11. An interesting rationalization by a worker occurred when the one Negro with long company service was cited as proof of the good qualities of Negroes in general. This white worker's reply was: "Oh, Hampton is different. We were brought up with him." Here the rationalization was one which tried to protect the community character of the institution, and it is interesting to

as compared with the large numbers who left after a short period of service—were those who seemed to believe in the charter and were willing to submit to the expectation implied in it.

The charter belief in "friendly cooperation" showed an effect in reducing antagonisms during the first union-management contract negotiations. At these meetings an appearance of friendliness, even of camaraderie, was maintained. The outside union representative, a man in his late sixties, who would normally have been called "Mr." on account of his age alone, insisted on being called by his first name and made a point of calling the others by theirs, thus setting the style for all the negotiators. Members of both management and employee committees, without denying that they were present to bargain over differences, stressed the good feeling which they evidently wanted to exist. Actually this good feeling became a reality. On one occasion, after the contract was made public, a union official who had been on the bargaining committee consulted a management member of the committee for an interpretation of a contract clause because, he said, "We fellows who were at the meetings kind of understand this thing better than most of the help do." This man also commented upon the new feeling of respect he had for one of the management members whom he had previously disliked. "You have to get up early in the morning to beat that guy," he declared, "He's a pretty smart apple at that."

In addition to supplying a common framework of purposes and a set of re-enforcements for cooperation, the charter provides a basis for rationalizing antagonisms. The officials who persuaded themselves that recognition of the union merely continued the tradition of talking things over with the workers demonstrated this mechanism. They had felt that unionism was inherently dangerous and that workers promoting it were traitors. Having once made the rationalization, however, they were able to accept the union with relatively little revulsion and to carry on subsequent negotiations in an atmosphere of good will. Many workers who joined the union made corresponding rationalizations. They told themselves that,

---

note that outside Negroes who remained for a considerable time with the company tended to be exempted from prejudice on the grounds that they were good workers.

after all, the union would prove to be a good thing for the company. It would make things go more smoothly and would enable workers to deal directly with high executives. In the same period, both officials and workers drew upon ideals not specifically in the institution's charter but rather in the community or national charter. The president of the company, who was opposed to maintenance of union membership, hit upon the idea that workers signing up with the union were in effect making a bargain which they ought to keep. "It's no different from signing a lease when you rent a house," he said. "You don't expect to back out on that halfway through the year just because you change your mind about wanting to live there." [12] In a like way, some workers believed that they should "go along with the union" if the majority wanted it, because in a democracy the majority rules. In all of these cases, the rationalizations smoothed the way for cooperative action. They made the participants willing to cooperate. In fact, in the case of maintenance of membership, the rationalization came very close to making the president a proponent of an idea which he had opposed.[13]

Thus the charter serves to promote cooperation, to provide a basis for rules and norms which prevent or relieve friction, and to supply rationalizations for working agreements when antagonisms come out into the open. Ideally, this last function would scarcely

12. E. Wight Bakke tells of a similar case he witnessed when he was acting as conciliator in bargaining negotiations of another company. Here the president of the company declared that he would never accept maintenance of membership because it was contrary to his principles. Asked what these principles were, he said that from his office window he could see a famous Revolutionary War memorial. It was his custom to look at it several times a day and to reflect that he conducted his business in accordance with the principles of freedom for which the Revolution was fought. Maintenance of membership, he believed, violated these principles. He was reminded that another American principle was to stick by a bargain and not to renege if the bargain hurt a little. Members of the union, it was pointed out, joined of their own free will and hence should stand back of their contract as long as it was in force. As in the case cited above, this argument was conclusive.

13. A year later he used the same argument, and others like it, to justify drawing the new contract for two years and retaining maintenance of membership for that period.

be needed if the purposes, principles, and values of the charter were held and interpreted in exactly the same way by all members of the institution. Such a common sense of charter depends upon an unhampered system of communications among all employees, a system extending from the officials to the workers. The importance of free communications, of a system which fosters ready interchange of ideas, information, and other charter re-enforcements, can scarcely be overemphasized.

Forty years ago such a system was in effective operation at the New Freedom Products Company. Communications were easy and personal. Office employees, including the officials, worked within earshot of each other. Plant employees found plenty of time for gossip. Officials visited the plant regularly and often. Everybody knew everybody else. Officials knew the problems of the workers at first hand, and they spoke in language which workers understood.[14] Workers heard the story of James Freedom and others which re-enforced the charter. They learned about the use of the products from officials who had been "in the field" and of the importance of quality to users. Officials commented to workers on the state of the business, not in specific terms [15] but with the authority of those who knew the facts better than anyone else. Safety and the related "good housekeeping" were always uppermost in the minds of officials, and they did not hesitate to reprimand employees who seemed to be neglecting safe practices. They recalled the serious fires in the company's history, explained the reasons for safety devices, and, so it seemed to some of the younger men, harped on such subjects endlessly. They made a ritual of certain machine tests designed to protect the quality of the product. Indeed, these tests were conducted exclusively by officials until World War I, when they were delegated with a show of solemnity and secrecy to one of the two superintendents. Both officials and older workers frequently recalled in-

14. Recently an employee stated that he supposed the word "influence" meant to twist things around, to "put something over on somebody." Since influence is a word used frequently by management, one can easily imagine the misinterpretations which may result from misunderstanding this and other words.

15. The company books were regarded as private information, as sacred as a man's personal finances.

cidents which proved the company's interest in employee welfare and security; and workers, in their conversations with each other, supplemented the charter re-enforcing activities of the officials.

The function of personal contacts in binding the institution together by reducing antagonisms and enlisting common interests was probably understood only dimly, if at all, at the time. Officials said that the reasons they visited the plant were to check on production, equipment, and "housekeeping," to discharge such specific duties as marking cases for shipment, adjusting testing devices, and the like, and to see that everybody was " 'tending to business." Hence this function was not clearly appreciated during the period when officers' plant visits were diminishing in number. Checking equipment and production and similar duties were delegated to subordinates, but little attention was given to "personnel problems." This is indicated by the minutes of early foremen's meetings in 1928 and 1929. By then it was believed that the foremen's task had become important enough to deserve special attention, but the expressed purpose of the meetings was to improve efficiency.

The foremen's meetings were, however, the first step in the development of management's modern program for reducing antagonisms. Personnel problems were injected into these meetings by degrees. Within a few years after they began, safety and accident prevention were placed on the agenda, and a foremen's safety committee was organized. It was not until 1940, however, that much attention was given to the foremen's role in handling grievances, and by that time friction in the plant was too widespread to be overlooked. In 1940 a series of slide films was purchased and placed on the program for foremen's meetings. These stressed, in addition to safety and accident prevention, the need for handling grievances effectively, for knowing workers and their troubles, for letting workers "know where they stand," and for taking responsibility for personnel matters in other ways. The attitude of most of the foremen was ambivalent at the time. They felt that much improvement was needed in the "handling of help," but they did not believe that they had the authority to do much about it. Nor could they understand the techniques presented. Since that time, emphasis on this phase of the foreman's work has increased steadily until now "handling the help" is regarded as the foremen's principal duty. Several foremen have been given clerks and other assistance to free them for "supervision."

If foremen are genuinely part of management, as higher management says, then it can be said that there are still personal contacts between management and the hourly-paid workers in all industries. The questionable efficacy of such contacts in joining top management and workers on common grounds of understanding has already been discussed. Certainly employees accustomed to more direct means of communication look upon such intermediaries as foremen with some distrust, and the problems of reaching substantial accord on purposes, principles, and values are reflected throughout industrial literature and in innumerable talks at meetings of industrialists. Sometimes it seems as though employees and employers do not even speak the same language and that foremen have one language for the shop and another for the office.

Doubtless the development of an industrial relations division at the New Freedom Products Company was a response to the growing separation between the points of view of workers and management. Steps in this development, it will be recalled, were irregular and, when they involved too explicit a recognition of the decline of the old personal system, reluctant. Moreover, they were not conceived in the light of a broad recognition of functions, although safety, promotion, the hospital, and the like catered more or less successfully to needs. Presumably establishment of the personnel department rests more directly on recognition of functional requirements, that is, on an understanding of the needs of people and of the institution. This department is supposed to supplement the activities of the line organization, especially the foremen, to train foremen, and to supply employee services including some, like attention to housing requests, which were formerly in the hands of officials. Some of these services, among them publication of the employee manual and the plant newspaper, stress charter and aim at communications. Evidently this program is not complete. There is a somewhat cryptic heading in the box devoted to "labor relations" on the organization chart which says "management sharing." Precisely what this means is not clear, but it is left there as a reminder of something to be attended to some day. Also, one official believes that only when employees are enabled to obtain any fact they want about any phase of the business will relations be entirely satisfactory. To date, a little, but not much, progress has been made in this direction.

Whether such a program—one which was entirely management's —could ever have recemented relationships will never be known. Organization of the union local in effect inaugurated an employee program directed at the same ends. Although hopes for higher pay, longer vacations, and other benefits played a part in the success of the union organizing campaign, leaders in the organization and other employees believe that the union victory owed more to the fact that the workers had little confidence in foremen, managers, and others below official rank. They wanted to do business directly with "the boys at the top."

The union agreement is plainly a cooperative device designed, in part, to serve as a bridge between the point of view of the workers and that of management, and in this it was successful during the first year after it was signed. Whether it will continue to perform this function is an open question. In theory, at least, it places the employees in another institution and could conceivably involve loyalties to two separate charters. Company officers have expressed fear of this, but representatives of the national union claim that there is no such possibility: "We are as much interested in the prosperity of the company as you are. If you don't make money there will be no pay envelopes; no pay envelopes, no dues."

The fact that the line dividing the balance of interests between the higher and the lower status groups in the personnel falls on the foremen, rather than above or below their level, is especially interesting in view of national efforts to unionize foremen. The company is making strenuous efforts to "make the foremen part of management," that is, to bring them around to the management's point of view. Foremen feel the strain but so far have been receptive to the management's overtures. Late in 1945 they urged occasional meetings between company officers and themselves to discuss company affairs and "to get to know each other better." The officers

thereupon invited the foremen to a dinner party, and soon afterward they determined to hold meetings quarterly. After the first
two, several executives spoke of them as "our regular foremen's
dinners," and several foremen declared that the meetings marked
the point where they really began to believe they were part of
management.

In summary, it can be said that the most important antagonisms
at the New Freedom Products Company are related to divergent
interpretations of the charter and to differences in emphasis placed
upon charter elements by the subdivisions of the personnel. The
other antagonisms, arising from interpersonal friction and conflicts
between isolated individuals and the institution, are common
enough, but institutional norms seem to be able to cope with
them satisfactorily so long as they are not compounded by more
important antagonisms related to the charter. In any event, such
antagonisms are probably inevitable in any association of human
beings, as the prevalence of mores, folkways, laws, rules, customs,
rituals, and conventions indicates. Serious charter divergencies
may occur more rarely, but in the view of some students at least,
such divergencies are at the root of many of the ills of complex
societies. Other aspects of the problems associated with complexity,
change, and depersonalization at the New Freedom Products Company are discussed in the next chapter.

CHAPTER NINE: *Depersonalization*

One of the commonest and most persuasive explanations for the deterioration of personnel relations in modern industry is the statement that this is due, primarily, to depersonalization, which in turn is an outgrowth of the increased size and complexity of industrial operations. It is frequently asserted that when employers and employees knew each other intimately and conversed frequently the problems of human relationships were negligible, whereas today these problems are the most difficult in the whole industrial picture. Certainly a quick look at the history of the New Freedom Products Company would seem to confirm this opinion.

Moreover the problems which arise when organized groups grow so large and complex that people can no longer deal with each other in simple face-to-face meetings are neither new nor confined to modern industry. Moses [1] was confronted by such problems in the wilderness and, on the advice of his father-in-law, attempted to solve them by delegating authority and drawing up policies and

1. *The Holy Bible,* Exodus 18:13–27. Here Jethro, Moses' father-in-law, emerges as the prototype of the modern management engineer. He admonished Moses not to wear out himself and the people by trying to judge all their problems and tells him to appoint "captains" of thousands, hundreds, fifties, and tens. These were to judge all minor problems and bring only important ones to Moses. At the same time Moses was to "be for the people to God-ward" and to teach them ordinances and laws. Many years later the management of the New Freedom Products Company paid handsomely for the same advice and proceeded to appoint "captains" and to promulgate rules, although they hardly equaled the long lists in the next four or five books of the Bible. Jethro,

rules. Primitive tribes also know these problems and meet them in similar ways.[2]

The comments of sociologists, also, strengthen the conclusion that face-to-face relationships are almost, if not quite, essential for preserving effective cooperation. Among these, one of the best known is C. H. Cooley's discussion of primary groups.[3] In essence, what Cooley says is that primary groups are those in which people have intimate, face-to-face contacts; that such groups, as exemplified by the family, are "the nursery of human nature"; and that such groups on the adult level are especially conducive to harmonious relationships. This view has, of course, been followed by many others. Selden D. Bacon,[4] for example, emphasizes the unfortunate results for individuals and argues that while the advantages of a complex society are numerous there is a price to pay for them in "tensions, fears, sensitiveness, feelings of frustration, which constitute . . . insecurity."

Especially interesting in this connection are the works of two French sociologists, both of whom were more or less directly concerned with industrial conditions. These are Frédéric Le Play, an engineer who spent a long lifetime trying to discover the sources of happiness and unhappiness among European workers, and Émile Durkheim, who combined anthropological and sociological inter-

however, grasped a principle which New Freedom officials have not grasped quite so clearly. When he told Moses to "be . . . to God-ward," he evidently meant he should emphasize the tribal charter. At any rate Moses certainly did not neglect the purposes, principles, and standards of his people.

2. Analysis of 66 tribes in the Human Relations Area Files, Inc., shows that of 36 tribes with a population of less than 10,000 17 delegated authority in the administration of justice, while in 19 authority remained entirely in the hands of the chief or other supreme functionary. In 30 tribes with larger populations, this type of authority was delegated in every case. Statistically the possibility that this is a chance correlation is practically nil (personal communication from J. W. M. Whiting).

3. Cooley, *Social Organization*, p. 23.

4. S. D. Bacon in *Alcohol, Science and Society; Twenty-nine Lectures with Discussion as Given at the Yale Summer School of Alcohol Studies*, pp. 179–195.

ests. Le Play, among other considerations, stressed the relationships between persons of prestige and those on lower status levels [5] and concluded that long-established community leaders and employers are tremendously important in preserving the happiness of their neighbors. They enjoy the respect of subordinates; they transmit the customs which serve as guides for the people; they decide questions which might otherwise lead to friction; and they establish harmony of opinion. However, when, as Le Play says, they are "seduced by luxury" which comes with industrialization, they cease to deal directly with the people, and the delegates whom they appoint do not satisfactorily discharge the functions which the "social authorities" performed.

Durkheim [6] traces the history of industry from the Middle Ages, when workers and masters labored side by side and conflicts were rare, to modern times, when specialization separated employers and employees and quarrels became numerous. Indeed, Durkheim bases much of the discussion of his famous concept of *anomie* upon this ristory. *Anomie,* as Durkheim defines it, represents an aimless, disorganized, frustrating situation, and he attributes these ills to the divisive effects of specialization and to ceaseless change which prevents new patterns of cooperation from developing.

Accounts of modern industry frequently sound like case studies from which some of these sociological ideas might have been deduced. The following is an example:

> The growth of huge concerns has ever widened the gap between employers and employees. When once they were of one class and one mind, they are now miles apart—members of two different classes and motivated by different folkways and *mores*. It is these deep-seated, unconsciously followed customs and beliefs that emphasize the present wide-spread lack of understanding between workers and employers, where once there was usually a common bond of mutual

5. Le Play, *Les Ouvriers européens,* Vol. VI; and *The Organization of Labor,* especially pp. 121–122.

6. Durkheim, *De la Division du travail social,* pp. 397–417.

good-will enlisted for a common purpose. Lack of knowledge and understanding is the root of multitudinous maladjustments in human relationships. Nowhere is this fact more aptly substantiated than in the impersonalization of industrial relations, where it is often impossible for managers to possess even meager knowledge about their thousands of employees and where face-to-face contacts are precluded by the many other duties and problems of management, such as keeping accounts and coping with credit situations, market fluctuations, and change in processes. The employers live in a different world from that of the employees, face different problems. It was the belated recognition of this fact that led to the establishment of personnel departments in the attempt to restore personal contacts with wage earners.[7]

The following excerpt also describes as generally true of American industry certain elements which are found in the history of the New Freedom Products Company:

> The complexity of operating relations is due largely to the growth of industrial organizations, which has made it more and more difficult for management to keep in touch with the individual. As personal intercourse becomes less feasible, the danger of submerging the human equation increases; rules and regulations become necessary; supervisors must be appointed; and reliance must be placed upon them to maintain the proper relationship with the supervised. In order that the ideas of employees may not be lost sight of, suggestion systems may be invoked. An effort may be made to ascertain the employee's thoughts—to measure his morale.[8]

In reviewing such accounts of industry, and the preceding generalizations of sociologists as well, there is a temptation to infer that increasing complexity and size, with consequent depersonalization, are, at least from the point of view of the people involved,

7. C. R. Daugherty, *Labor Problems in American Industry*, p. 58. See also Dale Yoder, *Personnel and Labor Relations*, p. 49.

8. Felix E. Baridon and Earl H. Loomis, *Personnel Problems*, p. 321.

always unfortunate. The old New Freedom employee with his reminiscences of the "good old days," the writer who speaks (in the quotation above) of "submerging the human equation," as well as the sociologist who mentions "personal insecurity," all suggest this opinion. This inference is not necessarily justified either for the New Freedom Products Company or for industry in general. Some writers, as will be seen below, point out that the economies and productivity of large-scale enterprise are too great to be sacrificed and that other, perhaps better, adjustments than the system of personal contacts can be found. At the New Freedom Products Company, it appears that both size and specialization were necessary to maintain company prosperity and stability, without which neither purposes nor needs could be satisfied. Moreover, it can be argued that impersonality makes for impartiality. Of industry in general S. A. Lewisohn [9] says:

> It is a mistaken and romantic notion to believe everything was rosy when industry operated in small-scale units, and that all our troubles are due to the fact that the owner no longer has personal contact with his men . . . The small family enterprise is, in a way, somewhat analogous to the old feudal ownership and is not so much in keeping with the spirit of our national life as the large depersonalized institutions. Stressing the advantages of small-scale units sounds suspiciously like the customary romantic reminiscences about "the good old times."
>
> It is certain that some of the worst exploitation and some of the most troublesome forms of unrest are associated with small-scale, sweatshop industry, where boss and wage earners work side by side.

Lewisohn, however, does recognize the difficulty of administering very large plants, since "it is hard to talk to five thousand foremen in an intimate manner." He suggests that the solution may lie in limiting the size of plants and in applying "modern ingenuity and knowledge of administrative principles" to large units of people.

9. S. A. Lewisohn, *Human Leadership in Industry,* pp. 13–15.

It may be said, then, that while personal contacts are not necessarily an unmixed blessing there is presumptive evidence, both
theoretical and experimental, that they do possess advantages. On
the other hand, large, complex organizations cannot expect to have
a complete set of such relationships which will include all members
of the personnel, and the advantages of size and complexity are too
great to ignore in many organizations. The pressing task for industry is to discover how to retain the advantages of large, highly
specialized organization and at the same time to achieve the results
attributed to the sort of organization described by Cooley in his
term, "primary group." And here the emphasis needs to be placed
on the functions of activities, whether they be on an intimate,
face-to-face basis or on an impersonal level. Simply to note that
growth in size and complexity have tended to go hand in hand with
decreased cooperation and lessened personal satisfaction from the
job will produce little more than nostalgia for a culture which
is no longer adjusted to the demands of modern life. This problem—that of finding adjustments which will discharge both the
organizational and individual functions of big enterprises—moreover, is not one which concerns management alone. Unions also
are industrial organizations, their size has grown even more rapidly
than has that of industrial concerns, and already there are symptoms that their problems of establishing morale, meeting the requirements of their organization, and satisfying the needs of their
members differ from management's only in detail.

There is a good deal of evidence which suggests that one of the
most fundamental problems associated with maintaining a closely
knit organization is to be found in the tendency for charters to
split or become fragmented when communications fail to convey
the information and ideas equally to all segments of the personnel.
This evidence, also, indicates that failure to establish unity of
purpose and agreement on principles, which are essential for group
cooperation and harmony, also represents a failure to meet needs
of individuals who require a sense of personal significance (respect
of fellows), of understanding, of belonging (integration), and of
security and justice.

We have seen in Chapter 8 that at the New Freedom Products

Company an important set of antagonisms was based on divergent emphases on charter elements, which developed as the communications afforded by personal contacts between officials and workers disappeared. Durkheim also suggests the importance of communications in establishing a sense that activities have *une fin en dehors d'elles mêmes,* and Jethro told Moses to be "for the people to God-ward," that is, a symbol and preacher of the tribe's religious charter. Alexander R. Heron [10] sees the problem of mutual understanding as affecting industry generally and extending to cleavages in American society. The following excerpts from his book, *Sharing Information with Employees,* are interesting for the solution he offers and for the way in which they relate to our discussions of charter, communications, and antagonistic cooperation:

> The ideas of the class struggle could gain no hearing among us until employers had, consciously or otherwise, provided a basis of classes and class barriers. And the principal way by which employers have fostered this idea has been by permitting the men and women who work for wages to become increasingly ignorant of the wider significance and importance of the work they are doing.
>
> . . . in the change from the local wagon shop to Colossal Motors, . . . we have lost the old sharing of information and understanding. With it we have lost the only internal force which impels a wage earner to give his best to the enterprise of which he is a part. We lost even the ability to demonstrate that he is part of the enterprise and that the enterprise is part of him and his life. And, finally, we lost the attitude on the part of the employer which enabled him to permit every fellow worker to know the business facts as a normal and personal right.
>
> There is no turning back to the small unit as a pattern of organization and production . . . But the restoration of an understanding unit *within* even the largest of our mass organizations can be accomplished.

10. Alexander R. Heron, *Sharing Information with Employees,* pp. 27, 29, 34, 195–198.

This unit, he suggests, could be a lead man associated with a small number of fellow workers. Thus his system would recognize the span of control [11] but would nonetheless retain face-to-face personal contacts as media for the dissemination of the information. This, he believes, is vital for mutual understanding or what we would call a common sense of charter.

The history of the New Freedom Products Company, as we have indicated, possesses elements similar to those described above as typical of American industry. Early in the present century peregrinations of the officials comprised a set of customary norms of behavior or folkways which permitted free and easy intercourse with the employees in the plant. For their part, plant employees also had customs which facilitated meetings with the officials. Together those corresponding practices constituted an essential part of the institutional organization, which discharged its functions so well that there was a state of near equilibrium. The institutional charter, with its emphasis on security and friendly cooperation, became firmly entrenched in traditions and in the minds of workers and officials alike. Both were in essential agreement on purposes, principles, and values. Employees saw how sales, quality, reliability, and similar factors were related to their personal goals almost as clearly and in very much the same way that management did. The personal contacts were channels for communications which enabled both management and employees to see each other's points of view and to unite them in a mutually acceptable charter.

These personal contacts, it may be noted, had additional functions which should not be disregarded. For individuals they enhanced feelings of respect, control, and the satisfaction of similar needs. Officials, for instance, clearly drew satisfaction from the trust and admiration given them by workers, while the workers were impressed by being able to talk to the men at the top. Moreover, the officials felt that by knowing the workers they could control them, and workers felt that by being able to bring personal and moral pressure to bear on the men who ran the company they,

11. Heron says it is a "crude" recognition of the span of control. This span refers to the theory that a superior functionary can deal directly with only a limited number of subordinates.

too, exerted a measure of control. For the organization, personal contacts facilitated several functions. Communications, as we have seen, were greatly simplified, not only with respect to the ideas contained in the charter but in the more technical matters of conveying orders, receiving grievances, and so on. Regulation, likewise, was not dissipated or distorted by the indirect channels of the larger organization, and authority flowed directly from the most powerful members of management to workers at the lowest levels. Officials were able to participate in training, and workers, being aware of the subtle requirements suggested by the charter, regularly went well beyond mere job instruction as they initiated new employees. Technological requirements, too, came directly into the purview of the officials, and it is interesting that these men were responsible for a number of inventions and improvements in equipment and products. Finally, welfare requirements—aid to needy workers, pensions, and so on—were met in a highly personal way.

While all functions listed in the last paragraph are important, several of them are incidental to the argument we are making. No one would deny, for instance, that the shift of technological controls can be and frequently should be transferred to engineers, chemists, and other technical specialists or that the purely technical aspects of communications and regulation—the transmission of orders and direction, for instance—can be delegated to such intermediate functionaries as foremen and supervisors. Indeed such functions are usually clearly recognized as organizational objectives and are handled in a more or less rational manner. In fact, at the New Freedom Products Company the approach to them may be so rational that it obscures the more subtle but equally important functions concerned with morale and satisfaction of individual drives other than that for money.

One of the weaknesses to be found in such discussions of the shift from primary group relationships to a formal and impersonal structure is that they fail to explore fully the whole gamut of functions of the personal contacts of an earlier day. Cooley's remark about intimate, face-to-face contacts causing kindliness to flourish seems to have set the tone for many such discussions. One sometimes gets the impression that intimacy has a magical quality inherently capable of eliciting the nobler sentiments of man. This is as unfortunate as it is false. Intimacy can breed all sorts of sentiments including distrust and dislike as well as kindliness, and dwelling on the pleasant aspects tends to obscure the really practical problem, which is to discover new means for achieving old results. Only communications, of all the functions facilitated by personal contacts, seems to have received much attention, and even here the question of what is communicated and why it is important is left at best only half answered.

To understand fully the functions of relationships between officials and workers it is necessary to view them in the light of the institutional charter, that is, the purposes, principles, and values held more or less in common by the whole personnel. Basically the first task of an institution, as a cooperating group, is to prevent antagonisms from destroying cooperation—in other words, to prevent uncoordinated or conflicting personal interests from interfering with or thwarting attainment of common interests. The charter, in its purposes, holds the common interests. In its principles it outlines the fundamental means for realizing the purposes; and in its system of values it provides a basis for judging the propriety of decisions, policies, rules, and activities. Reduced to its essentials the charter sets forth incentives to joint activity and includes guides and moral standards to govern this activity.

Charter, however, has meaning only to the extent that it exists in the minds of individuals. For each individual, charter is a conception of what the institution is and how it does and should operate. Unless he is in rebellion against the charter, this conception helps to determine his behavior in the institution. For the institution, the charter consists of a general, though frequently tacit, agreement among the individual conceptions. The charter has, however, an existence over and above individuals since it is embodied in policies, stories, precepts, and other statements of value and purpose which pass from person to person and may outlive the individuals who at various times give them expression. Ideally, each individual receives and retains a replica of the institutional charter. In practice these replicas are not exact; they vary considerably. If, nevertheless, the charter is successfully to unite the entire personnel, the correspondence of individual conceptions must be fairly close.

Possibly, in an institution where all members performed exactly the same tasks and encountered exactly the same conditions, there could be uniformity of charter conceptions without much linguistic re-enforcement. Indeed, according to Durkheim,[12] there are two kinds of social solidarity. One, found in primitive societies, depends upon similarity of activities of the people. Presumably individuals are bound together by the ease with which they can identify with one another—by what Giddings called consciousness of kind.[13] The other kind of solidarity depends upon the interdependence of people as specialization develops—although they grow progressively more different from each other, they cannot get along without one another. As Durkheim suggests, however, mere interdependence is not enough to guarantee effective social organization. There must be rapport, another kind of consensus, which in turn depends upon effective communication of charter and upon indoctrination or training.

Thus when company or union officials can converse daily with workers they know the questions which are troubling the personnel and can prevent the workers' interpretations of charter from diverging radically from their own. Conversely, the workers can present their own views and problems and thus shape the conceptions of their superiors. When the officials of the New Freedom Products Company stopped visiting the plant regularly, effective communications between them and the workers ceased. As a result, officials and workers came more and more to interpret charter in the divergent ways which their respective experiences emphasized. In this case, neither group entirely lost sight of any of the charter elements, but in effect the charter was split. Officials emphasized those things which had to do with the strength of the company as a business firm and resisted suggestions which seemed to threaten its stability. Workers, on the contrary, stressed things which concerned their own well-being, notably income and se-

12. Durkheim, *De la Division du travail social,* especially pp. 188, 397–417.
13. F. H. Giddings, *The Principles of Sociology.*

curity. They were convinced that the company could do more for them; management believed that the workers' demands were dangerous to the company and failed to see the context from which these demands arose. The differences between the two groups corresponded to the differences in knowledge available to them, and the two groups were those between which communications had become most imperfect.

In this case, as we have noted, the split was not very wide. One can readily call to mind more serious breakdowns of charter, cases, for example, where only the chance to earn a living holds workers on the job and where strife is frequent and violent. Or, to take another sort of example, one can readily conceive of workers whose loyalty is divided between irreconcilable union and company charters. In the case of the New Freedom Products Company, the purposes of the union and the company were in several respects identical, and there was little difficulty in reaching agreement.[14] But some unions are committed to socialistic objectives which hold that private enterprise should be destroyed, and obviously, in such cases, agreement between the union and the company must be tenuous at most.

At this point, a reasonable query arises. Cannot individuals or groups manipulate communications for their own ends? Cannot knowledge of charter and the way it enlists loyalty be used disingenuously to hoodwink people? The answer to this question is undoubtedly yes. One need only consult Machiavelli to find instructions for doing this, and it is necessary to go no farther than the nearest political meeting to find ringing appeals to ideals which citizens hold dear and politicians regard as expedient. Management handbooks which counsel understanding employees aim at enhancing management's control. Unions use the knowledge they have to advance their ends. Social workers, revolutionists, and nearly all others who try to influence behavior use this technique to some extent at least. The goals of these people may or may not be ideal; it is not our purpose to pass judgment upon them. There is, however, one realistic check on unscrupulousness. It appears

14. For an even more striking case, see Donald B. Straus, *Hickey-Freeman Company and Amalgamated Clothing Workers of America: A Case Study.*

that the more closely charter and its re-enforcements are confirmed by experience the less likely the institution of which they
are part will be to encounter shocks which will weaken or destroy
its organization. For the long pull, hoodwinking people is a risky
business, even though they may cherish mistaken but honestly
held beliefs for generations. Lincoln said hoodwinking could not
be done consistently on a broad scale.

At the bottom of all human organization lie the needs of individuals and the needs of society. As far as industry is concerned,
there is one prime social function—to manufacture goods which
society wants at a cost which society is willing to pay—and no
matter how the charter is framed or how well it is communicated,
no industrial plant can survive unless it meets this realistic requirement. At the level of individual needs, moreover, one encounters dynamic forces which are beyond the reach of mere words.
To be sure, individuals will make tremendous sacrifices for ideals
which they hold dear; some will even die for them. In the end,
however, the proof of the pudding is in the eating, and this is
particularly true of industry where the ideals are closely connected
with material rewards. The man who is hungry or afraid or in-
sulted or rejected or deeply frustrated in any way is a rebellious
man. He discards first the norms and then the ideals which seem
to punish him, and he strikes out for other norms and other ideals
which promise better. This, of course, is a lesson which industry
might have learned during the depression. In those days plenty of
"100 per cent" Americans lost faith entirely in capitalism and em-
braced ideologies which promised them a glittering new system
in which they would have control and through which they could
avenge themselves for the wrongs they felt so keenly. Countering
this, management tried hard to appeal to such ideals as "rugged
individualism" and "free private enterprise." Often enough, however, they lost sight of the fact that the words they used had lost
meaning and the speakers had lost respect. Happily the depression
did not last, and the workers went back to their jobs. They went
warily, however, and they took strong unions with them.

The preceding paragraph is intended mainly to suggest that
there are limits to the results which can be gained by manipulat-

ing communications. Other very real factors are present in every social situation. Or, to phrase the matter in another way, all the elements of an institution help to determine behavior. This conclusion is obvious from the history of the New Freedom Products Company. There the personal system of interaction which had made the charter strongly felt throughout the organization failed and was not, at least for a long time, replaced by an alternative system. This fact in itself, however, was not responsible for the division between the management and the shopworkers. Each of these groups responded to real factors in its respective environment, and its behavior was in response to felt needs as defined and guided by the ideas, knowledge, principles, and purposes as it saw them. Undoubtedly more effective communications could have kept these views much closer together, could have held the charter more or less intact. But the fact remains that the officials *had* to respond to the demands of a growing business in an increasingly complex economy and the employees *had* to do something about restoring their sense of security, respect, control; and the rest of the needs which were unsatisfied as change progressed.

To this point in this chapter, the line of thought has pretty much indicated that depersonalization per se is not the basic problem in industry or even in other organizations, such as communities or schools and the like which have also grown large and complex. Instead the focus has been shifted to the functions of personal organizations and to the possibility that other means for discharging these functions without sacrificing either size or specialization can be found. The conclusion implied by this shift in attention, however, cannot confidently be left unqualified.

It is conceivable that Cooley's idea that primary groups are the nursery of human nature strikes at the heart of the recurrent problem of depersonalization. If in all their important relationships children learn how to behave through intimate personal contacts with other people—parents, sisters and brothers, teachers, and neighbors—can impersonal contacts ever be as satisfactory to them as personal ones? To this the answer is probably yes—sometimes. Cooley himself preferred books to going into the field to study people at first hand. Some people, scholars for example, learn to commune with others most comfortably by reading and writing. They do not have to see the gestures and expressions of other people or to hear vocal inflections. They evidently do not require the kind of rapport which can only be had by the give-and-take of conversation. Such people, however, are not typical of those found in industry. They may be psychologically aberrant, so shy that association with other people is painful; or they may have had special education in reading, writing, or other impersonal media of communications. The shy hermit does occasionally find a job in industry—one or two such eccentrics held positions at the New Freedom Products Company—but he is exceptional. Most people in industry can read and write, to be sure, but for them reading and writing are likely to have been confined largely to school exercises in their formative years and to have declined rather than increased in importance in adulthood. One cannot, of course, be dogmatic upon a matter which has not been clearly demonstrated by the appropriate science, which is psychology, but one can at least base a reasonable case upon Cooley's contention. Most industrial workers are probably much more comfortable in personal, face-to-face relationships with people who are important to them than they are in dealings through writing or through intermediaries. Their relationships with their parents, their teachers, and, as far as older New Freedom Products Company employees are concerned, with their bosses have been mostly on a personal basis. One can at least guess that the intimate, face-to-face relationships of primary groups have an advantage as a basis for organization, a kind of head start over other possible types of relationships, because the earliest socialization of every individual occurs in such groups.

Modern psychology adds support to such a speculation. It requires no very tenuous deduction from learning theory [15] to extend the principle of generalization to the cooperative activities of human beings. According to this theory, habitual behavior is learned and reinforced by rewards which follow upon successful activities; and, at the same time, cues associated with the successful activities are also learned. The individual learns to distinguish the

15. Cf. Miller and Dollard, *Social Learning and Imitation*.

elements in a situation and to act when the appropriate elements are present. Thus the motorist approaching an intersection observes a clear road ahead and a green light and feels free to proceed, or if he sees pedestrians and cars moving across his path and a red lights he stops. The novice may be awkward in making these responses, but for the experienced driver they become second nature. The individual may also learn to generalize from one social situation to another—from one with which he is familiar to one which is new to him. In such cases, similar cues will elicit similar behavior; and the more closely the new situation resembles a familiar one, the more assurance the individual will feel. On the other hand, if familiar cues are absent, the individual is faced with the uncomfortable necessity of learning new behavior from scratch. His needs impel him to act, but he does not know what to do. Or, if familiar cues do not lead him to rewarding activity, he is frustrated. Assuming, then, that for most people observation of the cues present in personal intercourse becomes second nature, one may suppose that individuals will be likely to feel more at home and to act more successfully in primary groups.

These observations are not set down as proof that primary groups are necessarily the most advantageous basis for industrial or other organizations. They simply seem important enough to be borne in mind in this discussion and, on a practical level, in dealing with personnel problems. This will, of course, not come as a startling revelation to students of industry. The "human touch" is familiar enough. Occasionally it is even proposed as a sort of magic rite which will solve all problems.

We return, then, to the dilemma we noted earlier in this chapter. The large industrial plant cannot operate as a primary group in the sense that every individual has intimate personal relationships with all other individuals. On the other hand, communications, training, and other functions would be more readily discharged if it could. The choices implied by these two statements are not, however, mutually exclusive. There is a good deal of evidence that both personal relationships and large-scale operations can be retained together.

Actually, of course, people seldom work in isolation, and the evidence of the Hawthorne studies,[16] of Walker's *Steeltown*,[17] and of a considerable body of other research makes it plain that large plants include a veritable network of primary groups, some of them informal in terms of the official organizational structure and some of them included in the organization chart.

Essentially the problem of unifying large organizations consists of integrating such subgroups. One solution for this is to create interlocking primary groups which, so to speak, climb the organizational hierarchy. Thus, the operating department can be regarded as a primary group which includes the foreman who is in frequent face-to-face contact with the workers. Above this, there may be another primary group including foremen and managers. The managers may, in turn, belong to a primary group including chiefs of divisions, and so on up to the higher levels where in various ways—committee meetings and informal associations alike—other primary groups knit the whole organization together. Such a system is said to have been successful in a number of instances where it was consciously planned,[18] and to some extent it probably exists in many organizations in which little rational planning has been directed toward it. At least on the management level, the so-called multiple management scheme originated at the McCormick Company [19] appears to realize this interlocking system of primary groups.

Despite the success of some of these schemes, however, there remains a question as to whether such interlocking groups can achieve the level of interaction of the single primary group. It appears that they offer opportunities for discussion, for the give-and-take of conversation, and for utilizing the cues of face-to-face contact, provided communications and other functions are not inhibited by barriers of rank and differing points of view. More-

16. Cf. F. J. Roethlisberger and W. J. Dickson, *Management and the Worker*, as one of the several reports on these studies.

17. C. R. Walker, *Steeltown*, especially the emphasis on the formation of working teams.

18. S. Avery Raube of the National Industrial Conference Board has told the writer that he regards this as a prime means for overcoming depersonalization.

19. Charles P. McCormick, *The Power of People*.

over, it is evident that considerable care, forbearance, and enthusi-asm has had to go into such schemes and that they require a degree of organizational and social skill not necessary in simpler groups. Nevertheless, the raw material for programs of this sort is present in most if not all organizations, and the success of some of them is encouraging.

This idea of interlocking primary groups represents essentially an elaboration of the organizational system usually indicated by organization charts, an attempt, so to speak, to supplement the formal lines of communication and authority between boxes on such charts by emphasizing personal interchanges. Of a somewhat different order are other means for weaving face-to-face relation-ships into organizations. Among these may be mentioned labor-management committees, suggestion committees, and similar groups in which individuals from different departments or dif-ferent organizational levels participate.[20] Even dealings between union locals and management sometimes serve this purpose. In fact, in the six years following organization of the union at the New Freedom Products Company, it seems that the union has effectively restored a number of the functional lines which, more or less unconsciously, the employees and even the management sought.

So much for the opportunities which exist for personal interac-tion. While it may be true that for most people face-to-face con-versations are the easiest channels for communications, it it not true that they are the only ones which will work. To date, industry has evidently not discovered how to use impersonal media of com-munications very successfully. In fact, management publications have devoted a great deal of space to discussing how to make house organs, letters to employees, bulletin boards, and the like more effective. Even the unions, which at times have seemed to solve this problem better than management has, are often puzzled as to how to reach their members effectively. In moments of crisis—when,

20. For two interesting discussions of such committees, see W. H. Scott, *Joint Consultation in a Liverpool Manufacturing Firm; a Case Study in Hu-man Relations in Industry,* and Ernest Dale, *Greater Productivity through Labor-Management Cooperation; Analysis of Company and Union Experience.*

for example, a strike is impending—union speakers and publications seem to be extremely effective, but in the day-to-day routine of normal times they seem to succeed not much better than management's efforts. Nevertheless, there is reason to suppose that impersonal media can be highly impressive. Such figures as Roosevelt, Churchill, and many other public leaders have been able to grip the hearts of millions whom they never saw by using techniques of expression and mass media of communications and to inspire whole nations to almost inconceivable heights of patriotic devotion. There is, therefore, no reason to suppose that there are inevitable psychological barriers to distant communications despite the advantages which intimacy may be supposed to possess.

To conclude this chapter with these remarks on communications would be deceptive. Effective communications are, to be sure, of inestimable importance for every phase of industrial operation, but other functions are no less essential. Several of these may, apparently, be facilitated by the personal sort of organization which once obtained at the New Freedom Products Company, but others, such as the production of goods and services in modern society, quite obviously require both the size and specialization which inhibit face-to-face contacts. This productive function, moreover, is vital. The other functions, including those which serve to satisfy the various needs of the people who work in industry, are contingent upon it. Thus the problem to be faced is how to retain the advantages of size and complexity and at the same time to meet all the needs—both those of individuals and those inherent in organization. To say that anyone has yet solved this problem would, of course, be ridiculous. But we can say that there is evidence enough to indicate that it can be solved, provided all the elements which theory suggests are taken into account and provided, also, that each organization, indeed each situation, be understood in its own as well as in theoretical terms.

CHAPTER TEN: *Conclusions*

In its inception, the study which provides most of the factual data for this book had two main purposes. These were, first, to demonstrate to sociologists that they could improve the theoretical structure of the science by studying industry at first hand and, second, to show practical persons in industry that they could profitably use sociological theory in attacking their practical problems. This last chapter is devoted primarily to the first of these purposes. It is the writer's conviction that, to the ingenious mind which is possessed both of a sound grasp of theory and of the elements of the practical problem in hand, theory is the most useful tool which can be commanded. Hence, although in this summary practical applications are not discussed separately they are not forgotten. Indeed, to do more than allow specific applications to suggest themselves as they relate to and emerge from the discussion of theory would be unwise, for each situation, each industrial plant, possesses its own complex elements which require study in themselves. The theoretical implications touched upon here are offered as a means of unraveling and evaluating these complexities.

Perhaps the first consideration in studying the New Freedom Products Company was to investigate the utility of Malinowski's concept of institutions as a tool for analyzing the human relationships in industry. This concept has the virtue of outlining clearly and concisely all the factors which must be taken into account in interpreting the behavior in any organized group, and it seemed

plain that this company qualified as such a group just as certainly
as did the primitive organizations which Malinowski studied. The
point was to put this tool to work and find out whether it was as
good as its inventor claimed. This was, as far as the writer knows,
the first time this theory had been taken into the field for such
a test. Whether or not it has proved itself is, of course, a judgment
which should properly be left to the reader and to other social
scientists who will test it further. However, in the writer's opinion,
although, for industrial purposes at least, it needs some clarification and elaboration, the concept comes very close to justifying
Malinowski's rather sweeping claim that it is indispensable.

Its first advantage is that it outlines the structural elements
which determine the behavior within any organized group. These
are described and illustrated in Section II. They include personnel, charter, rules and norms, material apparatus, activities, and
functions. In other words, the theory consists of a concept, or a set
of related concepts, which defines an institution and outlines in
broad terms the various sorts of factors which must be taken into
account in interpreting or explaining behavior. To be sure, these
concepts appear to neglect certain other pertinent factors, mainly
those which are concerned with the broader setting within which
any organized group exists—that is, such things as its historical
setting and its relationships with other groups in society. History,
however, is suggested by the ideas which are summed up in charter, and the significance of historical influences is suggested by the
manner in which they have continued to make themselves felt in
such an institution as the New Freedom Products Company. Relationships with other institutions are suggested in the concept of
function, especially the functions which an institution performs
for society in general or for other groups not included within the
institution. Moreover, function plants the roots of behavior firmly
in the soil of human motivation since it holds that, in the last
analysis, people act to satisfy their needs.

In essence, then, Malinowski's institutional conquest provides a
chart or check list for research. To some extent this must be regarded as a device primarily suited for static analysis, but it leaves
the doors open for other theories which bring in dynamic con-

siderations and thus make it possible to study the changing structure of patterns and ideas. In other words, Malinowski helps to throw light on both uniformities and deviations in behavior and, for this reason, gives some sort of basis for predicting the results of experimental activities. This last contribution, of course, is the eminently practical one, and it is made even more practical by the emphasis the concept places on a complete analysis of all pertinent areas of information. That is, the concept precludes the limited approaches, which sometimes seem to promise relatively easy results but which usually fall short in that they leave out genuinely important factors. All the elements of an institution are linked like the interdependent parts of a machine, and a change in one will inevitably be reflected through activities in some or all of the others.

Malinowski died before he completed work on institutions, and what he left consists mainly of broad concepts expressed in sweeping terms. The first theoretical contribution which it is hoped this book makes is in the nature of amplification or refinement of some of these in ways which were suggested by the facts discovered at the New Freedom Products Company and by other studies of modern industry. These elaborations are described in Section II, and they may be summarized as follows:

First, it is proposed that the content of charter can be usefully classified into three principal parts: purposes, principles, and standards. Purposes are the goals which the personnel of an institution, more or less tacitly, agree upon as the ends of their joint endeavors and the ultimate reasons for participating in institutional activities. These may, at times, constitute a more or less exact consensus, and, to the extent that the institution remains an organized whole, they bear closely upon the incentives which cause individuals to "work together." On the other hand, differences in conceptions of these goals make for friction and disorganization. | Principles are the general means to the ends represented by purposes, the broad and often only informally expressed policies upon which the more specific norms and rules and even nonconforming activities may be based. Like purposes, principles provide a rationale for activity, and the degree of agreement upon them is closely related to cooperation. Standards are modifying values, which are not regarded primarily as ends or means but by which behavior is judged to be proper or the reverse. And finally, closely associated with charter we have noted re-enforcements which are verbal and symbolical norms that strengthen and convey the ideas which charter includes. To the philosopher, perhaps, this attempt to systematize a value system may appear considerably less than adequate, but for purposes of sociological analysis it seems to be useful and reasonably complete. To it might be added the beliefs which the group takes to be facts of nature or "facts" of faith, but beyond these categories this study indicates no important need for further clarification or amplification.[1]

A second clarification suggested by this study is a rather simple distinction which can be made between "rules" and "norms," terms which Malinowski uses interchangeably. It seems appropriate to use "norms" as equivalent to folkways and mores, i.e., customs or informal group-behavior patterns, and to restrict the word "rules" to those norms which have been put into formal or written statements and for which or to which official or organizational sanctions are attached.

Third, it seems advisable to divide the complex element of functions into the various types of functions which appeared in the course of analysis. These are *a*) the outging or extrainstitutional functions, which represent the services that the institution performs for the whole society or, at any rate, for persons and groups outside the institution; and *b*) the ingoing or intrainstitutional functions which the institution discharges in meeting its own operational requirements and in satisfying the needs of its own personnel. This latter category can be further subdivided into instrumental functions—that is, those which fulfill operating needs—and consumatory functions, which minister to the needs of personnel. In the case of industry, the consumatory needs have

1. It is recognized, of course, that abstract definitions such as those given above are difficult and not entirely satisfactory. Much of Section II is devoted to an effort to give them an operational basis by illustrating them from observations made in studying the New Freedom Products Company

been taken as including such things as the "desire for creature comforts," the "desire for the respect of fellows," and others which follow, in general, a list proposed by Bakke, although for other types of institutions this list would have to be altered. The principal instrumental functions, however, are listed as including communications, recruitment, training, regulation, protection, technology, and welfare, which are proposed as representing requirements which must be met in any organization. In this connection, it can be argued that needs can be felt only by individuals so that to speak of institutional needs is incorrect. This argument, however, is met by the term "instrumental," which implies that ultimately activities, such as communications or regulation, facilitate the satisfaction of individual drives but also makes it clear that such activities may minister only very indirectly to such drives. The act of enforcing a rule, for example, may be onerous to the enforcer and frustrating to the person who is being regulated.

These elaborations of Malinowski's concepts are presented somewhat tentatively. They follow the thought that putting the tools of scientific theory to work should lead to improvements in them, a notion which is especially true of analytical tools such as the institutional theory. From a sociological point of view, the attempt to designate the principal types of organizational instrumental functions is perhaps the most pertinent. A list of consumatory needs typical of any particular type of organization is, to be sure, a most useful device, but such a list represents a compilation of acquired drives which has to be established empirically for given circumstances. The establishment of a list of universal drives from which the acquired drives observable in activity are derived is primarily the task of the psychologist. Determination of requirements which can be shown to be essential for any kind of organization is, on the other hand, a task for the sociologist, and the list here given is an attempt in this direction.

To Malinowski's second statement—that no organized human activity can be analyzed except in terms of his conceptual scheme—no single case study can expect to contribute much in the way of confirmation. Yet the New Freedom Products Company has been here so analyzed and, it seems to the author, effectively. Moreover the additional fact that the company is an institution in a culture far removed from the primitive societies which furnished Malinowski with the materials from which he constructed the concept is clearly significant.

That an industrial firm has personnel, rules and norms, and material apparatus and engages in activities which function to satisfy needs of one kind or another is surely not news, although the full implications of these elements are not always well understood. Plenty of industrial studies have dealt with these as subjects. The subject of charter, however, has not been so specifically treated by students of industry although, particularly in writings by people who have worked in industry, the importance of this concept may be inferred. The insistence by experienced personnel that the newcomer should "get the feel" of a plant or that he must be aware of its objectives is always striking. However, the idea that objectives may go well beyond official pronouncements or that "the feel" may consist of a more or less consistent body of purposes, principles, and standards which are transmitted from member to member of a group through communications and are perpetuated by training is not so clear in industrial literature. Another point, also, which emerges plainly in this study is that frequently discussions of morale leave this quality in a realm which is tinged with something of the mystery which surrounds vague but powerful supernatural forces. Here the charter concept seems to make a very definite contribution, since it may well be that morale can be defined as the result of a strong and mutually consistent sense of charter on the part of an institution's personnel. Or, to consider the reverse of this picture, lack of morale, friction, and relative disorganization can be regarded as, at least partly, the result of failure to grasp charter or of diverse conceptions of charter in an institution.[2]

2. To some readers, this emphasis on charter may appear to be either a laborious effort to fit the facts to the concept or a bit of idealism inspired by too close study of a peculiar little factory in an old New England town. To such skeptics, the following excerpts from a variety of sources may be convincing:

"Show your men the main objective toward which your organization is di-

One of Malinowski's claims for his concept is that no cultural element can be defined except in its institutional setting. This means both that each institution stands, so to speak, as a self-

rected. Keep this objective constantly before them . . . Then put each individual's part in the enterprise before him and release him into action." Erwin Haskell Schell, *The Technique of Executive Control*, p. 53.

"The morale factor in an organization will always elude precise measurement, yet it is one of the most important elements in attaining maximum effectiveness . . . Of two organizations with the same technical advantages at their disposal, the one whose entire organization is filled with enthusiasm for what the company is trying to do is bound to forge to the front." A. R. Wiren and C. Heyel, *Practical Management Research*, p. 22.

"Underneath the stop watches and bonus plans of the efficiency experts, the worker is driven by a desperate inner urge to find an environment where he can take root, where he belongs and has a function, where he sees the purpose of his work and can take pride in achieving it." Stuart Chase, *Men at Work*, pp. 26–27.

An interesting description of how a small group within a factory created and later was forced to alter what amounted to a charter is to be found in Whitehead's *The Industrial Worker*, pp. 124, 152 ff., 205. In this book Whitehead reports on a small group of women workers studied by representatives of the Harvard Graduate School of Business Administration over a period of years. This group built up "routines and sentiments around the work situation," and these were influenced by the operators' belief that the experiment was of great importance to themselves and to workers in general. They felt they were collaborators in research of high future significance, and their morale was reflected in continued increases in production. When, however, the experimenters lost interest in the group and it became apparent to the workers that they were no longer working for their original broad goals, their production fell below its peak levels, and the group reoriented itself toward maintaining its "social activity [i.e., its identity as a work group] in the face of a continuously crumbling situation."

"The drive for a more equitable share of the national income for the worker is a fixed star in the union horizon, a generally accepted point of departure. It gives the expert a clear mandate within which to exercise his economic selectivity and an assurance that any facts which do not contribute to the ends described are hardly relevant . . . The adjusted individual in the labor movement is he who understands what policy is and how to work within its framework. Once he has learned, he is both restricted and freed; restricted in attempts to deviate from it, and freed to use his imagination to advance it." Kermit Eby, "The Expert in the Labor Movement," *The American Journal of Sociology* (July, 1951), p. 30.

contained unit and that no custom or rule or other organized behavior can be understood except in its relationship to all elements of the institution. In other words, one cannot understand the behavior in any institution unless he studies that particular institution carefully. In a sense each organization is unique, for while certain general facts obtain in all, and certain principles of individual and social behavior are true of all, it is impossible to tell how these influence each other and combine to produce activities until their specific nature in specific situations is known. This is especially true in diagnosis, for here the social scientist or practitioner differs not at all from the physician, who has to examine each patient before he can tell what is wrong and what treatment is indicated. This does not mean that in every situation everything about the institution must be explored thoroughly. Criteria of relevance must be established, although it is unsafe to omit at least a preliminary survey of all the areas suggested by the theory. In the office of the New Freedom Products Company, for example, there are voluminous files filled with blueprints and specifications for buildings and machines; in the laboratory the composition and characteristics of many materials are described in great detail. There is a wealth of detail on the single element of material apparatus. Information of this kind, however, while it might be intensely interesting to the technologist would add little to the study described earlier in this book. Some aspects of material apparatus—the fact that there are dangerously inflammable materials, for example, and the fact that in the plant changes in equipment have been, in the view of workers, slight and unaccompanied by layoffs or downgrading—are important both because they illustrate the interrelationship of institutional elements and because they clarify the events under investigation.

The interrelationship of elements may be further illustrated by referring to the connections between charter, rules and norms, and activities. In the New Freedom Products Company, it will be recalled, there is a high emphasis on security, especially for old employees. The genesis of this resulted from the isolated act of pensioning the first employee who reached an age which prevented further work. Later—and here the element of personnel, in this

CTORY FOLKWAYS

instance an aging personnel, enters the picture—this act was taken as a precedent for other pensions, and before long the practice of granting pensions became an informal rule. This, along with other considerations for old employees such as keeping them on the payroll as long as possible, a practice facilitated by light machine operations, tended to create an unusually high average age in the work force, and this in turn tended to strengthen the incipient charter values favoring security for elderly employees. Here, incidentally, one is tempted to conclude that values grow from activities rather than vice versa. This conclusion, however, tempting though it may be, would be misleading. Even in this factory one can point to activities which grew from charter ideas, and even the continued consideration for older workers is carried along by the charter.

Another of Malinowski's claims for the institutional concept is that the institution is the "real isolate of culture." This, of course, does not mean that an institution can in reality be severed from the rest of society and held in suspension, so to speak, in the way a biologist can detach a segment of living tissue and keep it alive. Malinowski recognized this fact implicitly, if not explicitly, when he asserted that a culture is composed of semiautonomous, semi-integrated institutions. Malinowski, moreover, stressed the integration of culture and society through the "integral functions" of institutions, that is, through what we have designated the principal outgoing or extrainstitutional functions. Thus society can be looked upon as being composed of a network of institutions which specialize more or less in supplying, as outgoing functions, satisfaction for the basic consumatory needs and for the seven instrumental needs which we have codified. For example, the family, which is a comprehensive institution, discharges most if not all consumatory functions and has as main instrumental functions the "recruitment" or production of new members for society and the basic training or socialization of these members. Similarly, government in modern societies has, as prime instrumental functions, regulation and protection, while industries discharge technological functions in that they supply material goods and closely related services.

Despite Malinowski's emphasis on integral function as the point at which an institution is integrated with the rest of culture, other elements in institutions also represent bonds which tie any particular organized group to the rest of the society in which it exists. Charter, for instance, may be regarded as an element existing solely within an institution and can be so defined, but it is nevertheless true that a charter borrows much of its content from ideas held by the personnel as members of other institutions. In fact, in some respects, a given charter appears almost as a segment of a community or societal charter. Thus the humanitarian ideas of John Freedom with their implications for safety and quality and the neighborly attitude of the community in which the New Freedom Products Company was founded were incorporated into the developing charter of the young company. Later there were striking instances of the influence of ideas of democracy in the reluctance of officials to accept union security and in the attitudes of second-generation immigrants as contrasted with those of their parents. The charter of an institution shares the community or societal charter—that is, the ethos [3] of the society of which it is a part—but also adds particular values of its own and shapes the borrowed values to fit its own conditions.

Similarly, an institution is integrated with other organized groups through its personnel. While it is convenient to regard roles as separate compartments of personality—compartments which can be looked upon as creating separate individuals for each of the institutions to which a person belongs—individuals generalize from one role to another. Moreover, the kinds of individuals which a community can supply directly affect the institution. Thus, the fact that Teasville residents have risen in education and in their general level of aspiration has meant that the town no longer supplies enough new employees, and there is a tendency for the least desirable jobs to be taken over by nonlocal Negroes—the people in our society whose aspirations and skills have been kept at low levels. Viewed from a different angle, also,

3. See Sumner, *Folkways*, pp. 36–37, 70–74. S. W. Reed has suggested that ethos may be regarded as the residual core of values common to all institutions in a society.

it can be said that the integration of an institution with the community is to be found in the activities of individuals. The recreational activities of company officials constitute a case in point, for they tended to reduce the hours they spent at the factory and thus to influence the number of personal contacts they could have with plant employees. Similarly, the opportunity for Teasville residents to find employment outside the factory has increased the necessity for hiring out-of-town workers.

It seems unnecessary to labor the point that an institution is integrated with society through all its elements. In addition to functions, charter, and personnel, one need only cite the effect of federal and state laws on company norms and rules and to recall the ramifying effects of technological change to bring material apparatus into the picture. It is clear, therefore, that no institution can be understood without reference to its setting in society.

This does not mean, however, that using the institution as an isolate is not a valuable procedure. It makes it possible to focus attention, to describe the elements of an institution as parts of a discrete entity, and at the same time to view them as connected with or influenced by factors outside the institution. In important ways, also, it leads to a realistic view of behavior and culture. For example, social scientists have spent a good deal of time trying to designate mores and folkways of whole societies, but many mores and folkways can be properly described in institutional terms only. Smoking, for instance, has often been mentioned as an American folkway, but smoking is contrary to the mores in the New Freedom Products Company plant and within the edifices of many churches.[4] For several reasons, then, the institution as

4. The way in which institutional analysis clarifies the concepts of folkways and mores is striking. These, as they are defined by Sumner (*Folkways*, pp. 30–39), are usages which are backed by varying degrees of sanction by public opinion. Mores are supposed to be vital to societal welfare and are sternly sanctioned, while some folkways are held lightly and are sanctioned only by ridicule. Sumner refers to "notions of societal welfare," a somewhat vague term which is considerably sharpened by the concept of charter. Thus, on account of the fire hazard, smoking could cause accidents dangerous to many in the personnel at New Freedom Products, and its relationship to charter ideas

CONCLUSIONS   253

Malinowski defines it is an extremely useful isolate. It represents
a concrete entity—a group of people rather than a disembodied
system—and clearly designates the cultural and other conditions
which bear directly upon their activities.

It is obvious that a static view, such as the one provided by
analysis according to the institutional scheme, cannot fully answer
the requirements of the sort of problem posed by the history of the
New Freedom Products Company. In this the question was one
of changing relationships among the personnel of the company,
changes which were bound up with the manner and effectiveness
of cooperation. Whereas the evidence pointed to a relatively harmonious acceptance of goals, principles, and standards shared by
all the personnel in the past and to a high degree of personal satisfaction and company prosperity, it also showed that complete identification of interest on the part of the entire personnel did not
exist.

The picture was one of antagonistic cooperation in which conflicting interests were—and are—held in check in order to realize
important common goals. Hence, although the institutional scheme
seems to suggest smooth operations based on a common charter and
established rules and norms, the concept of antagonistic cooperation makes it clear that organization is at best a successful com-
promise. Elements of antagonism are present, side by side with
incentives to cooperation, in any institution.[5] Simply to recognize
this fact, however, is not of much value. Therefore, it is useful
to consider the incentives to cooperation, the types of antagonism
which can exist, and the means whereby antagonisms are reduced

---

of safety is obvious. Hence the prohibition of smoking is strongly rooted in
the charter and is both an officially sanctioned rule and an informally sanctioned norm. Even the humblest worker would not wait for the foreman to
enforce this rule; the smoker is regarded with horror, and any employee would
feel justified in stopping him. In fact, New Freedom employees share the common aversion to "squealing," but they would feel no compunction about re-
porting a smoker.

5. To say that there are elements of antagonism in industry may seem a
trifle less than necessary. Perhaps the emphasis should be on the fact that
there are also bases for cooperation. The point is that both are present and
more or less successfully balanced.

or controlled. In other words, it is necessary to go beyond the blanket definition of antagonistic cooperation given by Sumner and Keller [6] and to point up the elements within it as they are revealed by field research.

The most valuable clue to the first of these elements, the incentives to cooperation, is supplied by the charter concept. While undoubtedly individuals seek employment for reasons which are not provided by the charter of the institution where they work— because, for example, in our culture people are expected to earn a living, and in the Teasville community the company offered one of the opportunities to do this—the presence of motivations other than uncoordinated self-interest is obvious. The charter contains a set of purposes with which individuals are indoctrinated and which they come to accept as their own. The belief that the company makes products which are useful to society, for instance, transcends consciously held ideas of self-interest, although it probably also satisfies needs for prestige (respect of fellows). Charter re-enforcements such as stories, anecdotes, and even words like "quality," which possess affective significance, channel public opinion and exert pressure on individuals to conform. Thus charter purposes, principles, and standards are incorporated into each individual's thinking, and membership in the institution comes to be cherished for its own sake.[7]

The concept of charter, therefore, throws a positive light on the bases for cooperation by making it impossible to isolate in-

6. Sumner, *Folkways*, pp. 16–18; Sumner and Keller, *The Science of Society*, pp. 28–29.

7. A striking example of the way in which charter can lead individuals to act in ways apparently contrary to their selfish interests was provided by two union officers at the New Freedom Products Company in discussions of policy to be adopted when it became necessary to curtail working hours or to lay off a number of employees after V-E Day when the government canceled orders for company products. In this instance, the issue revolved around "sharing the work," which is a way of expressing the principle of cooperation in the institutional charter, especially as this is related to such purposes as income for the personnel and security and to such standards as friendliness and neighborliness. The two union men urged that hours be reduced so that employees would not have to be sent home, although they realized that this course would cut their own pay by a considerable weekly sum.

centives. This does not mean that the satisfaction of individual needs can be overlooked. Failure to satisfy these, whether they are consciously recognized or not, lies at the root of variations which lead to change. Nevertheless, a prime function of charter is to make people *want* to cooperate.

Antagonisms, like incentives to cooperation, can also be usefully analyzed, and it is possible to separate them into four different kinds in a manner which makes it easier to observe intrainstitutional conflicts. These categories of antagonisms are: interpersonal friction; conflicts between individuals and the institution; conflicting or poorly defined rules and norms; and conflicts arising from significant differences in the interpretation of the charter.

By interpersonal friction are meant antagonisms between individuals for reasons not primarily arising within the institution. To be sure, the institution brings the individuals together and their quarrels may be over matters concerned with the institution, but generally their differences are regarded by the rest of the personnel as personal in nature. If individuals are unable to prevent a quarrel from affecting operation of the institution, the antagonism then moves into the second class listed above. Presumably, uncontrolled personal antagonisms could, if they grew numerous enough, inhibit cooperation of all kinds; but such a conclusion could at best be only inferred from the evidence provided by the New Freedom Products Company.

The second class of antagonisms is also concerned with individuals as such. Presumably again, if enough individuals believed that they could not reconcile their own goals with the opportunities provided by the institution, the group would disintegrate and cooperation would cease, unless means were found to enforce participation. Such means are not available to modern industry,[8] although individuals may often continue to work as the lesser of evils, as, for example, when the choice lies between uncongenial employment and none at all. The potential significance of such

8. Even under the manpower controls of World War II, the government did not attempt to force individuals to work. Instead, it resorted to appeals to patriotism and tried to make it difficult to leave one job and obtain another.

antagonisms for an organization like the New Freedom Products
Company is to be seen in the cases of individuals who are discouraged by this institution's emphasis on security rather than advancement or opportunity for full utilization of capacities. Such
individuals are reluctant to seek employment in the company or
are impelled to leave it. While in this particular case the effect
on the institution is not yet marked, it is possible that rising
educational standards in the community and other considerations
may make this kind of antagonism a serious factor.

The third type of antagonism is well illustrated by the situation
at the New Freedom Products Company in the period immediately
preceding reorganization of management's duties. At that time
conflicting rules and norms led to a crisscrossing of authority and
communications which reflected not only in inefficiency but in
personal irritation and hostility.

The final type of antagonism is that which had the most significant effects upon the New Freedom Products Company and
probably affects most industrial concerns in varying degrees. It
consists in divergent emphases placed on various elements in the
charter and even in what amount to splits in charter, and it is
reflected in a division between upper and lower status levels. It
has aligned two important segments of the personnel in opposition to each other and has to some extent canceled the unifying
function of the charter. Company officials and higher executives,
reinforced by their more intimate view of the problems of the
institution as a whole, tend to emphasize the welfare of the company and its stability. Workers, on the other hand, lacking full
information regarding company problems, tend to place a higher
valuation on their own income and security. Thus the union has
emerged as an organization of workers which presses for the goals
held more important by the workers, while the management tries
to protect the company from what it looks upon as excessive costs.

This last type of antagonism has seriously affected American
industry,[9] both in individual plants and as a part of the national

9. Cf. Yoder, *Personnel and Labor Relations*, pp. 48–49; Daugherty, *Labor
Problems in American Industry*, p. 58; P. Pigors, L. C. McKenney, and T. O.
Armstrong, *Social Problems in Labor Relations*, p. 6; F. J. Roethlisberger,

economic system. Further, it may be at the root of problems in other institutions. It seems not unlikely that members of institutions generally cherish common goals and that their differences may arise from disagreement as to the relative emphasis which should be given to various goals and to the principles for attaining them.[10] Basically, perhaps, the same problem—or perhaps the larger one of building a charter—is inherent in international relations. E. B. White [11] suggests:

> One of the curious difficulties in the way of world federation is the necessity of developing a planetary loyalty as a substitute for, or a complement to, national loyalty. In the United Nations of the World there will be no foreigner to make fun of, no outsider to feel better than. A citizen of the U.N.W. must take pride in the whole world; that, for some people, is going to be a very large thing to get excited about. A man will have to pledge allegiance not only to a national flag but to a universal banner, the colors of which will be rather unfamiliar.

Although one may join with Linton in being pessimistic about such large projects,[12] it is still possible to test the utility of scien-

---

Management and Morale, p. 111; Heron, *Sharing Information with Employees,* p. 34; Lewisohn, *Human Leadership in Industry,* p. 95; E. M. Queeny, *The Spirit of Enterprise,* p. 29; Warner and Low, *The Social System of a Modern Factory,* p. 71.

10. Cf. *Recent Social Trends in the United States,* pp. lxxiv–lxxxv: "Unless there can be a more impressive integration of social skills and fusing of social purposes than is revealed by recent trends, there can be no assurance that these alternatives with their accompaniments of violent revolution, dark periods of serious repressions of libertarian and democratic forms, the proscription and loss of many useful elements in the present productive system, can be averted . . . The clarification of human values and their reformulation in order to give expression to them in terms of today's life and opportunities is a major task of social thinking. The progressive confusion created in men's minds by the bewildering sweep of events revealed in our recent social trends must find its counterpart in the progressive clarification of men's thinking and feeling, in their reorientation to the meaning of the new trends."

11. E. B. White, *The Wild Flag,* p. 10.

12. See Linton, *The Study of Man,* p. 490: "We have come to a door be-

tific theories in smaller institutions. The systematization of antagonistic cooperation outlined here has been of assistance in analyzing one such institution; possibly it is capable of broader application.

While it was hoped that study of the New Freedom Products Company would lead to some positive conclusions as to whether or not primary group relationships—that is, intimate, personal association among the members of a group or institution—are essentially the most effective basis for organization, no such result was achieved. Although it is clear that the company has changed from a primary group into one in which relationships between officials and workers are indirect and impersonal, it cannot be asserted that growing impersonality was, in itself, the reason for personal dissatisfaction and institutional disorganization. Cooley and other writers mentioned in Chapter 9 suggest that this might have been the case, as do some older employees of the New Freedom Products Company. But considerations involved in the concepts of strain toward consistency, cultural lag, and *anomie* indicate that the difficulties experienced by this institution may have been owing simply to the dislocations occasioned by change.

In either event, the functions of the personal contacts which characterized the earlier organizational system of the company must be taken into account. There is no reason to suppose that intimacy or "fusion of personalities" possesses a mystical power to generate kindliness [13] or that consistency in the folkways springs from a sense of proportion or from any conscious desire for "well-rounded integration." [14] In the case of the New Freedom Products

yond which lies a store of knowledge that promises to give man a better life than any he has known, but there seems little chance that we will be allowed to pass through."

13. Cf. Cooley, *Social Organization*, p. 23.

14. Such a view is suggested by Nathan Miller in "Primitive Economics," *Studies in the Science of Society*, pp. 424–426. Miller speaks of culture as "the mode or the attempts by which a people actually seeks for its own satisfaction to secure an inner adjustment or integration of its folkways . . . Morals, so-called, ethics, social values—all these encased in the supernatural trappings of the cult or in the philosophical, mystical envelope of organized religions—have been the chief external vehicles representing the strain toward consistency . . .

Company, personal contacts answered instrumental needs of the institution and of its members as individuals. Through such contacts, for example, officials controlled technical operations, and workers received assurances which strengthened their sense of security. Essentially, moreover, the system of personal contacts between officials and workers represented corresponding and complementary sets of folkways or norms. Or, to express the matter differently and to strike directly at the heart of the problem, the roles of the officials changed at points where they integrated with the roles of workers, and need for readjustment was felt by the workers. They sought to re-establish institutional equilibrium or consistency because they felt the pain produced by maladjustment.[15]

Important among the functions of the folkways which previously brought workers and officials into intimate association were those of communication. They facilitated full and effective exchange of information and thus tended to maintain a common sense of charter. Each group was trained in and kept familiar with the facts and ideas held important by the other. Later, the strongest and most pervading kind of antagonism between these groups— that based on divergent interpretations of the charter—arose largely because of the differences in information available to them; and the antagonistic groups were those between whom communications had broken down most badly.

Thus the problem of depersonalization resolves itself into a question of whether the functions of the folkways of personal interrelationship can be discharged successfully in other ways. Several variations intended to replace the older folkways have developed at the New Freedom Products Company, as they have in other industries. These include the appointment of intermediaries between "top management" and workers—such as foremen, minor executives, and union functionaries—and the development of such media as the office newspaper. Whether these will succeed no one can yet be sure. One is tempted to believe that personal relation-

---

it is apparent that the notion of consistency in the mores is always inextricable from certain value-judgments."

15. Cf. Sumner, *Folkways*, p. 5.

ships of some kind cannot with safety be entirely eliminated, but what evidence we have indicates that, at least in the few years they have existed, the newer adjustments—the union and the reorganized management—have been reasonably successful.

Much of the history of society has been a pageant of increasingly large and complex institutions. Almost by definition "primitive" means small and simple, while "civilization" implies size and complexity. Dotted over the face of the earth are the ruins of civilizations which have perished, some of them, perhaps many, because they were unable to solve the problems which accompany size and complexity and the problems of assimilating change without falling into *anomie*. These are the problems with which, on a smaller scale, American industry is wrestling today and with which, on a minute scale, the New Freedom Products Company is faced.

The structure of American society sometimes seems so vast and complicated that it is hard to know how to begin studying it. The factory and other small institutions offer, perhaps, one solution to this problem.[16] A factory is a functional social group. In it behavior is, to some extent, controlled and predictable; and in some factories social phenomena are observable on a relatively comprehensible

16. Cf. Gabriel Tarde, *Social Laws,* p. 198: "If we wish to make sociology a truly experimental science and stamp it with the seal of absolute exactness . . . Let twenty, thirty, or as many as fifty sociologists . . . write out with the greatest care and in the greatest possible detail the succession of minute transformation in the political or industrial world . . . in their own native town or village . . . within such a highly instructive body of monographs there cannot fail to appear . . . truths most valuable for the sociologist and the statesman to know."

Also C. H. Cooley, "Case Study of Small Institutions as a Method of Research," *Publications of the American Sociological Society,* XXII, 123–132: "While persons and families are the usual objects of case study, the method may be extended to other constituents of the social process, to the life histories of groups and institutions not too large to be treated in direct and total fashion . . .

"Suppose we have captured one [small institution] and have it under observation: What shall we observe? I presume that our aim is to understand what part the form of life we have before us plays in the social process, and also, perhaps, to foresee its operation, know how to influence it, and by comparison, extend our knowledge to other forms more or less similar."

scale. It is not likely that sociologists will be permitted very soon to perform their own experiments in factories, but they can observe the experiments of others and, using the "tools" of the science, contribute to the general body of sociological theory.

Man has come a long way toward understanding and being able to control two of the "life conditions"—his natural environment and his own physical constitution. He has been less successful with two others—his social and conceptual environments. In studying the first two, scientists have profitably used small isolates—molecules, atoms, or cells. This book is concerned primarily with the third and fourth, and its subject, the New Freedom Products Company, can be regarded as a tiny isolate of society, possessed of its own cultural conceptions. The findings presented here, though in detail probably not universally applicable to human society or to all institutions everywhere, will, it is hoped, prove to be of some value in the solution of practical problems of industrial relations, in the development of the new and growing field of scholarly investigation which has come to be called industrial sociology, and, optimistically perhaps, in the general expansion of knowledge about man and his society and culture which is the goal of the science of sociology.

APPENDIX: *Note on "Institution"*

Among the particularly valuable concepts in the study of an organized group such as an industrial plant is that of "institution." This word has both advantages and disadvantages. The main disadvantage lies in the fact that it is used by sociologists in a confusing variety of meanings and contexts. The principal advantage is that, around this key concept, there has been developed an inclusive and significant theoretical framework. Appropriately elaborated, the concept readily stands the test of specific application, serves as a guide for study and exposition, and contributes to the understanding of social structure and group dynamics.

Definitions of the term "institution" are of two principal kinds: those which deal with abstractions, such as property or religion; and those which are applied to a specific, organized group, such as *a* school or *a* church. By the latter kind of definition the factory itself is an institution. By the former it might be regarded as a part of the economic institution or, perhaps, a part of the property institution.

The dichotomy of meanings is described by L. T. Hobhouse [1] as follows:

> The term institution then covers (1) recognized and established usages governing certain relations of men, (2) an entire complex of such usages and the principles governing it, and (3) the organization (if such exists) supporting such a complex. On

1. Hobhouse, *Social Development*, pp. 49–50.

263

the one side the reference is to certain relations of human beings; on the other to the human beings themselves united by
the fulfillment of some particular function. It is convenient to
divide these meanings in our terminology and retaining "institutions" for relations, their complexes and their principles,
to find another term for human beings united for a specific
purpose or in the performance of a specific function. Such a
union might be called an association.

In this he is followed by McIver, as will be explained below.

Even more abstract is Walton H. Hamilton's definition in *Encyclopaedia of the Social Sciences:* [2]

Institution is a verbal symbol which for want of a better
describes a cluster of social usages. It consists of a way of
thought or action of some prevalence and permanence which
is embedded in the habits of a people. In ordinary speech it
is another word for procedure, convention or arrangement; in
the language of books it is the singular for which mores or folkways are the plural . . . Arrangements as diverse as the money
economy, classical education, the chain store, fundamentalism
and democracy are institutions.

In the same vein is Veblen's earlier definition: [3]

The institutions are, in substance, prevalent habits of thought
with respect to particular functions of the individual and the
community. Institutions must change with changing circumstances, since they are in the nature of an habitual method of
responding to stimuli which these changing circumstances
afford.

Veblen's examples include the monogamic family, the agnatic
system of consanguinity, private property, theistic faith, ancestor
worship in China, and the leisure class.

Although a complete list would be pointless, the following names
of writers who have used the term "institution" in approximately

2. *Encyclopaedia of the Social Sciences,* VIII, 84 ff.
3 Thorstein Veblen, *The Theory of the Leisure Class,* p. 202.

this same way are interesting: Keller,[4] Cooley,[5] McIver,[6] Ogburn,[7] Panunzio,[8] and Williams.[9]

Sumner's conception of institution seems, at times, to include the the idea, as described above, that institutions are more or less abstract crystallizations of mores and folkways. He mentions property as an institution. Nevertheless, as he develops the concept, it seems rather to apply to groupings of people. His principal discussion of it centers around "wedlock" or "a family." His most explicit explanation of what he means by the term follows: [10]

> An institution consists of a concept (idea, notion, doctrine, interest) and a structure. The structure is a framework, or apparatus, or perhaps only a number of functionaries set to cooperate in prescribed ways at a certain conjecture. The structure holds the concept and furnishes instrumentalities for bringing it into the world of facts and action in a way to serve the interests of men in society. Institutions are either crescive or enacted. They are crescive when they take shape in the mores, growing by the instinctive efforts by which the mores are produced. Then the efforts, through long use, become specific. Property, marriage, and religion are the most primary institutions. They began in folkways. They became customs. They developed into mores by the addition of some philosophy of welfare, however crude. Then they were made more definite and specific as regards the rules, the prescribed acts, and the apparatus to be employed. This produced a structure and the institution was complete. Enacted institutions are products of rational invention and intention. They

4. A. G. Keller, *Societal Evolution*, pp. 61–62.

5. Cooley, *Social Organization*, pp. 313–314. It is interesting that Cooley apparently swung at times to the alternative view, especially in his "Case Study of Small Institutions as a Method of Research," *Publications of the American Sociological Society*.

6. R. M. McIver, *Society; a Textbook of Sociology*, pp. 11, 14–15.

7. W. F. Ogburn and M. F. Nimkoff, *Sociology*, p. 46.

8. C. Panunzio, *Major Social Institutions*, pp 6 ff.

9. R. M. Williams Jr., *American Society*, pp. 28–29.

10. Sumner, *Folkways*, pp. 53–54.

belong to high civilization. Banks are institutions of credit which can be traced back to barbarism.

This conception is made somewhat clearer by the following statement: [11]

> The relations of men to each other consist in mutual reactions (antagonisms, rivalries, alliances, coercions, and cooperations), from which result societal concatenations and concretions, that is more or less fixed positions of individuals and subgroups towards each other, and more or less established sequences and methods of interaction between them, by which the interests of all members of the group are served. . . . men, each struggling to carry on existence, unconsciously cooperate to build up associations, organizations, and institutions . . . These concretions of relations and act . . . are attended by faiths, doctrines of philosophy (myths, folklore), and by precepts of right conduct and duty (taboos) . . . The structure which is built is not physical but societal and institutional, that is to say it belongs to a category which must be defined and studied by itself. It is a category in which custom produces continuity, coherence, and consistency, so that the word "structure" may properly be applied to the fabric of relations and prescribed positions with which societal functions are permanently connected.

Elsewhere Sumner places more stress on the idea of function.[12] He speaks of the "function" of the family as the formation and handing down of folkways and mores. Also he refers to "a family" as an institution.

On the basis of this discussion it is possible to list the following factors as part of Sumner's conception of institutions:

1). *Concept:* This includes the goal (interest), beliefs (faiths), principles (doctrines), and precepts.

2). *Structure:* This includes persons and their separate interests

11. *Ibid.*, pp. 34–35.
12. W. G. Sumner, "The Family and Social Change," *American Journal of Sociology.*

(as distinct from the goal or common interest included in the concept), rules including prescribed acts and definitions of the interrelationships of individuals and subgroups (fixed positions with relation to each other), and apparatus and instrumentalities.

3). *Function.*

Possibly this analysis does some violence to Sumner's conception. Thus "persons" and "function" are included somewhat by inference. Moreover, Sumner was obviously much more interested in the types or general forms of institutions than he was in individual examples of these institutions, despite the fact that his generalizations were based on accounts of specific groups. It is interesting to see, however, that Sumner noted many of the points later developed more systematically by Malinowski.

An effort to define institution in terms of a more closely integrated system of concepts is to be found in Chapin's *Cultural Change.*[13] This may be summarized as follows:

Institutions arise as a result of the responses of social groups of interacting human beings to elemental needs or drives. From this process of interaction, common reciprocal attitudes and conventionalized behavior patterns develop (affection, loyalty, cooperation, domination, subordination). Cultural objects embodying symbolic value are invented and become "cue stimuli" to behavior. Utilitarian culture objects are invented and become the means of supplying creature wants for shelter, etc. Specifications for the behavior patterns of interrelationship among the factors mentioned above (drives, attitudes, and "cultural traits") are put into words and are handed down through the generations. "We may say that the structure of social institutions consists in the combination of certain related parts into a configuration possessing the properties of relative rigidity and relative persistence of form, and tending to function as a unit in a contemporary field of culture." Institutions are family, state, religion, and industry, each of which exhibits the "elements of the institutional complex," which have been described above. Thus industry has: attitudes and behavior patterns such as fair play, loyalty, cooperation, conflict, workmanship, and thrift; symbolic culture—for example, trade-mark, patent sign, and ad-

13. F. Stuart Chapin, *Cultural Change,* pp. 46, 48–49.

vertising emblem; utilitarian culture traits like stores, shops, factories, ships, railroads, and machinery; and oral and written specifications including franchises, licenses, contracts, partnership papers, and articles of incorporation. The significance of these, Chapin says, becomes clearer when they are used as criteria to analyze institutions, especially particular institutions, such as a definite industrial enterprise. The similarity of Chapin's concept to that of Malinowski is obvious.

Bibliography

General References

Arnold, Thurman, W. *The Folklore of Capitalism*. New Haven, Yale University Press, 1937.

Bacon, Selden D. "Alcohol and Complex Society" in *Alcohol, Science and Society; Twenty-nine Lectures with Discussion as Given at the Yale Summer School of Alcohol Studies*, pp. 179–195. New Haven, Quarterly Journal of Studies in Alcohol, 1945. Emphasizes the effects of stratification upon individual stability.

Benedict, Ruth. *Patterns of Culture*. New York, Penguin Books, 1946 (original edition, Boston, Houghton Mifflin, 1934). Description of Zuñi religion cited as an example of institutional equilibrium.

Chapin, F. Stuart. *Cultural Change*. New York, Appleton-Century, 1928.

Cooley, Charles Horton. "Case Study of Small Institutions as a Method of Research" in *Publications of the American Sociological Society*, XXII (1928), 123–132.

——. "The Development of Sociology at Michigan" in *Sociological Theory and Social Research*, pp. 3–14. New York, Henry Holt, 1930.

——. *Human Nature and the Social Order*. New York, Charles Scribner's Sons, 1902.

——. *Social Organization; a Study of the Larger Mind*. New York, Charles Scribner's Sons, 1909.

——. *Social Process*. New York, Charles Scribner's Sons, 1927 (original edition, 1918).

Dickinson, Henry Douglas. *Institutional Revenue; a Study of the Influence of Social Institutions on the Distribution of Wealth*. London, Williams and Norgate, 1932.

Durkheim, Émile. *De la Division du travail social; étude sur l'organisation des sociétés supérieures*. Paris, Ancienne Librairie Germer Baillerie, 1893.

Giddings, Franklin Henry. *The Principles of Sociology; an Analysis of the Phenomena of Association and of Social Organization*. New York, Macmillan, 1896.

Hamilton, Walton H. "Institution" in *Encyclopaedia of the Social Sciences*, VIII, 84–89. 15 vols., New York, Macmillan, 1932.

Hobhouse, L. T. *Social Development*. New York, Henry Holt, 1924.

Keller, Albert G. *Societal Evolution*. New York, Macmillan, 1931.

Kluckhohn, Clyde, and Kelly, William H. "The Concept of Culture" in *The Science of Man in the World Crisis* (ed. Ralph Linton), pp 78–106. New York, Columbia University Press, 1945.

Le Play, Frédéric. *Les Ouvriers européens; études sur les travaux, la vie domestique et la condition morale des populations ouvrières de l'Europe d'après les faits observés de 1829 à 1855 avec des épilogues indiquant les changements survenus depuis 1855.* 2d ed., 6 vols., Tours, Alfred Mâme et Fils, Libraires-Editeurs, 1878.

———. *The Organization of Labor; in Accordance with Custom and the Law of the Decalogue with a Summary of Comparative Observations upon Good and Evil in the Regime of Labor, the Causes of Evils Existing at the Present Time, and the Means to Effect Reform; with Objections and Answers, Difficulties and Solutions* (translated from the French by G. Emerson from the 2d ed., Tours, 1870). Philadelphia, Claxton, Remson, and Heffelfinger, 1872.

Linton, Ralph. *The Cultural Background of Personality.* New York, Appleton-Century, 1945.

———. *The Study of Man; an Introduction.* New York, Appleton-Century, 1936.

Lippert, Julius. *The Evolution of Culture* (translated from the German and edited by George Peter Murdock). New York, Macmillan, 1931.

Lynd, Robert S. and Helen Merrell. *Middletown.* New York, Harcourt, Brace, 1929.

———. *Middletown in Transition; a Study in Cultural Conflicts.* New York, Harcourt, Brace, 1937.

Malinowski, Bronislaw. "An Anthropological Analysis of War" in *The American Journal of Sociology,* XLVI, No. 4 (Jan., 1941), 521–550.

———. "Culture" in *Encyclopaedia of the Social Sciences,* IV, 621–645. New York, Macmillan, 1931.

———. "Culture as a Determinant of Behavior" in *Factors Determining Human Behavior,* pp. 131–168. Harvard Tercentenary Publications; Cambridge, Harvard University Press, 1937.

———. *The Dynamics of Culture Change; an Inquiry into Race Relations in Africa* (ed. Phyllis M. Kaberry). New Haven, Yale University Press, 1945.

———. "The Group and the Individual in Functional Analysis" in *The American Journal of Sociology,* XLIV, No. 6 (May, 1939), 938–964.

———. "Man's Culture and Man's Behavior" in *Sigma Xi Quarterly,* XXIX (Oct., 1941), 182–196, and XXX (Jan., 1942), 66–78.

———. "The Scientific Approach to the Study of Man" in *Science and Man* (ed. Ruth Nanda Aushen), pp. 207–242. New York, Harcourt, Brace, 1942.

———. *A Scientific Theory of Culture; and Other Essays.* Chapel Hill, University of North Carolina Press, 1944.

————. "Social Anthropology" in *Encyclopaedia Britannica; a New Survey of Universal Knowledge,* 20, 862–870. 14th ed., 24 vols.

McIver, R. M. *Society; a Textbook of Sociology.* New York, Farrar and Rinehart, 1937.

Mead, Margaret. "Sex and Temperament in Three Primitive Societies" in *From the South Seas; Studies of Adolescence and Sex in Primitive Societies.* New York, William Morrow, 1939.

Miller, Nathan. "Primitive Economics" in *Studies in the Science of Society in Honor of Professor A. G. Keller* (ed. G. P. Murdock), pp. 424–426. New Haven, Yale University Press, 1937.

Miller, Neal E., and Dollard, John. *Social Learning and Imitation.* New Haven, Yale University Press, 1941.

Murdock, George Peter. "Bronislaw Malinowski" in *American Anthropologist,* 45, No. 3 (July–Sept., 1943), Pt. I, 441–451.

Myrdal, Gunnar. *An American Dilemma.* 2 Vols., New York, Harper, 1944.

Ogburn, W. F. (with the assistance of Gilfillian, S. C.). "The Influence of Invention and Discovery" in *Recent Social Trends in the United States; Report of the President's Research Committee on Social Trends,* pp. 122–166. New York, McGraw-Hill, 1933.

Ogburn, William F. *Social Change; with Respect to Culture and Original Nature.* New York, Viking, 1922.

————, and Nimkoff, Meyer F. *Sociology.* Boston, Houghton Mifflin, 1940.

Panunzio, Constantine. *Major Social Institutions; an Introduction.* New York, Macmillan, 1939.

Steiner, J. F. "Recreation and Leisure Time Activities" in *Recent Social Trends in the United States; Report of the President's Research Committee on Social Trends,* pp. 912–957. 1-vol. ed., New York, McGraw-Hill, 1933.

Sumner, William Graham. "The Family and Social Change" in *American Journal of Sociology,* XIV, No. 5 (March, 1909), 577–591.

————. *Folkways; a Study of the Sociological Importance of Usages, Manners, Customs, Mores, and Morals.* Boston, Ginn, 1906.

————. "Purposes and Consequences" in *Selected Essays of William Graham Sumner* (eds. Albert Galloway Keller and Maurice Rea Davie), pp. 1–7. New Haven, Yale University Press, 1924.

————, and Keller, Albert G. *The Science of Society.* 4 vols., New Haven, Yale University Press, 1927.

Tarde, Gabriel. *Social Laws; an Outline of Sociology* (translated from the French by Howard C. Warren). New York, Macmillan, 1899.

Tuck, Ruth D. *Not with the Fist; Mexican-Americans in a Southwest City.* New York, Harcourt, Brace, 1946. Illustrates the cultural relativity of motivations.

Veblen, Thorstein. *The Theory of the Leisure Class.* New York, B. W. Heubsch, 1918 (original edition, New York, Macmillan, 1899).

White, E. B. *The Wild Flag; editorials from the New Yorker on Federal World Government and Other Matters.* Boston, Houghton Mifflin, 1946. By inference White suggests the necessity for developing a "planetary" charter (although he does no more than hint at Malinowski's use of this term) as a prerequisite for world peace.

Williams, Robin M., Jr. *American Society; a Sociological Interpretation.* New York, Alfred A. Knopf, 1951.

Wilson, Godfrey and Monica. *The Analysis of Social Change; Based on Observations in Central Africa.* London, Cambridge University Press, 1945. Includes statements on how impersonality has increased the difficulty of administering tribal justice.

Witmer, Helen Leland. *Social Work; an Analysis of a Social Institution.* New York, Farrar and Rinehart, 1942. Miss Witmer uses Malinowski's institutional concept as a means for relating social work to "the total social life."

Young, Kimball. *Sociology.* New York, American Book Co., 1942. General textbook; includes views on primary groups as basic factors in socialization and on cooperation and conflict.

The Holy Bible; Containing Old and New Testaments Translated out of the Original Tongues and with the Former Translations Diligently Compared and Revised, by his Majesty's Special Command; Appointed to be Read in Churches (Authorized King James Version). Oxford, Oxford University Press. Exodus 18: how Moses' father-in-law helped him plan a system of administration.

Recent Social Trends in the United States; Report of the President's Research Committee on Social Trends. 1-vol. ed., New York, McGraw-Hill, 1933.

The Shorter Oxford English Dictionary; on Historical Principles (prepared by William Little, H. W. Fowler, and J. Coulson; revised and annotated by C. T. Onions). 2d ed., 2 vols., Oxford, Clarendon Press, 1936.

United States Department of Commerce, Bureau of the Census. *Religious Bodies: 1936,* Vol. I: Summary and Detailed Tables. 2 vols., Washington, D.C., United States Government Printing Office, 1941.

———. *Sixteenth Census of the United States: 1940; Population,* Vol. III, The Labor Force; Occupation, Industry, Employment and Income, Pt. I, United States Summary. Washington, D.C., United States Government Printing Office, 1943.

Industrial References

Arensberg, Conrad M. "Industry and the Community" in *The American Journal of Sociology,* XLVIII, No. 1 (July, 1942), 1–12.

———. "Behavior and Organization: Industrial Studies" in *Social Psychology at the Crossroads* (eds. John H. Rohrer and Muzafer Sherif). New York, Harper, 1951.

Babchuck, Nicholas, and Goode, William J. "Work Incentives in a Self-determined Group" in *American Sociological Review, 16,* No. 5 (Oct., 1951), 679–687.

Baker, Helen. *Company Plans for Employee Promotions.* Princeton, Industrial Relations Section, Department of Economics and Social Institutions, Princeton University, 1939.

———. *The Determination and Administration of Industrial Relations Policies.* Princeton, Industrial Relations Section, Department of Economics and Social Institutions, Princeton University, 1939.

Bakke, E. Wight. *Bonds of Organizations.* New York, Harper, 1950.

———. *Citizens without Work; a Study of the Effects of Unemployment upon the Worker's Social Relations and Practices.* New Haven, Yale University Press, 1940. Includes interesting comment upon the neighborhood as a primary group (p. 3): "The normal type of neighborhood associations . . . are not of the face-to-face sort which would exercise a very strong . . . force in the determination of attitudes or behavior."

———. *Principles of Adaptive Human Behavior* (reprint from Bulletin 4, *Training and Research in Industrial Relations: II,* Industrial Relations Center, University of Minnesota). New Haven, Labor Management Center, Yale University, 2d ed., July, 1946, also processed revision, 1950.

———. *The Unemployed Worker; a Study of the Task of Making a Living without a Job.* New Haven, Yale University Press, 1940.

Baridon, Felix E., and Loomis, Earl H. *Personnel Problems; Methods of Analysis and Control.* New York, McGraw-Hill, 1931.

Barnard, Chester I. "Functions and Pathology of Status Systems in Formal Organizations" in *Industry and Society* (ed. W. F. Whyte), pp. 46–83. New York, McGraw-Hill, 1946.

———. *The Functions of the Executive.* Cambridge, Harvard University Press, 1938.

Bell, Daniel. "Adjusting Men to Machines; Social Scientists Explore the World of the Factory" in *Commentary, 3,* No. 1 (Jan., 1947), 79–88.

Brown, Alvin. *Organization; a Formulation of Principle.* New York, Hibbert Printing Co., 1945.

Cabot, Philip. *Addresses 1935–1941.* Cambridge, Riverside Press, 1942.

Chase, Stuart. "A Generation of Industrial Peace" in *The Lamp* (house magazine of the Standard Oil Co. of New Jersey), Oct., 1946.

———. *Men at Work; Some Democratic Methods for the Power Age.* New York, Harcourt, Brace, 1945.

Collins, Orvis; Dalton, Melville; and Roy, Donald. "Restriction of Output and Social Cleavage in Industry" in *Applied Anthropology; Problems of Human Organization, 5,* No. 2 (Summer, 1946), 1–14.

Dale, Ernest. *Greater Productivity through Labor-Management Cooperation;*

Analysis of Company and Union Experience. New York, American Management Association, 1950.

Daugherty, Carroll R. *Labor Problems in American Industry.* Boston, Houghton Mifflin, 1936.

Dodge, Martin. "Does Management Get Its Message Across to Employees?" in *Management's Internal Public Relations,* Personnel Series No. 102. New York, American Management Association, 1946.

Eby, Kermit. "The Expert in the Labor Movement" in *The American Journal of Sociology,* LXVII, No. 1 (July, 1951).

Eskin, Leonard (assisted by Irving Gedankin). "The Labor Force in the First Year of Peace" in United States Department of Labor, Bureau of Labor Statistics. *Monthly Labor Review, 63,* No. 5 (Nov., 1946), 669–680.

Feis, Herbert. *Labor Relations; a Study Made in the Proctor and Gamble Company.* New York, Adelphi, 1928.

Gardner, Burleigh B., and Moore, David G. *Human Relations in Industry.* Chicago, Richard Irwin, 1950.

——, and Whyte, William Foote. "Methods for the Study of Human Relations in Industry" in *American Sociological Review,* II, No. 5 (Oct., 1946), 506–512.

Gillespie, James J. *The Principles of Rational Industrial Management.* London, Sir Isaac Pitman, 1938.

Halsey, George D. *Supervising People.* New York, Harper, 1946.

Heron, Alexander R. *Sharing Information with Employees.* Stanford, Stanford University Press, 1942.

——. *Why Men Work.* Stanford, Stanford University Press, 1948.

Hicks, Clarence J. *My Life in Industrial Relations; Fifty Years in the Growth of a Profession.* New York, Harper, 1941.

Jones, Frances M., and Buschman, E. K. "Postwar Increases in Basic Wage Rates" in United States Department of Labor, Bureau of Labor Statistics, *Monthly Labor Review, 63,* No. 3 (Sept., 1946), 342–345.

Lewisohn, Sam A. *Human Leadership in Industry; the Challenge of Tomorrow.* New York, Harper, 1945.

Mayo, Elton. *The Social Problems of an Industrial Civilization.* Boston, Division of Research, Graduate School of Business Administration, Harvard University (Andover Press), 1945.

McCormick, Charles P. *The Power of People.* New York, Harper, 1949.

McNaughton, Wayne L. *Employer-Employee Relations.* Los Angeles, Golden State Publishers, 1946.

Miller, Delbert C., and Form, William H. *Industrial Sociology; an Introduction to the Sociology of Work Relations.* New York, Harper, 1951.

Moore, Wilbert E. *Industrial Relations and the Social Order.* New York, Macmillan, 1946.

Myers, Richard R. "Interpersonal Relations in the Building Industry" in *Ap-*

plied Anthropology; Problems of Human Organization, 5, No. 2 (Spring, 1946), 1–7.

Niles, Mary Cushing Howard. *Middle Management; the Job of the Junior Administrator.* New York, Harper, 1941.

Petersen, Elmore, and Plowman, E. Grosvenor. *Business Organization and Management.* Chicago, Richard D. Irwin, 1942.

Pigors, Paul; McKenney, L. C.; and Armstrong, T. O. *Social Problems in Labor Relations; a Case Book.* New York, McGraw-Hill, 1939.

Pope, Liston. *Millhands and Preachers; a Study of Gastonia.* New Haven, Yale University Press, 1942.

Queeny, Edgar M. *The Spirit of Enterprise.* New York, Charles Scribner's Sons, 1943.

Reynolds, L. G., and Shister, Joseph, *Job Horizons; a Study of Job Satisfactions and Labor Mobility.* New York, Harper, 1949.

Roethlisberger, F. J. *Management and Morale.* Cambridge, Harvard University Press, 1941.

——, and Dickson, William J. (assisted by Harold A. Wright). *Management and the Worker; an Account of a Research Program Conducted by the Western Electric Company, Hawthorne Works, Chicago.* Cambridge, Harvard University Press, 1939.

——, and ——. *Management and the Worker; Technical vs. Social Organization in an Industrial Plant,* Publications of the Graduate School of Business Administration, George F. Baker Fund, vol. XXI, No. 9 (Oct., 1934). Harvard University, Graduate School of Business Administration, Bureau of Business Research, Division of Research, Business Research Studies No. 9.

Roper, Elmo. "What American Labor Wants" in *The Management Review,* XXXIII, No. 3 (March, 1944), p. 75; an excerpt from the *American Mercury* (Feb., 1944).

Schell, Erwin Haskell. *The Technique of Executive Control.* New York, McGraw-Hill, 1926.

Scott, W. H. *Joint Consultation in a Liverpool Manufacturing Firm; a Case Study in Human Relations in Industry.* Liverpool, University Press of Liverpool, 1950.

Seybold, Geneva. "Company Organization Charts" in *Conference Board Reports; Studies in Personnel Policy No. 64.* New York, National Industrial Conference Board, 1944.

——. "Organization Standards and Practices" in *Studies in Business Policy No. 18.* New York, National Industrial Conference Board, 1946.

Shumard, Frederick Warren. *Primer of Time Study.* New York, McGraw-Hill, 1940. Describes the incentive system used at the New Freedom Products Company.

Smith, Charles Copeland. *The Foreman's Place in Management.* New York. Harper, 1946.

Spriegel, William R., and Schulz, Edward. *Elements of Supervision*. New York, John Wiley, 1942.

Stowers, Harvey. *Management Can Be Human*. New York, McGraw-Hill, 1946.

Straus, Donald B. *Hickey-Freeman Company and Amalgamated Clothing Workers of America; a Case Study* (case study no. 4 in the series on "Causes of Industrial Peace Under Collective Bargaining"). Washington, National Planning Association, 1949.

Strong, Esther B. "Industrial Adjustment in Industrial Society" in *American Sociological Review, 14*, No. 3 (June, 1949), 335–346.

Taylor, Frederick W. *The Principles of Scientific Management*. New York, Harper, 1911.

Tead, Ordway. "Industrial Relations 1939 Model" in *Personnel Journal, 17*, No. 5 (Nov., 1938), 160–167.

————. *Instincts in Industry; a Study of Working Class Psychology*. New York and Boston, Houghton Mifflin, 1918.

Urwick, L. G. *The Elements of Administration*. New York, Harper, 1943.

Walker, Charles R. *Steeltown*. New York, Harper, 1950.

Ward, Russell. *The Personnel Program of Jack and Heintz*. New York, Harper, 1946.

Warner, W. Lloyd, and Low, J. O. *The Social System of a Modern Factory; the Strike a Social Analysis*. New Haven, Yale University Press, 1947.

Watkins, Gordon S., and Dodd, Paul A. *The Management of Labor Relations*. New York, McGraw-Hill, 1938.

Watts, Frank. *An Introduction to the Psychological Problems of Industry*. London, George Allen and Unwin, 1921. Includes a discussion of the "herd instinct" as a factor in the psychological make-up of industrial workers.

Weiss, Abraham, and Hussey, Edith L. "Grievance Procedure under Collective Bargaining" in United States Department of Labor, Bureau of Labor Statistics, *Monthly Labor Review, 63*, No. 2 (Aug., 1946), 175–185.

Whitehead, T. N. *The Industrial Worker; a Statistical Report of Human Relations in a Group of Manual Workers*. 2 vols., Cambridge, Harvard University Press, 1938.

Whyte, W. F. (ed.). *Industry and Society*. New York, McGraw-Hill, 1946.

————. "Small Groups and Large Organizations" in *Social Psychology at the Crossroads* (eds. John H. Rohrer and Muzafer Sherif). New York, Harper, 1951.

Wiren, A. R., and Heyel, C. *Practical Management Research*. New York, McGraw-Hill, 1945.

Wolman, Leo, and Peck, Gustav. "Labor Groups in the Social Structure" in *Recent Social Trends in the United States; Report of the President's Committee on Social Trends*, 1-vol. ed., pp. 801–856. New York, McGraw-Hill, 1933.

Worthy, James C. "Organizational Structure and Employee Morale" in *American Sociological Review, 15*, No. 2 (April, 1950), 169–179.

Yoder, Dale. *Personnel and Labor Relations.* New York, Prentice Hall, 1948.

100-Years; the "New Freedom Products Company" and the "Products" Industry in America. "Teasville," "New Freedom Products Company," 1936.

Retirement Plan. "Teasville," "New Freedom Products Company," 1946.

Union Agreement between the "New Freedom Products Company" and the Textile Workers Union of America, CIO and Local No. ———. "Teasville," May, 1946.

Union Agreement between the "New Freedom Products Company" and Local No. ——— of the Textile Workers Union of America, CIO. "Teasville," May, 1945.

United States Department of Commerce, Bureau of the Census, *Sixteenth Census of the United States: 1940; Manufacturers, 1939,* Vol. I, Statistics by Subjects. Washington, D.C., United States Government Printing Office, 1942.

War Manpower Commission, Training Within Industry, *Job Instructor Training; Training Sessions Outline and Reference Manual.* Washington, D.C., 1942.

Working Together, "Teasville," "New Freedom Products Company," 1944.

INDEX